EDIBLE IDEOLOGIES

Edible Ideologies

Representing Food and Meaning

Edited by
Kathleen LeBesco
and
Peter Naccarato

WITHDRAWN

STATE UNIVERSITY OF NEW YORK PRESS

Published by
State University of New York Press, Albany

For information, contact State University of New York Press, Albany, NY
www.sunypress.edu

Production by Kelli W. LeRoux
Marketing by Anne M. Valentine

Photo/illustration credits: Figure 9.2—reproduced with the permission of
Norman Rockwell Family Agency, Inc.; Figure 9.3—reproduced with the
permission of Trans High Corporation

Library of Congress Cataloging in Publication Data

Edible ideologies : representing food and meaning / edited by: Kathleen
LeBesco, Peter Naccarato.
   p. cm.
  Includes bibliographical references and index.
  ISBN 978-0-7914-7287-3 (hardcover : alk. paper) — ISBN
978-0-7914-7288-0 (pbk. : alk. paper) 1. Food—History. 2.
Food—Social aspects. I. LeBesco, Kathleen, 1970– II. Naccarato, Peter,
1970–

TX353.E35 2008
641.3—dc22

                                2007007754

10 9 8 7 6 5 4 3 2 1

To Fede Mauro Naccarato and Brooks LaRose,
our grandparents, perched on whose windowsills
and countertops we learned to love food

"One cannot think well, love well, sleep well, if one has not dined well."

—Virginia Woolf, *A Room of One's Own*

Contents

Illustrations

Acknowledgments

We must beg to differ with the sentiment behind the adage that "too many cooks spoil the broth." In fact, we have a great many people to thank for stirring the pot.

Our nine contributors worked diligently to provide the raw material for this collection, flexibly reworking their pieces under tight deadlines with great skill.

Partial funding for the project was generously granted by the late Margaret Sokol, a vibrant longtime supporter of faculty development.

A number of faculty, staff, and students at Marymount Manhattan College were supportive of this endeavor. In particular, we appreciate conversations with our undergraduate students in "Edible Ideologies: The Politics of Food" both in fall 2002 and spring 2006. Henry Blanke and Tammy Wofsey assisted with a never-ending series of requests for interlibrary loans. Ryan Cunningham provided heroic administrative support. Kelsey Crittenden, Louise Mattarelliano, Margaret Westby, and Laura Young served capably as editorial/research assistants. David Linton and Dawn Weber championed funding for the project through administrative channels.

We first dreamed up the project after attending the "Eat, Drink and Be Merry: Food and Drink in the 21st Century" conference at the Amsterdam School of Cultural Analysis in 2002. Subsequent food studies-related presentations at the annual meeting of the Popular Culture Association in Atlanta (2006), the "Politics and/in Aesthetics" conference at the University of Veliko Turnovo, Bulgaria (2005), and the International Communication Association annual conference in San Diego (2003) cemented our knowledge base and our commitment. We thank the many scholars who provided fine feedback on our ideas at these varied venues.

At SUNY Press, we thank Larin McLaughlin for recognizing the potential of this project and shepherding it to fruition, and Kelli Williams LeRoux for guidance during the production phase. The comments of two anonymous reviewers also shaped the collection, and to them we express gratitude.

Our families and friends have also been enthusiastic about the project. (After some of our earlier research topics, food is a relatively easy sell!) "Grazie" to Peg Leahy, Kurt LeBesco, Pauline Franz, John Shields, Pete Naccarato and Laura Naccarato.

Introduction

Kathleen LeBesco and Peter Naccarato

> When he buys an item of food, consumes it, or serves it, modern man does not manipulate a simple object in a purely transitive fashion; this item of food sums up and transmits a situation; it constitutes an information; it signifies.
>
> —Roland Barthes, *Mythologies*

As Roland Barthes suggests, buying, consuming, and serving food are acts of signification through which people construct and sustain their identities. At the same time these acts—and the broad range of cultural representations that support and are supported by them—also serve as vehicles through which ideological expectations about those very identities are circulated, enforced, and transgressed. While on the surface food culture offers its consumers education, entertainment, and escape, it implicitly invites them not only to appreciate the beauty and pleasure of well-prepared food, but also to consume the subtle messages embedded within these representations. However, food representations are not simply tools of seduction or devices for the exercise of repressive power—they are also occasions for resistance that provide opportunities for pleasure.

The twentieth century has seen a boom in the industry of representing food and foodways, culminating in the present era of celebrity chef worship, culinary boot camps, lush food magazine spreads, gastroporn imagery on television and in film, stores selling nothing but cookbooks, and heavily traveled chowhound websites. However, at the same time that we have become fascinated by food and food culture, we hear cries from all quarters about the growing American waistline. Both sides of the political aisle have linked food representations and their presumed physical consequences: policy makers have sought to ban the advertising of sugary "junk food" to children, public health officials have fretted over the appropriateness of fat health care providers as role models, and government agencies have attempted to more closely regulate claims about the health benefits of food products as touted in media and even on their wrappers. It is evident that representations that would presume to shape the American diet in a repressive manner—as various as the Food Pyramid, diet cookbooks, and antiobesity public health campaigns—in fact simultaneously produce pleasure and knowledge when transgressed.

Thus, we want to move beyond stale objections to the state of our food culture, present and past. We'll neither frame the fast-food industry nor big agriculture as nefarious villain and the consuming citizen as unwitting victim (as the political left is fond of doing), nor impugn the individual for lacking the God-given strength to resist the temptation fobbed upon her/him by the decadent structures of modern living (as the political right is fond of doing). Our contemporary preoccupation with food makes little sense when viewed as the plight of a docile citizenry at the mercy of Big Food and its alluring representations. But a clearer picture starts to crystallize when we consider how these representations produce both power and pleasure.

This book begins from the premise that representations of food and foodways, when closely examined, illuminate both the repressive power and the productive potential of representation, in a Foucauldian sense.[1] Food representations have historically been understood as mere barometers of cultural sensibilities; instead, we contend that these representations actively *produce* cultural sensibilities and the possibility of transgression. One of the ingredients that flavors this book is a dash of Marxist theory, as we do want to think (in part) about how food and foodways serve as vehicles for the deployment of repressive ideologies. However, we are concerned that past scholarship on the culture industries has focused almost exclusively on the ways in which ordinary people are manipulated into adopting specific ideologies through pleasurable means; one could easily imagine Louis Althusser rejecting delectable representations of food as serving the needs of the State as their viewers and consumers digest dominant ideologies. But ideology must be considered in a more nuanced manner than that pursued by Althusser or Theodor Adorno, to take into account the productive nature of those representations. What pleasures and knowledges do those representations afford in the consuming citizen?

In asking this question, we seek to balance this deterministic streak with one that more robustly imagines the affordances of these representations as well as their constraints. The work of reception theorists like John Fiske and Michel de Certeau, while not attended to directly by the chapters that follow, provides an appropriate counterbalance.[2] Obviously aware of structural constraints, Fiske and de Certeau nonetheless championed the meanings made by audience members of popular representations and rejected the notion of false consciousness. It is this spirit that informs our shift to Foucault as a theoretical guide throughout the book. Although Fiske and de Certeau demonstrate that pleasure is important, Foucault shifts the terms of the discussion as he recognizes discourse as a vehicle for exercising both repressive and productive power.

It is this theoretical framework that flavors our particular foray into cultural studies, which has taken as a central objective the critical examination of "culture" as a means of producing and regulating economic and social power.[3] While this work has moved in a myriad of directions, this book follows from a tradition that dismisses the privileging of "high culture" as the only site of intellectual investigation and, instead, considers texts and genres from across the cultural spectrum. This shift towards "cultural populism" has widened the scope of intellectual inquiry from established literary canons to an open-ended list of cultural texts and practices.[4] Janice Radway's work on romance, Dick Hebdige's work on subculture, Ien Ang's work on soap operas, and Alexander Doty's work on queer mass culture are only a few examples of such scholarship on popular representations.[5] At the same time, there has been a growing focus on food practices and foodways as sites of cultural production. Bob Ashley, Joanne Hollows, Steve Jones, and Ben Taylor have recently released work that theorizes food(ways) through the prism of semiotics, while other scholars like Arlene Avakian, Carole Counihan, Marion Nestle, Warren Belasco, and Sherrie Inness (to name but a few) have interrogated the politics of food in an array of situated contexts—from U.S. government debates about the food pyramid, to the gradual deskilling of the American home cook, to a close-up look into the kitchens and dining rooms of denizens of a startling variety of cultures.

Edible Ideologies extends this line of inquiry specifically to the realm of representation, hoping to help readers digest that how a culture decides to (re)present itself tells us far more about that culture's dominant ideological underpinnings (and the fun people can have in transgressing them) than some "naturalized," purportedly nonconstructed version of it does. We begin with questions about ideology that concern, for instance, whose interests are served by a particular food practice or habit, and what political ends were fulfilled by the historical change that led from one practice to another. This allows us to look beneath the surface of the stories that groups tell about themselves, revealing not only underlying political ideologies, but also, and perhaps as importantly, the tenuous, socially constructed quality of those stories and the pleasurable ends to which they are put.

Our focus on representation as a specific vehicle through which a culture's ideology is shaped and circulated is informed, first and foremost, by the work of Roland Barthes. In *Mythologies*, Barthes defines myth as "a system of communication" that "can consist of modes of writing or of representation; not only written discourse, but also photography, cinema, reporting, sport, shows, publicity" (Barthes, 109, 110). As such, myth is sustained by a series of oral and visual representations that can be read semiotically. In this way, for instance, the decadent chocolate cake in a late-night television commercial is not simply an incitement to salivate (or to head to the nearest grocer); with dulcet-toned voice-over and gastroporn imagery, it is also an offer of sensuality, of erotic comfort to the solitary viewer, available for mere cents. It also provides a promise of resistance to food norms in a society with an inconsistent attitude toward indulgence. In addition to employing semiotic analysis to understand the structure of myth, Barthes acknowledges that myth also functions within an historical and cultural context.

Consequently, Barthes shifts his focus from semiology to ideology "to explain how [myth] corresponds to the interests of a definite society" (Barthes, 128). One of myth's central functions, Barthes argues, is to mask historically and culturally specific ideologies as it "transforms history into nature" (129). The chocolate cake does not merely remind the viewer of the essential human need for food; instead, it plays upon sexual desire and culturally ingrained fantasies of attainment through consumption, thus keeping our economic machinery well-oiled while disguising this ideological work behind the mask of a seemingly natural appetite. Myth, then, plays a central role in the circulation of bourgeois ideology by "giving an historical intention a natural justification, and making contingency appear eternal" (142). But myths also produce pleasure. This book follows Barthes' lead through its focus on representations of food and foodways. Each chapter demonstrates how such representations are not just about nourishment or pleasure, but are instead sophisticated producers of both repressive and resistant ideologies and practices.

In approaching this book, readers will encounter ten chapters that explore how various modes of representation, reflecting prevailing attitudes and assumptions about food and food practices, function to circulate and transgress dominant cultural ideologies. With this as the thread that connects them, each chapter offers its own perspective as it charts the sophisticated interconnections between particular cultural texts, certain aspects of food culture, and specific ideological values. Taken together, these chapters offer a rich historical narrative that moves from the construction of the nineteenth-century English gentleman to the creation of two of today's iconic figures in food culture, Julia Child and Martha Stewart. Along the way, readers will encounter World War I propaganda, holocaust and Sephardic cookbooks, the Rosenbergs, German tour guides, fast-food advertising, food packaging, and chocolate! What unites these disparate topics is the complex methodology employed by each chapter for illuminating the power and politics of representation and underscoring the potential of food and foodways as sophisticated ideological signifiers.

Within the borders of Western, primarily North-American culture, this book offers its readers a rich buffet of culinary choices inasmuch as it examines a range of food products and modes of representation. While very serious and insightful books have focused on the history and significance of particular food products—from chocolate, to cod, to salt—our readers will encounter a fuller menu. Rather than focusing on specific foods or food groups, this book includes chapters that cover a rich variety of foods and food practices within a Western, largely U.S. context. Readers who have given little thought to the meanings of everything from Camembert to Velveeta, from spotted dick to blood sausage, from salads to burgers, from tikka masala to Campbell's Soup and from healthcake to porridge will find food for thought here. At the same time, readers will find that our authors engage a broad range of cultural texts as they examine the ideological impulses behind various representations of food. While other books have focused on food and literature, food and film, or food and television, this book offers a array of textual analysis. From literature and popular fiction to cookbooks and travel guides; from war propaganda and women's magazines to television and print advertisements; this book covers a broad range of cultural texts, highlighting their unique role in utilizing representations of food to circulate and transgress specific ideologies.

This range of textual forms is vital in response to earlier cultural critics who limited their studies of ideology and ideological manipulations to a number of dominant social institutions and to a set of privileged artistic venues, like literature and film. Following Michel Foucault's cue, we contend that less obvious, more subtle forms of discourse are perhaps even more vital sites for the production of knowledge, and thus further exploration and analysis of them is warranted. Discourse moves in multiple directions, and is articulated through a disparate range of cultural sites. Thus, it is incumbent upon us to examine not only great works of literature (as Annette Cozzi and Celia Kingsbury do in the chapters that follow), but also the minutae of food packaging (Elliott), advertising (Retzinger; Nutter), cookbooks (Drews; Mason), news reports (Abrams), travel guides (Fallwell), and cooking shows (LeBesco and Naccarato) to round out our comprehension of the ways in which food and foodways are productive sites of discourse.

The Volume

The ten chapters in this collection are arranged roughly chronologically, beginning with Annette Cozzi's chapter on Charles Dickens, which establishes the framework that structures the entire book. By revealing how nineteenth-century English culture utilized specific food practices to maintain social stratification during a period when it was promoting a national identity based on the illusion of equality and then exploring how fictional representations of these culinary customs and rituals both circulate and normalize them, Cozzi underscores the role of food and foodways in sustaining cultural ideologies during periods of significant political, economic, and social change. Her specific analysis of several novels by Charles Dickens reveals how nineteenth-century English society utilized food and food practices to define and promote certain gender and class ideals. As subsequent chapters shift the historical moment, the cultural context, the modes of representation, and the specific food customs and practices, each of them advances the central goal of the book that is initiated in Cozzi's chapter, namely, to reveal the ways in which representations of food and foodways are utilized to negotiate social change and protect dominant ideologies.

In the second chapter, Celia Kingsbury shifts the focus to World War I as she explores how propaganda from that period—including posters, books, and popular magazines—was used to recruit women as "culinary soldiers" in support of the war effort by encouraging them to conserve food and to adopt the modern tenets of domestic science that emphasized the nutrition, health, and moral well-being of the nation. In making this argument, Kingsbury also examines representations of various food and food practices in wartime fiction, including works by Willa Cather, Ford Madox Ford, H. G. Wells, and Helen Zenna Smith. Like Annette Cozzi, Kingsbury reads a range of cultural texts to understand food's vital role as a powerful political force that serves the cause of social control during a period of change and upheaval.

Marie Drews also explores the power of food as she considers a number of crucial questions that emerge from the publication of *In Memory's Kitchen: A Legacy of Women of Terezín*, a cookbook that houses recipes collected by concentration camp victims. Drews uses this specific text as a springboard for analyzing the important intersections of cooking, story, history, and memory, arguing that *In Memory's Kitchen* memorializes a set of culinary practices and rituals that serve as vital sites of individual and cultural identification. By asking what is at stake when we publish and produce the recipes in *In Memory's Kitchen*, Drews, like the other authors in the book, explores the ways in which specific representations of food and food practices carry with them complex ideological messages.

For Nathan Abrams, media representations of the Rosenbergs leading up to their conviction for atomic espionage serve as an unexpected site for the convergence of ethnic and gender ideologies with particular food and food practices. In particular, Abrams distinguishes between those kosher foods and food practices through which Jewish-Americans communicated their loyalty to America and those nonkosher foods, such as Jell-O, that came to symbolize un-Americanism. By analyzing the role of food and food practices in the media's representations and the court's prosecution of the Rosenbergs, Abrams utilizes this specific historical moment to explore a number of themes that resonate throughout the book. First, the deployment of food practices to establish and police the boundaries between Self and Other plays a central role not only in Jewish culture, but also in a broad range of other contexts (see Cozzi, Mason, Fallwell, Elliott, LeBesco and Naccarato, in this volume). Second, Abrams' particular discussion of the condemnation of Ethel Rosenberg as a bad mother highlights a connection between food practices and gender that is taken up at a number of other points in the book (see Kingsbury, Drews, Retzinger, Nutter). Third, by situating his discussion in the broader context of the Cold War, Abrams teases out the subtle connections between food practices, cultural identity, and national politics, thereby offering his own slant on a number of themes that run throughout the book (see Cozzi, Kingsbury, Drews, Mason, Fallwell, Elliott).

In chapter five, the focus returns to cookbooks as Eric Mason explores how they enshrine particular culinary practices and, consequently, contribute to the production of national, ethnic, and individual identities. To support this argument, Mason focuses specifically on the modern interest in Sephardic cuisine, the cooking of the descendants of the large Jewish community that lived in Spain and Portugal during the Middle Ages. He reviews a number of popular cookbooks to expose how they circulate particular ideological values while masking this work behind the everyday practices of food preparation and consumption. While Mason's focus on cookbooks aligns his chapter most overtly with Marie Drews' discussion of *In Memory's Kitchen*, his work connects with other chapters that focus on the deployment of "ethnic" food as a vehicle for designating the boundary between Self and Other, both individually and culturally (see Cozzi, Abrams, Fallwell, Elliott, LeBesco and Naccarato).

This is certainly one of the links that connects Mason's chapter with Lynne Fallwell's investigation of how German food and culture is represented in English-language travel guides. In particular, Fallwell is concerned with how such representations function to help readers/travelers define and reinforce their own familial, communal, regional, and national identities by establishing the food taboos through which the boundary between them and this foreign "Other" is demarcated. While her analysis of this particular mode of cultural and culinary representation is unique, it nonetheless furthers the overall exploration of the political and ideological function of food and foodways that guides the entire book. In particular, Fallwell's chapter connects with others in the book that explore the links between food practices and national identity (see Cozzi, Kingsbury, Mason, Abrams, Elliott). At the same time, by framing her discussion around the concept of "culinary tourism," Fallwell's analysis bridges the individual and the nation by demonstrating how the assumptions, expectations, and practices of individual tourists both inform and are informed by broader national politics.

Broad national and cultural values and assumptions also serve as the backdrop for Jean Retzinger's examination of contemporary print advertisements and television commercials for fast-food salads. While such advertising is geared toward satisfying our desire to exercise individual choice as consumers, Retzinger argues that it simultaneously exploits contemporary anxieties and stereotypes about sexuality, body image, ethnicity, and gender. Through her analysis of specific print and television advertisements, Retzinger exposes how they deploy the discourse of health in a purely narcissistic fashion laced with innuendo and double entendre. By exposing the discursive maneuvers and manipulations in these advertisements, Retzinger works to reclaim the concept of "health" by framing individual health within the context of social and environmental health. Retzinger's sharp analysis of the cultural assumptions and messages that inform the fast-food industry's advertisements for salads provides another perspective for understanding the complex connections between specific representations of food and the broader ideological values that they circulate.

Charlene Elliott deploys a similar framework even as she shifts focus from food advertisements to food packaging. Specifically, she utilizes Edward Said's notion of "Orientalism" in her analysis of the powerful implications that food packaging has for perceptions of one's own and other cultures. To accomplish this task, Elliott turns to the *President's Choice* product line sold in Canada's Loblaw-owned supermarkets. She explores representations of the "exotic" in *President's Choice* packaging to reveal how such packaging circulates particular stereotypes of race, class, and culture. Like Retzinger, Elliott is also interested in the discourse of health as she contrasts the packaging and marketing of the exotic through *PC's* "Memories of" product line with that of its "blue menu" of "health" foods. While Elliott's particular focus on food packaging adds another mode of representation to those that are discussed in the book, it simultaneously merges with other chapters that explore how such representations promote cultural assumptions about race, class, and ethnicity (see Cozzi; Drews; Abrams; Mason; Fallwell; LeBesco and Naccarato).

In chapter nine, Kathleen Banks Nutter returns to a focus on print and television advertising to explore how advertisements for chocolate reflect shifting assumptions about women, gender, and sexuality in American culture. By assuming a broad historical perspective, Nutter contrasts advertisements from the beginning of the twentieth century, in which women assumed the demure role of fulfilling the needs of others rather than acknowledging their own needs and desires, to more contemporary ads, where women delight in consuming chocolate in order to fulfill their own cravings. As such, Nutter argues that female empowerment and feminist liberation have, themselves, become marketing strategies for selling a range of products, including chocolate. By using changes in chocolate advertisements as a lens for reading shifts in gender ideology, Nutter makes her own contribution to the larger analysis of how representations of food and foodways produce and sustain cultural and individual identities.

In the final chapter, Kathleen LeBesco and Peter Naccarato shift the focus from particular cultural texts to a consideration of how such texts function to create the ultimate representation of food and foodways, namely, the culinary icons of Julia Child and Martha Stewart. LeBesco and Naccarato frame the Child and Stewart oeuvres in the context of lifestyle programming that encourages have-nots to daydream of class mobility, suggesting that while lifestyle experts maintain their privileged class status through their knowledge and appreciation for food, they simultaneously offer their viewers an otherwise elusive taste of this privileged position through the food products they buy, consume, and serve. While acknowledging that both women can be read as gender outlaws as they each manipulate cultural expectations for women as a means of transgressing those limits, LeBesco and Naccarato ultimately use class as the lens that frames their analysis of these iconic figures. From this perspective, they contend that while the overt message of both Child and Stewart is one of class mobility as they invite their readers/viewers to emulate their practices and, thus, share in their privileged status, they ultimately serve to maintain the very class hierarchy that contributes to their iconic status. After close examinations of both women's cookbooks and lifestyle books, biographies, and television shows, LeBesco and Naccarato conclude that each of these texts contributes to the construction and circulation of the ultimate cultural production, the iconic figures of Child and Stewart, themselves, both of whom come to represent and circulate a set of ideologies that sustain the prevailing class hierarchy. This final chapter, then, ties together a number of arguments that have been made throughout the book and highlights the multiple and productive ways in which these ten chapters intersect with each other.

Notes

1. See Michel Foucault, *Power/Knowledge: Selected Interviews and Other Writings, 1972–1977,* ed. Colin Gordon (New York: Pantheon, 1980).

2. See Michel de Certeau, *The Practice of Everyday Life,* trans. Steven Rendall (Berkeley: University of California Press, 1984); and John Fiske,

Understanding Popular Culture (New York: Routledge and Kegan Paul, 1989).

3. See Pierre Bourdieu and Jean-Claude Passeron, "Cultural Reproduction and Social Reproduction," in *Knowledge, Education and Social Change*, ed. R. Brown (London: Tavistock, 1973); and Theodor Adorno and Max Horkheimer, "The Culture Industry: Enlightenment as Mass Deception," in *The Cultural Studies Reader*, 2d ed. Ed. S. During (London: Routledge and Kegan Paul, 1993).

4. See Jim McGuigan, *Cultural Populism* (London: Routledge and Kegan Paul, 1992).

5. See Janice Radway, *Reading the Romance: Women, Patriarchy, and Popular Literature* (Chapel Hill, NC: University of North Carolina Press, 1991); Dick Hebdige, *Subculture: The Meaning of Style* (London: Routledge and Kegan Paul, 1981); Ien Ang, *Reading Dallas* (London: Routledge and Kegan Paul, 1985); and Alexander Doty, *Making Things Perfectly Queer: Interpreting Mass Culture* (Minnesota: University of Minnesota Press, 1993).

Works Cited

Althusser, Louis. 1971. "Ideology and Ideological Apparatuses (Notes towards an Investigation)." In *Lenin and Philosophy*, 127–186. London: New Left Books.

Barthes, Roland. 1957. *Mythologies.* Trans. A. Lavers. Reprint, New York: The Noonday Press, 1972.

———. 1997. "Toward a Psychosociology of Contemporary Food Consumption." In *Food and Culture: A Reader*. Eds. Carole Counihan and Penny Van Esterik, 20–27. New York: Routledge and Kegan Paul.

CHAPTER 1

Men and Menus

Dickens and the Rise of the "Ordinary" English Gentleman

Annette Cozzi

When Henri Misson de Valburg, a Frenchman, visited London in 1698, he waxed eloquent on the subject of, of all things, pudding: "BLESSED BE HE THAT INVENTED pudding, for it is a manna that hits the palates of all sorts of people. . . . Ah, what an excellent thing is an English pudding! To come in pudding time, is as much as to say, to come in the most lucky time in the world" (qtd. in Tames, 23). While one is inclined to think that the Frenchman was being sarcastic, he appears to have been perfectly earnest. Misson's rhapsody encapsulates much that the British like to declaim and disseminate about their national identity: that pudding is manna that appeals to all palates, regardless of rank or station; that Londoners are the most fortunate citizens in the world; and that the British are the beneficiaries of providential grace. While the purveyors of pudding may have liked to believe the fantasy that all Britons were equal, the dining habits, places, foodstuffs, and tastes of the metropolis reveal how stratified and segregated society really was—and how national identity depended upon such equalizing illusions to sustain its self-image as the protectors of Parliamentarian and civil freedoms and the guarantors of modern liberalism.

British identity is often defined externally, against the quaint or the exotic, the long-ago or faraway; but it is also defined internally, in terms of class and gender. If the Other is often considered to be foreign or colonial, particularly Indian, African, Irish, or French, and if identity is also defined against a rural past, then the temporal and geographic point of origin around which these antiquated or alien satellites orbit is contemporary London. For the nineteenth-century Briton, London is indeed the center of the world, just as it is the zero hour of meantime. Throughout the eighteenth and nineteenth centuries, the population growth of London was explosive: although there was no census until the first decade of the nineteenth century, sources estimate that London's population increased from five hundred seventy-five thousand in 1700 to nine hundred thousand in 1800; its population reached more than a million by 1811; and it more than doubled again by the middle of the nineteenth century (Tames, 24, 29). Political philosophers such as Thomas Robert Malthus were concerned with this population growth and how to feed these rapidly reproducing citizens, fearing that, at the current rate of growth, the inhabitants of England would soon starve. Hunger is so anathematized by the British that it is the defining image of the grasping Other, not only the famished Irish and the agitative Chartists—that union of disenfranchised artisans and laborers who were particularly strident during the aptly named "hungry forties," and whose name is derived from their petitions to Parliament demanding the right to vote—whose undisciplined insatiability endangers the stability and depletes the resources of the nation, but also the grasping Jew, whose alleged hunger for money and tastes for strange or restricted food is excoriated in a variety of Victorian discourses. The image of the well-fed Englishman, weaned on beef and ale or bread and cheese, is such an integral part of British national identity that the male counterpart to the personification of Britannia is the stout and hearty John Bull, so well-nourished that his waistcoat strains at the seams. Foreign visitors often commented on the surprising bulk of the nation's citizens; according to J. C. Drummond, the "rich at all times, the poor when they could, were intemperate in meat and drink to an extent which made the English notorious all over Europe. The swollen limbs, bulging cheeks and pendulous paunches which nearly every artist and cartoonist of the time depicted tell their own story" (Drummond and Wilbraham, 299). But while hunger for the middle and upper classes was a dim prospect, the threat of and from a starving working class, whose growling stomachs dictated food riots and chartist agitation, was a very real and immediate problem.

For many writers, London is more than a place; it is a character in its own right, a mythical beast spewing diachronic narratives, spellbinding in its phantasmagoric enchantments. When David Copperfield—hero of the eponymous novel that most critics read as a thinly veiled autobiography of Dickens himself, and which delineates the story of the young boy's rise from penniless, working-class orphan to middle-class professional writer—first catches sight of the teeming city, he exclaims: "What an amazing place London was to me when I saw it in the distance, and how I believed all the adventures of all my favourite heroes to be constantly enacting and re-enacting there, and how I vaguely made it out in my own mind to be fuller of wonders and wickedness than all the cities of the earth . . ." (Dickens, 74–75). Ever-renewing and enthralling, London is, for the dispossessed rural poor, the site of a contemporary metropolitan fairy tale, where happily-ever-after might be achieved in the social restructuring afforded by industrialization. But fairy tales often depend upon something edible—magic beans, oven-baked orphans, poisoned red apples—to define and epistemologize its formal identity. Fairy tales also require a villain, and for British national identity, that trail of crumbs spills from the gaping mouth of the greedy Other, whether he be Indian or African, Irish or French, or a member of England's own starving working class. But in the novels of Dickens, no figure is as despicably dangerous, as pestilent and polluting, to the status quo as that of the Jew, who is perceived as a threat not only because of his strange and "un-English" tastes and appetites and his voracious craving for material gain, but also because of his ability to perform a version of Englishness at times so convincing that he (almost) fools the English themselves, thus rendering the nation vulnerable to contamination through miscegenation—or worse.

When the threat of domestic starvation became defused thanks to the repeal of the Corn Laws in 1846—laws intended to protect agrarian landlords, the repeal of which removed the tariffs on the importation of grain, resulting in a lowering of the price of bread—the threat of and from the working classes began to be rhetorically refigured; once physical starvation no longer loomed as the most immediate threat (although the famine in Ireland continued to actuate increasingly vicious depictions of the Irish as insatiable feeders), fears regarding the social transgression of the appetitive and discontented lower classes began to be substituted. In other words, the lower classes were now perceived as hungry not for sustenance, but status. One of the fears about the lower-class male was that, due to his animalistic slyness and cunning, he would cause the collapse of the social structure by transgressing his station through his monkey-like ability to mimic his "superiors." This fear was not entirely unfounded, as members of the middle class were experts at social performance themselves. The middle class elevated itself through social imitation of the aristocracy, just as the aristocracy aped the manners and fashions of the French court. Perhaps the most visible way that any class can announce its status is through food and the rituals of dining. It is at dinner time, in particular at the dinner party, that newfound wealth can be most spectacularly exhibited and that conspicuous expenditure can be most sumptuously displayed.

The exquisite encoding of dining etiquette is one way to assure the exclusion of the uninitiated, and these codes are in a constant process of revision. At the beginning of the century it was fashionable to dine *à la française*, a style that favored a table groaning with multiple courses displayed haphazardly and simultaneously, where soup tureens nestled against platters heaped with sugared fruits, and where pigeon pies sidled up to melting ices. But as the century wore on, and as food became cheaper and more plentiful, the middle and upper classes needed a new way to distinguish themselves from their inferiors, who could now, at least theoretically, afford such displays of abundance. Thus, the exhibition of wealth shifted from the variety of platters to the quality of plate. The sheer quantity of offerings would be streamlined and standardized, and dining would become encoded by its own set of rules that dictated that the soup come before the fish, and the salad after the roast. Now on display would be both the number of servants and the multiple utensils necessary to handle such service effectively and efficiently. Service *à la française* (essentially "family style") gave way to service *à la russe,* in which each diner was served individually and in which each course demanded new silver and specialized flatware and glasses. Ironically—or tellingly—this shift occurred around the time of the Crimean War, when France was finally Britain's ally, and when Russia had taken its place as its premiere enemy. The English, it seems, need to almost literally consume their rival's identity, as though they can gain knowledge and power by dining like their enemies. Not only were international differences reconciled at the table, but also gender differences were briefly erased. At least while the dinner lasted, women were on equal footing with men. But one category that remained inviolably excluded was that of the lower classes. In *Uneven Developments,* Mary Poovey argues that the construction of separate gendered realms was a strategy deployed to occlude class lines and defuse the threat of class warfare. But it is at the meal, when for a brief period men and women of the same social sphere share meat and drink, that class lines are reinscribed. For what enables the comfortable and abundant dinner is the invisible labor of the lower classes.

If middle-class notions of national identity prevailed and depended upon social imitation of the aristocracy, what was excluded from both imitation and definitions of national identity were the poor. In *Britons,* Linda Colley argues that British nationalism encompassed the entire isle and was an effective means of erasing class difference; in fact, "Britishness was superimposed over an array of internal differences in response to contact with the Other, and above all in response to conflict with the Other" (Colley, 6). While it is true that the working classes in England must be made to feel enough a part of the nation to fight for it, what Colley ignores is the fact that the Other often *was* the poor. Similarly, Poovey's claim that gender divisions were constructed and maintained in order to occlude class differences is problematized by the fact that class differences were very much in play, and what and how you ate was one indicator of status. Poovey claims that "the characteristic feature of the mid-Victorian symbolic economy [is] the articulation of difference upon sex and in the form of binary opposition rather than a hierarchically ordered range of similarities" (6). But if gender is arranged diametrically, then class is still a hierarchically ordered range of similarities. The difference between an aristocratic male, a middle-class male, and a working-class male, in other words, is not that one eats bread while the others do not; rather, all eat bread—it's just that some bread is made with coarser or more refined flour. Of course, what marks all classes as English is that their bread is made from wheat: "As the English prided themselves on eating white wheaten bread as a mark of national superiority the Scottish proclivity for oats . . . was equally mystifying" (Tames, 113). While such generalizations—wheat versus oats— helped to sustain the illusion of British superiority and a cohesive, inclusive national identity, internally there were degrees of separation that the socially encoded dinner helped keep discrete.

It is also at dinner time that the stratifications of the national hierarchy are most evident, for not only what, but also *where* one ate defined one's class. Upper-class men dined at parties or at their clubs, middle-class men supped at home or lunched at a chophouse, but the lower classes were forced to subsist upon food bought on the streets, thus further conflating the poor with the bestial, especially as the urban outdoors (in marked contrast to the romantic idealization of the rural countryside, which served as an antidote to repressive rationality and stiflingly exquisite civility) was quite literally a filthy and fetid environment, flowing with excrement from slop buckets emptied from windows overhead or from the droppings of horses and the ubiquitous unpenned pigs who jostled pedestrians for space. While the location of a meal thus reinforced class lines, social differences could be erased, however sketchily, through the appeal of national parochialism. To be poor and English might be a moral crime, wherein the starving were punished by being sentenced to imprisonment in a workhouse, but to be poor and foreign was almost a flagrant felony. While the rootless tenant farmer and the itinerant artisan were crowding the city and clamoring for rights, the foreign poor in London, particularly the reviled, red-haired Irish and Jewish, posed a more alarming—and potentially contagious—threat. The Irish and the Jew also served to defuse potentially explosive class-based tensions by constructing a foreign Other against whom—or, more appropriately, above whom—even the lowest classes, provided they were employed and English, could be superiorly positioned.

The novels of Dickens that I discuss below are all concerned with ideals of masculinity and gentility, the ascendancy of the working class, and the corrosive presence of the Other, especially the Jew, in the metropolis—and all describe and define such distinctions through food. According to John A. Taylor, "Benedict Anderson's notions of national identity find their best examples in the novels of Charles Dickens. Dickens subsumed the themes of the American Revolution into a British nationalism. Dickens also confirms [Linda] Colley: he founded national identity on secularized Anglicanism" (Taylor, 181). While Taylor is concerned with nationalism and popular literature, one secular avenue of British nationalism that Dickens explores and exemplifies is food. In Dickens' imagining of British national identity, even food is anglicized, and the heterodoxy of dining habits is enshrined. When Kit, in Dickens' *The Old Curiosity Shop,* woos the housemaid Barbara—and, with considerable foresight, Barbara's mother—he treats them to a night on the town: an evening at Astley's theater, followed by supper at an oyster house. As Kit is a mere household servant, Barbara is amazed at Kit's audacity in ordering; and this moment signals not only Kit's transition from voiceless affiliate of the working class to enterprising initiate in the middle class, but also his burgeoning claims to the status and imperatives of gentleman. In the nineteenth century—particularly after the passing of the Reform Bill of 1832, which extended the vote to include wealthier middle-class males—the definition of "gentleman" shifted from the idle aristocrat to the courteous, hardworking professional, a shift that is elucidated by proper "ordering," whether of servants, domestic comfort, or food.

If the middle-class family defined itself according to how many servants it could afford to keep, then the ability to order an inferior acts as a kind of substitute in which even the working classes could maintain an illusion of coercive, if temporary, power, a power that Kit both appropriates and relishes. After a thoroughly enjoyable night at the theater, the working-class party prolongs its revelries by dining out:

> What was all this though—even all this—to the extraordinary dissipation that ensued, when Kit, walking into an oyster-shop as bold as if he lived there, and not so much as looking at the counter or the man behind it, led his party into a box—a private box, fitted up with red curtains, white table-cloth, and cruet-stand complete—and ordered a fierce gentleman with whiskers, who acted as waiter and called him, Christopher Nubbles, "sir," to bring three dozen of his largest-sized oysters, and to look sharp about it. Yes, Kit told this gentleman to look sharp, and he not only said he would look sharp, but he actually did, and presently came running back with the newest loaves, and the freshest butter, and the largest oysters, ever seen. Then said Kit to the gentleman, "a pot of beer"—just so—and the gentleman, instead of replying, "Sir, did you address that language to me?" only said, "Pot o' beer, sir? Yezzir" and went off and fetched it; and put it on the table in a small decanter-stand. . . . In short, there never was a more successful supper; and when Kit ordered in a glass of something hot to finish with . . . there were not six happier people in all the world. (Dickens, 299–300)

Yet this innocent "dissipation" is followed by regret, the moral remorse sanctified by the anglicization of indulgence; Kit arises early the next morning, full "of that vague kind of penitence which holidays awaken . . ." (300). Kit is allowed to mimic the imperatives of the gentleman, but we're reminded that his performance is an imitation. Subdued and sorry, Kit regrets his social transgressions. In the fictional world of Dickens, one must not only earn his rise, but also sublimate his ambition. Unlike Pip, the protagonist of *Great Expectations,* whose own penance for his unearned wealth, his idleness, and his transgressive ambitions takes the form of self-banishment from the nation, Kit is rewarded at the end because he is both employed and inert. When others of his class actively strive to elevate their status, disregarding submission and worth, they are punished for it; and at times that punition demands expulsion from the nation itself.

In many ways, Pip is Kit's social superior; although he is a lowly apprentice, he is not a neutered household servant. In the novel, Pip's greatest expectation is the promise of wealth from an unknown benefactor. Unlike Kit, who earns his rise through dutiful hard work, Pip desires to be an idle gentleman, thus taking for his model of gentlemanliness the aristocratic, rather than the middle-class ideal. While the aristocratic gentleman is a man of leisure, the middle-class version is a mature and responsible man of moral worth, whose birth need not be genteel, only staunchly English. Pip tells Biddy, his family's household servant, and thus the figure who signals their own claims to middle-class status (albeit of the lowest rung), about his secret aspirations: "'Biddy,' said [Pip], after binding her to secrecy, 'I want to be a gentleman'" (Dickens, 131). Biddy is bound to secrecy for Pip recognizes something shameful, almost immoral in its repudiation of middle-class values, in his desires. That Pip's idea of the gentleman is an outmoded version of the aimless aristocrat is signified by not only his idleness, but also his desire to consume; he loiters "along the High-street, looking in disconsolately at the shop-windows, and thinking what [he] would buy if [he] were a gentleman" (122). Gentility glides along a minute scale in which there are subtle gradations between purpose and leisure, consumption and indulgence. As Pip's friend Herbert Pocket informs him, "[It] is indisputable that while you cannot possibly be genteel and bake, you may be as genteel as never was and brew. You see it every day." After Pip enquires whether a gentleman may keep a public-house, Herbert replies, "Not on any account . . . but a public-house may keep a gentleman . . ." (176). And indeed, in Pip's circle, drunkenness proves to be a sign of the morally incontinent, inutile gentleman, just as Pip's eventual industrious sobriety blazons the virtues of Protestant productivity and self-help.

Like Pip, David Copperfield also aspires to be a gentleman, but unlike Pip, his desires remain unvoiced; instead, David mimics the behavior and attitudes of the class he admires—and his performance is both more convincing and more sustained than Kit's. Kit represents the confessional servant, and David the ambitious professional, but both states are still aspects of vocational Anglicanism. When the death of his mother forces the orphaned boy to work for his meager supper at Murdstone and Grinby's warehouse, the young David, self-contained and preternaturally savvy, recognizes that the lower classes are contagious and declines to asso-

ciate with his peers, choosing instead to spend his free time wandering the
streets and ogling the fruits of gentility. He reminisces, "We had half an
hour, I think, for tea. When I had money enough, I used to get half-a-pint
of ready-made coffee and a slice of bread-and-butter. When I had none, I
used to look at a venison-shop in Fleet Street; or I have strolled, at such a
time, as far as Covent Garden Market, and stared at the pine-apples"
(Dickens, 156). Here food, especially exotic and rare food such as tropical
produce, serves as a sign of exclusion (as well as an oblique reminder of off-
stage British imperialism); the fruits that David covets can be earned and
attained only after literal and metaphorical labor.

While David must chasten and sublimate his desires in order to
become a productive, middle-class gentleman—and, paradoxically, finally
be able to earn and afford those desires—it is his youthful mismanage-
ment of food and its purveyors that announces his immaturity and dimin-
ished status. In order for David to achieve professional status and enjoy the
fruits of his labors, not only must he earn more than his current insuffi-
cient pittance, but also he must learn mastery. For most of the novel,
David is taken advantage of by those he should govern: waiters, servants,
even his wife. He is repeatedly duped by waiters who recognize his awk-
wardness and who insult him with their disrespectful "familiarity" (274):

> I felt it was taking a liberty to sit down, with my cap in my
> hand, on the corner of the chair nearest the door; and when the
> waiter laid a cloth on purpose for me, and put a set of castors on
> it, I think I must have turned red all over with modesty.
> He bought me some chops, and vegetables, and took the
> covers off in such a bouncing manner that I was afraid I must have
> given him some offence. . . .
> I thanked him, and took my seat at the board; but found it
> extremely difficult to handle my knife and fork with anything
> like dexterity, or to avoid splashing myself with the gravy, while
> he was standing opposite, staring so hard, and making me blush
> in the most dreadful manner every time I caught his eye. . . . (70)

Not only does David's lack of control render him socially incontinent, as
he fumbles with flatware and splashes and spills, but also the waiter proceeds to drink David's ale, eat his chops, and finish his pudding, all the
while convincing David that he is condescending to do so. A gentleman is
not concerned with taking liberties; he *is* liberty. At school, David is

instantly taken advantage of by the cad Steerforth, who blithely cons David into spending the rest of his shillings on currant wine and almond cakes. David's hero-worship of a figure who has the manners but not the morals of a gentleman signifies his lack of both maturity and judgment.

Of course, David is still a child, but even as an adult, not only is David still fooled by friends, merchants, and waiters, but now he is swindled by his own servants as well. When planning a party, the slatternly Mrs Crupp "cooks" for him: "Mrs Crupp then said what she would recommend would be this. A pair of hot roast fowls—from the pastry-cook's; a dish of stewed beef, with vegetables—from the pastry-cook's; two little corner things, as a raised pie and a dish of kidneys—from the pastry-cook's; a tart, and (if I liked) a shape of jelly—from the pastry-cook's" (335). After ordering from the pastry-cook's, David buys several bottles of wine from a merchant, but when he comes home and finds "the bottles drawn up in a square on the pantry-floor, they looked so numerous (though there were two missing, which made Mrs Crupp very uncomfortable), that I was absolutely frightened of them" (335). The problem is not merely that David is intimidated and cheated by his inferiors (and even by inanimate objects), but that his lack of mastery feminizes and incapacitates him, weaknesses which he himself publicizes by his immoderate consumption and drunken display later that night.

David marries the object of his immature desire, his "child-wife" Dora, a decision unmitigated by rational considerations, and the unsuitability of his choice confirms and compounds his incompetence. David admits, "I doubt whether two young birds could have known less about keeping house, than I and my pretty Dora did. We had a servant, of course. She kept house for us. I have still a latent belief that she must have been Mrs Crupp's daughter in disguise, we had such an awful time of it with Mary Anne" (Dickens, 585). David's use of the phrase "of course" rests upon the elliptical assumption that the ability to keep a servant was so indicative of middle-class status that it needn't be said; David must say it only to reassert his worth. But it is not enough to have servants; middle-class propriety demanded that one manage them as well. The unruly lower classes are a contagion that must, for the good of the nation, be contained, both geographically, in areas designated as working class, such as the East End or the bowels of the manor, and domestically, their attitude and behavior unceasingly policed by their employers. David's lack of management is not merely uncomfortable, it's potentially pestilent as well. There is slippage between the strict separation of classes, and this seepage is due to David himself. He lectures Dora, "'The fact is, my dear,' I began, 'there is contagion in us. We infect every one about us. . . . It is not merely, my pet . . . that we lose money and comfort, and even temper sometimes, by not learning to be more careful; but that we incur the serious responsibility of spoiling every one who comes into our service, or has any dealings with us'" (638). David realizes that it is his obligation to set an example, for the lower classes are presumably too ignorant to know better, and his immaturity is signaled by his failure to manage not only others, but also himself: "I begin to be afraid that the fault is not entirely on one side, but that these people all turn out ill because we don't turn out very well ourselves" (639). In order to effectively quarantine undesirable elements and thus contribute to the maintenance of the class structure, David must distinguish himself from his inferiors, establishing appropriate boundaries between the self and the Other, especially those who would feminize him by their avidity and incontinence.

David and his wife are gulls—English slang for the easily duped—hoodwinked by those they should comprehend and control. He laments, "Everybody we had anything to do with seemed to cheat us. Our appearance in a shop was a signal for the damaged goods to be brought out immediately. If we bought a lobster, it was full of water" (590). But what's worse is that the same sort of disorder is occurring in his own home; the boundaries between superior/inferior, inside/outside, street/home, masculine/feminine, self/other are dissolving in a most uncomfortable (a word to which David often recurs) way: "All our meat turned out to be tough, and there was hardly any crust to our loaves. In search of the principle on which joints ought to be roasted, to be roasted enough, and not too much, I myself referred to the Cookery Book" (590). That David is being feminized, even emasculated, by his impetuous marriage and coercive failures is concretized by the fact that he is forced to delve into the women's realm, as the cookery book is, of course, the woman's domain. David's marriage is based upon sexual desire rather than pragmatic consideration, David having chosen his wife much like an aristocrat or a bestial pauper—or an irrational woman. David's choice does not necessarily preclude ascent into the middle class, but in order to do so he must learn how to manage his inferiors, which includes not only servants, but also, and especially, his wife. After chastising her for being childish and "talking nonsense," he scolds her, ". . . I was obliged to go out yesterday when dinner was half over; and . . . the day before, I was made quite unwell by being obliged to eat underdone veal in a hurry; to-day, I don't dine at all. . . . I don't mean to reproach you, my dear, but this is not comfortable" (587). Perhaps no illusion was more central to the construction and dissemination of national identity than the sanctification of the comforts of the domestic hearth. Unfortunately, David never does learn how to train his wife, and he is spared a lifetime of uncooked meals and stomachaches by her timely death.

Great Expectations is also concerned with seepage between gender and class and the unmerited claims to social mobility. Like David, Pip is also feminized, but whereas David's emasculation is the result of improper management, Pip is feminized by sentiment; according to Hilary Schor, "In some ways, there can be no freestanding, narrating woman because Pip views himself as the woman in the text: Pip has chosen to identify himself with the feminized; and all subjectivity in the novel, all sentiment, all narration, is female—or rather, the victimized, battered, self-emasculated male" (Schor, 547). While Schor is discussing Pip's failure to maintain gender boundaries, particularly regarding his identification with Estella, the cold and haughty object of his affection, Pip's impotent masculinity is a consequence of both his reluctance to establish and enforce class distinctions and his artificial worth. Pip too is performing, and, like David Copperfield, he is made manifestly uncomfortable by servants, who see through the transparency of his act. When he woos Estella by taking her to tea, his lack of mastery is painfully evident: "[The waiter] led us to the black hole of the establishment: fitted up with a diminishing mirror . . . an anchovy sauce-cruet, and somebody's pattens. . . . [H]e at length came back with a casket of precious appearance containing twigs. These I steeped in hot water, and so from the whole of these appliances extracted one cup of I don't know what, for Estella" (Dickens, 250, 253). Significantly, Pip appropriates the role of the woman—and doesn't even do a good job of it. Even Dora, in *David Copperfield,* discovers that there is at least one of her duties that she is able to successfully—or at least prettily—discharge: the service of tea.

The "black hole" in which Pip and Estella take their tea is the antecedent of the modern restaurant and the descendant of the old-fashioned ordinary. In 1667, Samuel Pepys makes up to his wife—after picking a petty fight with her for wearing "white locks"—by treating her to dinner in a "French house," an ordinary kept by his periwig maker "in an ugly street in Covent Garden," where the table is set "in the French manner" (Pepys, 771). While, as always, Pepys enjoys his food, what he relishes more is the service, recording that "to see the pleasant and ready attendance that we had, and all things so desirous to please, and ingenious in the people, did take me mightily. Our dinner cost us 6s" (771). Pepys' entry marks the intersection of class, gender, food, and nationalism in that one moment—his status is confirmed by the attentive service (that he is stolidly middle class is indicated by his attention to price), gender is reconciled by dining together, and Englishness is bolstered by contrast with the French—but whereas Pepys dined happily with his wife, a century or so later, women would be (at least until the end of the nineteenth century) effectively banished from all public eating establishments.

The term "ordinary" arose from the limited menu available in inns. London's inns provided a daily "ordinary," a fixed price offering "[g]enerally four spits, one over another, carry round each five or six pieces of butcher-meat, beef, mutton, veal, pork, and lamb; you have what quantity you please cut off, fat, lean, much or little done; with this a little salt and mustard upon the side of the plate, a bottle of beer and a roll; and there is your whole feast" (Misson qtd. in Tames, 124). A plate of meat, bread, salt, and mustard, with nary a sauce or garnish in sight. If dining *à la française* was the fashion at home, abroad the meal was still relentlessly English. Inns represent the past and a premodern definition of inclusive identity, an appealing image of cozy insularity, particularly to an urban and alienated population whose sense of community had been fractured and patched with precise social codes. In *The Old Curiosity Shop,* it is in inns that the itinerant performer Mr. Codlin experiences the comforts of home: "A mighty fire was blazing on the hearth. . . . [W]hen the landlord stirred the fire . . . [and] took off the lid of the iron pot and there rushed out a savoury smell, while the bubbling sound grew deeper and more rich, and an unctuous steam came floating out, hanging in a delicious mist above their heads—when he did this, Mr. Codlin's heart was touched" (Dickens, 142). Not only does the meal provided by the inn touch his heart with its simple English fare, but also it simultaneously confirms his very masculinity, as self-restraint (along with, for example, rationality, responsibility, and maturity) was one of the characteristics gendered male in Victorian discourse; Mr. Codlin refuses to eat "even so much as a biscuit" until the dinner is ready, and the landlord nods "his approval of this decisive and manly course of procedure" (143).

But inns also allowed for the undesirable mingling of classes. Pip's relationship with Abel Magwitch, the criminal deported to Australia who turns out to be Pip's mysterious benefactor, is initially forged over food—the bread, rind of cheese, mincemeat, brandy, meat bone, and the "beautiful, round, compact pork pie" (Dickens, 35)—that Pip steals from his sister Mrs. Joe in order to feed the escaped convict, forever linking the two in a relentless cycle of crime, remorse, atonement, and redemption. And it is in an inn, the Jolly Bargeman, that Abel begins to pay back his debt of gratitude by entrusting a fellow convict with Pip's monetary compensation: "He stirred his rum-and-water pointedly at me, and he tasted his rum-and-water pointedly at me. And he stirred it and he tasted it: not with a spoon that was brought to him, but *with a file*" (88). Both the convict's inappropriate utensil and his choice of drink—for rum, as opposed to good English ale, was associated with dehumanized outlaws and outcasts figured as even lower than the gin drinking working classes, such as pirates and slaves—alert Pip to the nature of his true identity, both as convict and as comrade of Magwitch, and also signifies the "dirty" and often unlawful transactions that occurred in inns. Dickens scorns the materialism of a society that allows one to buy his way up the ladder. In *Great Expectations,* imperialism allows Abel not only to atone, but also to prosper. He brags to Pip, "'I've been a sheep-farmer, stock-breeder, other trades besides, away in the new world,' he said: 'many a thousand mile of stormy water off from this. . . . I've done wonderful well. There's others went out alonger me as has done well too, but no man has done nigh as well as me. I'm famous for it'" (Dickens, 296). Abel's money allows him to purchase a form of respectable masculinity: his very own gentleman—Pip.

Described in the physical terms of brutish manhood as brown, veined, and muscular, the aging convict Abel, even if he were lawfully allowed back into the nation, could never pass for a gentleman. But if he can't be one, he can buy one: "If I ain't a gentleman, nor yet ain't got no learning, I'm the owner of such. All on you owns stock and land; which on you owns a brought-up London gentleman?" (299). If Abel's figure weren't enough to signal his status, his manner of eating certainly betrays him: "He ate in a ravenous way that was very disagreeable, and all his actions were uncouth, noisy, and greedy" (306). Pip describes how he is more beast than man, let alone gentleman: "[A]s he turned his food in his mouth, and turned his head sideways to bring his strongest fangs to bear upon it, he looked terribly like a hungry old dog. If I had begun with any appetite, he would have taken it away, and I should have sat much as I did—repelled from him by an insurmountable aversion . . ." (306). The finickiness of the middle classes is not for the likes of Abel, and it is his inability to regulate and moderate his appetite that signals his low status:

"'I'm a heavy grubber, dear boy,' he said, as a polite kind of apology when he had made an end of his meal, 'but I always was. If it had been in my constitution to be a lighter grubber, I might ha' got into lighter trouble . . .'" (306). In fact, how he eats identifies him as a criminal:

> In all his ways of sitting and standing, and eating and drinking . . . of taking out his great horn-handled jack-knife and wiping it on his legs and cutting his food—of lifting light glasses and cups to his lips, as if they were clumsy pannikins—of chopping a wedge off his bread, and soaking up with it the last fragments of gravy round and round his plate, as if to make the most of an allowance, and then drying his finger-ends on it, and then swallowing it—in these ways and a thousand other small nameless instances arising every minute in the day, there was Prisoner, Felon, Bondsman, plain as plain could be. (Dickens, 312)

But Abel *is* a criminal, and as such must not be allowed to prosper—at least within the nation space. Yet for Dickens, there is a marked difference between the impoverished English driven to crime—as well as the criminalization of poverty—and the crime of race; and in many of his novels, the real, unredeemable criminal is rendered in characteristics that the Victorians associated with Jewishness, from the foul contamination of contact with base money or "filthy lucre"—often described as "touching pitch"—to unwholesome or "adulterated" appetites, including irreligious trespasses upon dietary restrictions.

In *David Copperfield*, Jewishness is represented by the despicable character of Uriah Heep, a lowly clerk and David's unworthy rival for his eventual second wife, Agnes Wickfield, and who is, as Mary Poovey observes, "the site at which the traces of class issues return" (Poovey, 116). But Uriah, who is described as "stealthy" (Dickens, 223), and "cadaverous" (209), a "red fox" (479), a "vulture" (358), a "devil,"(357), and a "cheat, and a liar" (655), is the site of an even more corrosive presence. His very name—from the Old Testament associations of his full "Christian" name and his mother's nickname of "Ury," with its obvious echo of "usury," to his last name suggestive of "dust-heap," the Victorian euphemism for refuse and waste—his red hair, his "greed and cunning" (Dickens, 698), his "meanness, his craft and malice" (531), his manipulations of money, and his constant rubbing of hands alerted contemporary readers to not just his class status, but also his Jewishness, a Jewishness that is rendered contaminating, as though Heep were pitch itself. After shaking hands, David cannot get his "touch" off of him: "But oh, what a clammy hand it was! as ghostly to the touch as to the sight! I rubbed mine afterwards, to warm it, *and to rub his off*" (Dickens' italics, 215). Uriah is also persistently associated with fish, the significance of which as an indicator of Jewishness I discuss later in this essay. David's guardian, Miss Trotwood, asks him whether he is a man or an eel (478), and his snake-like, "slimy" (356), slithery repugnance is relentlessly emphasized; he is "a crawling imper-sonation of meanness" (476), with "damp fishy fingers" (530), who "writh[es] . . . like a Conger-eel" (569) and "who "jerk[s], like a convul-sive fish" (355).

When David takes tea with Uriah and his mother, he is aware that something essentially English is missing. The room they inhabit is "a per-fectly decent room, half parlour and half kitchen, but not at all a snug room" (242), and despite that fact that Uriah and his mother "respectfully plied [David] with the choicest of eatables on the table [there] was noth-ing particularly choice there, to be sure . . ." (242–43). As though to underline how unsavory both the uncomfortable room and the tea are, next to the tea table is Uriah's bag, "vomiting papers" (242). The Heeps appear to be mimicking a performance of Englishness, and not a very con-vincing one at that—a performance whose artificiality is betrayed by Uriah's misplaced appetites. He eats "'umble pie with an appetite" (531), and he calls Agnes an unripened pear, making "motions with his mouth as if the pear were ripe already, and he were smacking his lips over it" (156). What makes him so dangerous is not only his perverted appetite, but also a barely disguised ambition that will result in the reversal of roles, in which the worthy Englishman Wickfield, Uriah's employer and "master," will be held enthralled by Uriah's misbegotten power (a power that Uriah achieves by manipulating accounts and which he partly maintains by plying his boss with alcohol). Agnes admits, "His ascendancy over papa . . . is very great. He professes humility and gratitude . . . but his position is really one of power, and I fear he makes hard use of his power" (344). It is this misuse of power that not only marks Uriah as extraordinary, a word with negative connotations in Victorian discourse, but also identifies him as a threat to the nation. Yet characters such as Uriah also serve an impor-tant function, for not only does their "baseness" allow even the lowest members of the working class to be superiorly positioned, but also it is thanks to their extraordinary Otherness that Englishness can be rendered as transparently ordinary.

While my use of the word "ordinary" in the title of this article is a barely concealed pun on the original word for restaurants, it also points to the Victorian devaluation of the extraordinary, for the Victorians had a mania for taxonomization, and those figures who breached knowable categories, such as geniuses, were viewed with suspicion. In Victorian novels the Jew is often depicted as extraordinary, the most potent example being that of Svengali, who appears in George Du Maurier's *Trilby,* and whose extraordinary abilities, ancient blood, and acute mind allow him, through his powers of mesmerism, to enthrall the apparently transparent and guileless British, thus potentially debilitating and dominating the vulnerable nation. Uriah anticipates Svengali in his dangerous power over the "ordinary" English, a power that threatens to invert the social order, enslave the worthy Englishman, intermarry with the pure and defenseless Englishwoman, and produce a monster of miscegenation. It is significant that one of the most potent ways that Uriah holds Mr. Wickfield in his thrall, thus gaining financial control, is through enabling his alcoholism, for drinking ultimately begins to subsume the desire to eat, thus compromising the healthy English appetite. And while a fixation upon money—and the hoarding or lending of it—Dickens associates with Shylockian exploitation, an awareness of the value of money, necessary for the administration of both the household and the poor, is one of the sacred duties of the middle class.

While the starvation of worthy characters in Dickens' novels dangerously aligns them with the criminal class, which is usually conceived as a separate race, *Oliver Twist* explicitly deals with the criminalization of poverty. Perhaps no character in literature is as hungry as that "parish child—the orphan of the workhouse—the humble half-starved drudge," Oliver Twist (Dickens, 47). The Poor Law Amendment Act of 1834, passed three years before Dickens began the serialization of his "urban exploration" into poverty and crime, resulted in not only the incarceration of the impoverished, but also their socially sanctioned starvation, a tactic designed to discourage paupers from seeking relief. Oliver is a victim of the conditions of institutionalization, conditions so inhumane and dehumanizing that the workhouse board "established the rule, that all poor people should have the alternative . . . of being starved by a gradual process in the house, or by a quick one out of it" (Dickens, 55). Oliver survives on "three meals of thin gruel a day, with an onion twice a week, and half a roll on Sundays" (55). Dickens goes on to describe the meager pittance the boys are allowed:

> The room in which the boys were fed was a large stone hall, with a copper at one end, out of which the master . . . ladled the gruel at meal-times; of which composition each boy had one porringer, and no more—except on festive occasions, and then he had two ounces and a quarter of bread besides. The bowls never wanted washing. The boys polished them with spoons till they shone again . . . employing themselves, meanwhile, in sucking their fingers most assiduously, with the view of catching up any stray splashes of gruel that might have been cast thereon. Boys have generally excellent appetites. Oliver Twist and his companions suffered the tortures of slow starvation for three months: at last they got so voracious and wild with hunger, that one boy . . . hinted darkly to his companions, that unless he had another basin of gruel *per diem,* he was afraid he might happen to eat the boy who slept next to him. . . . (55–56)

In at attempt to stave off cannibalism, Oliver utters his plaintive request, "Please, sir, I want some more" (56), which results in Oliver being cast out of even this unwelcoming home. He is apprenticed to an undertaker, at whose abode Oliver is offered the "dainty viands that the dog had neglected" (74). As a hungry orphan, not only is Oliver's status reduced to less than a dog, but also his masculinity is compromised, as starvation is both dehumanizing and feminizing him: Oliver weeps so much in the novel that it is hard to believe that he hasn't drowned in his own river of tears.

Dining habits reveal the strict segregation not only between classes, but also between gender and "races." In his own urban exploration of London's street people, *London Labour and the London Poor,* Henry Mayhew observes, "The sole places that seemed to prosper amid the general blight of the place were the public-houses; and in them, the lowest orders of Irish were wrangling with might and main" (Mayhew, 103). While middle-class notions of national identity depended upon the sacredness of the domestic hearth, the poor had to rely upon street traders and open markets for their food. Mayhew classifies his "folk" not only according to "profession," but also according to "race": "Among the street-folk there are many distinct characters of people—people differing as widely from each in tastes, habits, thoughts and creed, as one nation from another" (9). Mayhew treats the poor as its own nation, with its own tastes, language, reading material, habits and entertainments. Mayhew describes the diet of those poor who have managed to escape the indignities of the workhouse, the "costermongers"—the Victorian term for street-sellers—who "form by far the largest and certainly the most broadly marked class. They appear to be a distinct race—perhaps, originally, of Irish extraction . . ." (9):

> They breakfast at a coffee stall. For a penny they can procure a small cup of coffee and two "thin" (that is to say two thin slices of bread and butter). For dinner . . . they buy . . . small dark coloured pieces of meat exposed on the cheap butchers' blocks. These they cook in a tap room. . . . If time be an object the coster buys a hot pie or two, preferring fruit pies when in season, and next to them, meat pies. Saveloys with a pint of beer or a glass of "shod" (neat gin) is with them another common weekday dinner. The costers make all possible purchases of the street dealers and pride themselves on thus "sticking to their own." On Sundays only might they have dinner at home—a joint and "taters" if the week had gone well, a stew made of offal if it hadn't. . . . (9)

Mayhew also notes similarities between the aristocracy and the poor, remarking that "there is a close resemblance between many of the characteristics of a very high class, socially, and a very low class" (18, 19), thus privileging the temperate middle class.

That the poorest of the poor, according to Dickens, is not unworthy—or un-English—but merely unfortunate is underlined, once again, by contrasting Oliver (and even unrepentant criminals such as the Artful Dodger, the pickpocket whose trial is a spectacle wherein he proudly, and uncontestedly, asserts his Englishness) with a Jew. One of the most repugnant characters in all of literature, belonging to no class at all, reviled and despised by even the underworld, is that cartoonishly evil Jew, Fagin. Fagin, who kidnaps Oliver Twist and traffics in stolen goods, is not only associated with the taint of "pitch," but also his abode is the sooty, inverted reflection of domestic order and comfort. In Fagin's hovel, the "walls and ceiling of the room were perfectly black with age and dirt. . . . There was a great deal table before the fire, upon which were . . . a loaf and butter, and a plate. In a frying-pan . . . some sausages were cooking; and standing over them, with a toasting-fork in his hand, was a very shriveled Jew, whose villanous-looking and repulsive face was obscured by a quantity of matted red hair" (Dickens, 105). Not only is he a shriveled, villainous-looking, and repulsive Jew, not only does his home mock English ideals of cleanliness and sanctity, not only is he disregarding strict gender categories by cooking, but also he is not even devout, for he is preparing "unclean" sausages in his filthy hole. Fagin is antediluvian, a vampiric night crawler who feeds upon misery and despair: "It seemed just the night when it befitted such a being as the Jew to be abroad. As he glided stealthily along, creeping beneath the shelter of the walls and doorways, the hideous old man seemed like some loathsome reptile, engendered in the slime and darkness through which he moved: crawling forth, by night, in search of some rich offal for a meal" (186). Even more slippery and slithering than Uriah, Fagin is as greasy and unctuous as the eels sold in the market stalls, as corrupt and unhygienic as one of the defiling pork saveloys that he eats. While Kit, David, Pip, and Oliver each attain varying degrees of gentlemanliness through atonement and the self-enforcement of appropriately male behavior—in particular through their management of the self and the domestic sphere, the regulation of their appetites, and their recognition of proper consumption—Fagin represents all that is un-English and ungentlemanly in Dickens' vision of masculinity: how, what, when, and where he eats reveals his refusal to remain quarantined in the discrete category of pauper and Jew allowed him; he is contagious and contaminating, secretive and sly, dishonest and dishonorable, greedy and grasping, unsavory and unclean—a bottom-feeder in every sense of the word.

Despite the fact that Fagin does not eat kosher, he is still associated with Jewish food. It is in *Oliver Twist* that one of the first literary references to fried fish is made: "Confined as the limits of Field Lane are, it has its barber, its coffee-shop, its beer-shop, and its fried-fish warehouse. It is a commercial colony of itself: the emporium of petty larceny" (235). In 1851, Mayhew estimated "that there were some 300 street-sellers of fried fish as opposed to 150 selling whelks and another 300 selling pea-soup and hot eels" (Tames, 151). Even amongst people not particularly known for being dainty, the vendors of fried fish were the lowest rung of the ladder, for not only was fried fish associated with Jews, but also "fried fish-sellers live in some out of the way alley, and not unfrequently in garrets; for among even the poorest class there are great objections to their being fellow-lodgers, on account of the odour . . ." (Mayhew, 70). Here again, lower-class Englishness is elevated by defining itself against, and positioning itself above, the Other who is so polluting that he contaminates not through contact, but stinking proximity. Yet, as I mentioned earlier, the English are adept at appropriating other cultures and making them their own.

Fish and chips have become so associated with British national identity that John K. Walton can confidently claim that the lack of scholarship on fish and chips is a "neglect of a national institution" (Walton, 4):
"Fish and chips is generally recognized as a great and quintessentially
British institution . . . [and] is often recognized as a constituent of a broad
and emotionally resonant national cultural identity, but always in a
vaguely allusive or nostalgic vein" (1). By recasting fish and chips in a
"nostalgic" vein, they become a revised memory in which their original
associations are obscured. Walton believes that fish and chips are symbols
of a democratic national identity:

> This set of perceptions attaches fish and chips to potent patriotic
> images of land and countryside, industrial might . . . and, above
> all, the notion of Britain as a gallant seafaring nation whose little
> ships do battle with the elements and the foreign enemy to feed
> and protect the people. The convivial, open, public nature of the
> purchase and often the eating of fish and chips also enables it to
> be appropriated in support of cosy visions of democratic solidar-
> ity of a kind that transcends divisions of class or status. (2)

By the twentieth century, fish and chips had been transmuted into something distinctly, and nostalgically, national—and unabashedly imperial:
"Have we another food-catering trade so national in character as the
fried-fish trade? I doubt it. Fish landed by British ships, manned by
British fishermen . . . potatoes grown on our home farms, dripping from
home cattle, ranges made by British labour in British factories, and the
fuel, coal or gas, from British mines" (John Stephen qtd. in Walton, 1).
Walton touts fish and chips as a social equalizer, claiming that "there was
about fish-and-chips a sound democratic touch that no other food pos-
sessed; the poorest person could shop alongside the poshest. . . . You were
all one in the kingdom of fish-and-chips" (2). However, just how many of
the "poshest" subjects dine in the kingdom of fish-and-chips seems
debatable, to say the least, but such assertions allow for the comforting
illusion of a classless society.

But the social climber aspiring to "poshness" soon learns what—and
where—it is acceptable to eat, and fish and chips is not exactly a symbol
of status, its availability and ease of consumption—standing at a counter
or walking down a street—marking it as fare unfit for a gentleman.

"Dining" is no longer *à la russe* or even *à la française,* but *à l'anglaise,* so ostentatiously unbound from class distinctions that neither servants nor plate are now necessary; rather, food is ready-to-eat while perambulating down city streets presumably made clean and safe, thus conflating it with a national identity that purports to be, like such food, readily available, widely accessible, plain, simple, and above all, ordinary. Wrapped, significantly, in one of the most potent promulgators of national identity, the newspaper, fish and chips can be redrawn, like the pudding that appeals to all palates with which I introduced this essay, as solidly democratic. Yet while pudding can have a broad identificatory appeal, thanks to the sheer indeterminacy of its meaning, from a particular custard to dessert in general, fish and chips still retains culturally specific associations that ultimately reinscribe the same class lines that Britons, whether Victorian or modern, so vigorously and vigilantly occlude. As Walton admits, fish and chips express "ethnic diversity as well as simplistic national solidarity, from the strong East End Jewish element in the early days of fish frying in London" (Walton, 2), but this national solidarity is almost immediately negated by associating fish and chips with those elements that vexed Victorian middle-class identity: the lower classes and Jewishness. As Walton grudgingly concedes, "[B]ecause the fish and chip shop was an open, democratic institution, it was also 'common,' as well as having enduring associations with decidedly ungenteel smells and behaviour, with dubious hygiene and an associated threat of poisoning and illness" (2). Thus, despite the insistence that fish and chips represent a democratic national identity, the mode and manner of eating them reinscribes both class lines and racial distinctions. Fish and chips are reassociated with contamination, with poisoning and illness, with the ungenteel working class and the domestic or foreign unemployed, with oil-smeared newsprint and the reek of rancid oil, with "lowlifes" such as Uriah and Fagin. Fish and chips reify all that is fetid, distasteful, and disturbing in a symbolic economy that proclaims class solidarity by constructing identity against race while simultaneously revealing, through dining, the fissures that threaten to rupture the comforting illusion of an "ordinary" democratic national identity.

Fish and chips. Roast beef and ale. Bangers and mash. Yorkshire pudding, plum pudding, spotted dick. Even as a youth, David Copperfield is able to distinguish between "classes" of food, distinctions that are particularly evident when he purchases his usual supper of pudding: ". . . I went without dinner, or bought . . . a slice of pudding. I remember two pud-

ding shops, between which I was divided, according to my finances"
(Dickens, 156). David recalls how the pudding at one shop was "made of
currants, and was rather a special pudding, but was dear, twopennyworth
being not much larger than a pennyworth of ordinary pudding" (156). He
describes "ordinary" pudding as "a stout pale pudding, heavy and flabby,
and with great flat raisins in it, stuck in whole at wide distances apart"
(156). His description could just as easily apply to John Bull or the "ordinary" gentleman: stout and pale, heavy and flabby. Ultimately, the depiction of food in the novels of Dickens reinscribes social distinctions: some
are flat and ordinary, some are special, and some are studded with jewels.
While a foreigner such as Henri Misson de Valburg assumes that pudding
represents a democratic national identity that reflects English liberalism,
the novels of Dickens reveal uncomfortable truths: the English-born gentleman knows that neither puddings nor men are created equally, and the
stratifications of society are sustained by the codification of dining and the
discrimination of food.

Works Cited

Barker, T. C., J. C. McKenzie, and John Yudkin, eds. 1966. *Our Changing
Fare: Two Hundred Years of British Food Habits.* London: MacGibbon &
Kee.

Briggs, Asa. 1969. *How They Lived: An Anthology of original documents written between 1700 and 1815, Vol. III.* Oxford: Basil Blackwell.

Burnett, John. 1979. *Plenty and Want: A social history of diet in England from
1815 to the present day.* London: Scolar Press.

Colley, Linda. 1992. *Britons: Forging the Nation 1707–1837.* New Haven,
CT: Yale University Press.

Dickens, Charles. 1996. *David Copperfield.* London: Penguin Books, 1850.

———. 1996. *Great Expectations.* Boston: Bedford, 1861.

———. 1998. *The Old Curiosity Shop.* Oxford: Oxford University Press,
1841.

———. 1966. *Oliver Twist.* London: Penguin, 1839.

Drummond, J. C., and Anne Wilbraham. 1939. *The Englishman's Food: A
History of Five Centuries of English Diet.* London: Alden Press.

Mayhew, Henry. 1985. *London Labour and the London Poor.* London: Penguin, 1861.

Miltoun, Francis. 1985. *Dickens' London.* London: Eveleigh Nash.

Pepys, Samuel. 1985. *The Shorter Pepys.* Ed. Robert Latham. Berkeley, CA: University of California Press.

Poovey, Mary. 1988. *Uneven Developments: The Ideological Work of Gender in Mid-Victorian England.* Chicago: University of Chicago Press.

Schor, Hilary. "'If He Should Turn to and Beat Her': Violence, Desire and the Woman's Story in *Great Expectations.*" In *Great Expectations.* Boston, MA: Bedford, 1996.

Tames, Richard. 2003. *Feeding London: A Taste of History.* London: Historical Publications.

Taylor, John A. 1997. *Popular Literature and the Construction of British National Identity, 1707–1850.* San Francisco: International Scholars Publications.

Walton, John K. 1992. *Fish and Chips and the British Working Class, 1870–1940.* Leicester: Leicester University Press.

CHAPTER 2

"Food Will Win the War"

Food and Social Control in World War I Propaganda

Celia M. Kingsbury

One of the most important areas of focus for World War I propaganda was that of food conservation. In both Great Britain and the United States, posters urged housewives to save flour and other staple items. In the U.S. Food Administration, director Herbert Hoover joined forces with the domestic science movement, a group of university-trained scientists and other professionals devoted to the application of the scientific method to the study, production, and preparation of food. Hoover used domestic science methods, as well as specific recipes designed to save wheat and meat, to enlist women in the war effort. In magazine articles and recipe booklets, he personally instructed them in ways to conserve food. In Great Britain, the Royal Society, an honorary association of British scientists, sought to influence government decisions affecting food prices and availability. In both cases, food became, first, the subject of scientific scrutiny, second, the subject of political debate, and finally as a result of these, a method of surveillance and social control.

The idea of food as a subject of scientific scrutiny is by now a fact of life as well as a focus of frequent controversy. The idea, for instance, of consuming irradiated fruits and vegetables is, to many of us, untenable. But the implementation of national food policies emerged with full force in Great Britain and in the United States during World War I. In the United States, domestic science had already established a foothold in universities and become the distinguishing feature of the "modern housewife." Laura

Shapiro, in her landmark history of domestic science, *Perfection Salad: Women and Cooking at the Turn of the Century*, argues that the goals of domestic scientists were to educate housewives in the new science of nutrition, to encourage the food industry to devise new food products that were at the same time nutritious, tasty, and easy to prepare, and to establish, as she explains, "the link between science and housework" (Shapiro, 4). Shapiro correctly reminds us that women were believed to be responsible for the moral well-being of the American character. Movements rooted in the superior morality of women such as the Temperance Movement, as well as later war propaganda campaigns, illustrate the truth of her assertions. When it came to new methods of housekeeping and food preparation, the use of "modern conveniences," housewives who refused, according to Shapiro, "bore the responsibility for the failings of the American home, failings that seemed to lead directly to poverty, disease, alcoholism, unemployment, and all the other social miseries apparent at the turn of the century" (4). Women, on the other hand, who had mastered the new calorie charts and understood the function of nutrition would become the nation's salvation. And, of course, men like John Harvey Kellogg, creator of the cornflake and founder of the Battle Creek spa, believed not only in the power of nutrition, but also in the role of food as a social force.

By the time the United States entered the First World War in 1917 and world food supplies became a political issue, the domestic science movement was fully entrenched in American life. World War I propaganda—posters, books, and magazine articles—asks women in the name of national security to conserve food, to resume preparing food from scratch, to use "foods obtainable near home," and to see that "large quantities of perishable foods [were] preserved for later use," that is, to can the produce from their victory gardens (Hoover, 25). The laborsaving products, commercially canned and prepackaged foods women had just learned to use, were earmarked for shipment to a badly war scarred Europe and to American troops. Using the language of domestic science, U.S. Food Administration propaganda brought women into direct contact with the war effort by urging them in wartime cookbooks to enlist in the "American Army of housewives" (*Selected Recipes*, 1). These new culinary soldiers who had once been held responsible for only the moral salvation of the country were now responsible for its military salvation as well.[1]

In a concerted effort to avoid food rationing which he vehemently opposed, U.S. Food Administration director Herbert Hoover took his appeal directly to American women, most often in ladies' magazines which appealed largely to a middle-class audience. Working-class women were also targeted in posters and other propaganda, but, as we shall soon see, appeals for food conservation were often moot, aimed at a working class that was stifled in its purchases by high prices and an already limited diet. In a feature published in the August 1917 issue of *Ladies' Home Journal*, "What I Would Like Women to Do," Hoover speaks of food shortages in Europe and goes on to demonstrate ways to rectify them in the home kitchen. Hoover echoes the idea here of the "American Army of housewives" as he issues the call for war service. "Every woman," he writes, "should feel herself definitely engaged in national service in her own kitchen and in her own home" (Hoover, 25). Employing the language of domestic science, Hoover maintains, "[t]he intelligent woman of America must make a proper study of food ratios, so that the most nutritious foods will appear in their proper proportions on the home table" (25). Since wheat was one of the commodities considered most necessary for success in war, Hoover's directive is followed by an article that includes recipes for baking bread from wheat substitutes. Accompanying the recipes and the patriotic call to duty was a pledge card for the housewife to fill in and mail directly to Hoover and the Food Administration.

Indispensable and responsible at the same time, the American woman became part of the war effort without once leaving her kitchen. She and her utensils, the weapons of domestic science, are brought, as the subtitle for both articles proclaims, "in Close Touch With Her Government." In honor of the first anniversary of Hoover's campaign, "Hooverization" as it was called, Mabel Dulon Purdy penned a feature article in the September 1918 issue of *McClure's Magazine*, in which she praises Hoover and the united effort to control food consumption. Purdy, author of *Food and Freedom*, alludes to "[t]wenty-two million housekeepers [who] have been appealed to, organized to no small degree, and to-day a people only one short year ago commonly without scientific knowledge—indifferently ignorant, in fact. . . . have to an encouraging extent been taught what there is to know about food" (Purdy, 28). The ultimate triumph of domestic science, however, is the additional news that twenty thousand graduating "college girls" have received diplomas from the Food Administration for completing an "authorized" course in food science, a detail which prompts Purdy to declare, "surely the Huns must waver!" (28).

Other magazines offered similar articles. The November 1918 issue of *The People's Home Journal*, published before the armistice on November 11, includes a Food Administration approved menu for Thanksgiving dinner, along with recipes for the preparation of the menu. According to Marion Harris Neal, the menu's creator, the "sensible economical, wholesome feast" is intended to maintain "the spirit of true economy necessary to be observed to help win the war" (Neal, 26). Opposite the Thanksgiving feature an advertisement for "Yeast Foam" boasts an attractive young woman dressed in the uniform of the Food Administration saluting over a perfect loaf of bread (27). In all of these attempts to Hooverize the American housewife, practitioners of domestic science join forces with the U.S. government and with industry in what amounts to a full media blitz. No "responsible" woman could ignore the call without risking the epithet, "slacker." Sheet music, a popular medium for propaganda, also reflects food service. The "Salvation Army Lassie," the subject for a ubiquitous poster as well, is the focus of the 1919 fundraising song, "Don't Forget the Salvation Army (My Doughnut Girl)." The smiling, helmeted woman on the cover of the sheet music holds a huge tub of doughnuts. The lyrics, "officially endorsed and adopted by The Salvation Army" tell of a woman who was "As brave as a lion but meek as a lamb" as she delivered coffee and doughnuts to "the sons of Uncle Sam." The doughnuts, provided as a result of food conservation at home, were admittedly an important part of Allied morale. For this reason, the song was, according to its publisher, "the only secular song number to which its unblemished seal has been affixed."[2]

Targeted for service at home and service abroad, women found themselves the subject of additional scrutiny in research devoted to female strength. Since women were being asked to perform in traditionally male areas aside from the kitchen, including the War Garden in both the United States and Great Britain, the image of women as the "weaker sex" needed to be overshadowed by that of a more robust figure capable of the war work she was expected to do. On October 21, 1917, the *Sunday Magazine* section of the *St. Louis Post-Dispatch* includes an article, "The Weaker Sex? No, Not Woman, But Man!" on the research of Dr. Dudley A. Sargent, a "noted authority" from Harvard who declares in an interview with the Post-Dispatch reporter that women are physically superior to men and only seem otherwise because they choose to hide their strength. Sargent's reasoning is specious; nevertheless, he argues that women could "make as good soldiers as men." Women are, he declares, "biologically . . . more of a savage than man, more of a barbarian, and she has therefore a greater proportion of physical endurance." The unnamed reporter calls this statement "one the fair sex may find rather unflattering" (*St. Louis Post-Dispatch*, 3). While this research does not aim directly at food consumption, it follows a cover drawing by Lee Conrey which depicts frontline soldiers opening "A Box From Home." In the drawing, two immaculately clean soldiers share a pie baked and shipped by what we can assume to be a Food Administration recruit. And in case anyone takes Sargent's argument too seriously, the back page of the magazine is devoted to the "Season's Latest Hats," in which no woman could possibly engage in physical activity (12). The kitchen here is still the most appropriate area of service, at least for the middle-class woman, and food conservation the most important realm of feminine endeavor.

Women, including those from the middle class, were nevertheless occasionally asked to perform physical labor as well. Since many farm laborers had enlisted, women were expected to take their places, as women had in factories, actions which undoubtedly Sargent would approve of wholeheartedly. An article by Edwin A. Goewey in *Leslie's Weekly* for March 30, 1918, suggests farm work is appropriate for three groups of women. Surprisingly, the first group listed is educated women, college students, and teachers who were free for the summer and wanted to do patriotic service. The second group, "working women, strong, but unskilled" make a logical choice for proposed farm work as do seasonal factory workers who make up the third. Such a "camp" at Bedford Hills, New York, overseen by Miss Ida H. Ogilvie, Professor of Geology at Columbia, according to the author, "proved beyond a doubt that women can do agricultural work," and that the presence of college women is crucial to maintain the morale of the working-class women (Goewey, 444).

In Great Britain, food control became part of a power struggle on the part of university scientists. Members of the Royal Society saw the war as a way of gaining a permanent position of importance in the British government and its decision-making process. The belief, according to historian Andrew J. Hull, was that "[a]ll policy questions were essentially scientific questions," a reflection of late nineteenth-century positivism and an extension, according to Hull, of public science, the belief that science should influence policy (Hull, 265). Royal Society members thus found their way onto committees involving the development of weapons and other war related research. In spite of the ulterior motive of control, the Royal Society became in a roundabout way the guardians of working class well-being when it came to food consumption. Their actions were based on the work of, among others, two members, D. Noël Paton and W. H. Thompson, who had, prior to the war, done dietary studies of the working class involving food consumption and metabolism (Paton and Thompson in Hull, 266). The purpose of these studies was to establish the number of calories, generally derived from bread, necessary to maintain a high level of productivity. Although Paton argued against the importance of vitamins in diet, these studies were scientifically important, if class-informed. In the words of William Bate Hardy, Biological Secretary of the Royal Society during the war, "food is fuel, and . . . the quality of fuel supplied fixes the output of work" (Hardy in Hull, 270). This let-them-eat-bread cynicism in relation to the working class did lead to a rejection of mandatory rationing of flour while other commodities—tea, margarine, bacon— were ultimately rationed. This thinking also ignored or failed to anticipate the obvious reality, reflected in earlier efforts at voluntary rationing—that the poor could not afford inflated war prices for meat, rationed or not. According to Arthur Marwick in his cultural history *The Deluge: British Society and the First World War*, during the war some heavy laborers ate as much as fourteen pounds of bread a week, the equivalent of a two-pound loaf a day (Marwick, 193). Mandatory rationing in Great Britain, never a reality in the United States during World War I, followed at least two efforts at voluntary rationing, including a propaganda campaign to limit that essential bread consumption by the working class. Established in late 1916, the British Ministry of Food, via the doomed efforts of highly unpopular Controller Lord Devonport, initiated the voluntary rationing campaign. A poster aimed at working-class women depicts an aproned housewife under the caption "She Keeps the Family to Victory Rations and Prevents Waste." She is, of course, measuring flour, the commodity so important to the maintenance of her family.[3]

Few publications based on the conservation methods of domestic science address working-class needs. Instead, most magazine articles and cookbooks were designed to recruit middle-class women as much as they were to instruct. Dorothy C. Peel, in her 1917 publication *The Eat-Less-Meat Book*, does cite two studies of the diet of British laborers—*Poverty, A Study of Town Life*, by Seebohm Rowntree, and *Life and Labour of the People in London*, by Charles Booth. Both, according to Mrs. Peel, draw the same conclusion: "'(1) The diet of the middle classes is generally more than adequate; (2) that of the well-to-do artisan is on the whole adequate; but (3) that of the labouring class is seriously inadequate'" (Peel, 19). These studies echo the findings of Paton and Thompson, but Mrs. Peel, after devoting several pages to these rather obvious statistics, goes on to address the needs of her middle and upper-middle-class readers by devising menus "which contain the ample quantity of nourishment to which well-to-do people are accustomed, which do not depart unnecessarily from the usual style of living demanded and appreciated in England, and which yet lessen the strain on the nation's supply of meat, wheaten flour and sugar . . ." (32).

Clearly, middle-class sacrifices were less severe and in both countries involved the use of newly devised recipes; Marwick calls them "culinary innovations" (196). On both sides of the Atlantic, science becomes the key to maintaining a middle-class lifestyle for the duration of the war, and in doing so, science also places war work within the confines of the home and the kitchen. Peel, who believes that any "intelligent" person can learn to cook "after a few weeks of scientific teaching," still prepares food largely from scratch, albeit with fewer eggs and less cream, although both are still present (Peel, 42). Many U.S. creations also begin with basic recipes, then recycle leftovers in combination with convenience items such as canned soup. Harbingers of the American favorite, tuna noodle casserole, these recipes not only reflected food science, they used relatively new products—Campbell's Soup and the new lard substitute, Crisco. Domestic scientists who devised these new recipes and promoted involvement in the war effort also wrote testimonials to the new products and published these in cookbooks devoted to wartime recipes. Janet McKenzie Hill, editor of *American Cookery*, a sort of semiprofessional journal of domestic science, published a cookbook called *War Time Recipes*, in which all the recipes call for Crisco. Coincidentally, the book is published by the Procter & Gamble Company. A *Saturday Evening Post* advertisement for Crisco offers "War Time Recipes" to readers for "10 cents in stamps," and praises Janet McKenzie Hill for "dedicating this new book to the American Woman" and creating recipes that "use successfully all the flours substituted for wheat" ("Ham," 2). Maude Marie Costello, whose connections include the University of Chicago and the Boston Cooking School, part of Hill's empire, sanctions Calumet Baking Powder in a booklet of war recipes. Other war cookbooks sanction nonfood products related to health. "War-Time Cook and Health Book" published by Lydia E. Pinkham Medicine Company declares on its back page, "Women's Service Requires Health and Strength." The way to achieve this freedom from headaches and other female ailments is to use Lydia E. Pinkham's Vegetable Compound. Each page of the cookbook includes recipes and testimonials from users who swear to the compound's value. And of course, printed at the very beginning of the book is the directive from Herbert Hoover to conserve food.[4] Science, industry, and government unite here to regiment the behavior of American and British women, to promote war service, but in a traditional and womanly manner.

Food also plays a role in wartime fiction, both British and American, reflecting both widespread concerns over its continuing availability and its place in war propaganda. And of course, food continues to serve as a delineator of social class, depicting the desire of middle-class housewives to conform, as culinary soldiers, to remain socially acceptable and perhaps upwardly mobile. Much literature published during the war lacks the cynicism of postwar works, which strip from war experience the jingoism of propaganda, as for instance poet Wilfred Owen did even during the war.[5] In postwar novels, propaganda becomes a source of conflict between those who remain safely on the home front and those who agree to "do their bit" without any indication of what they are about to face. Food as an instrument of propaganda, then, becomes an important part of the war experience as it begins to appear in literary works.

American author Willa Cather was herself a gourmet cook although she employed a French woman to do most of her cooking. In her 1922 antiwar novel, *One of Ours*, Cather uses the theories of domestic science, which she deplored, to create one of the novel's most negative characters, Enid Royce. In Enid, we see the relationship between housework and moral well-being to which Laura Shapiro alludes. A vegetarian and a teetotaler, Enid turns cooking and other aspects of homemaking into a system of extremely rigid morality. From raising virginal hens to serving a dinner of canned salmon and boiled eggs before embarking on a Prohibitionist mission, Enid is all about control. Her spotless kitchen is the envy of working farm women in the area. Hoover and the Food Administration are never an issue for Enid because she leaves the United States to become a missionary in China.[6] Religious zeal quashes patriotism here, but food becomes one of the areas where social control and conformity dominate.

The degree to which food plays a role in war fiction is in fact telling. Dorothy Peel's focus on maintaining acceptable standards of living in the midst of war portrays food rationing and shortages as more of a patriotic challenge than a life-altering issue. While the death and dismemberment of loved ones was both a private and public tragedy and Zeppelin raids disrupted civilian life, food consumption on the home front was above all political and, as we have observed, based on social class. In Ford Madox Ford's war tetralogy, *Parade's End*, which depicts the lives of upper-class characters, scarcity of food is never an issue. In fact food appears to be plentiful. In a pivotal scene in *Some Do Not . . .* , the first of the four novels that make up *Parade's End*, Christopher Tietjens, who suffers from memory loss as a result of shell shock, discusses at lunch with his wife Sylvia financial matters and related rumors about his relationship with the daughter of an old family friend. Bored and furious with Christopher for being the gentleman he is, Sylvia hurls a plate "contain[ing] two cold cutlets in aspic and several leaves of salad" at Christopher (Ford, 156). First, the menu here does not reflect any sort of deprivation on the part of Tietjens, who, while impoverished, is a member of the landed gentry. Further, Sylvia's salad, which falls on Christopher's uniform, is loaded with vinaigrette, a detail that forces Christopher to dry-clean the tunic. We are told that "Sylvia *knew* that she took too much of all condiments" (Ford's italics, 156). Sylvia is an especially careless and indulgent woman, but this meal seems to be business as usual.

H. G. Wells, in *Mr. Britling Sees It Through*, published during the war, also depicts upper-class indifference to possible food shortages. On August 4, 1914, the day war is declared, one of Britling's neighbors drives up in her car, which is loaded with food and other staples. Waving at the Britlings excitedly, she explains, "I thought I'd tell you. I've been getting food." The neighbor, Mrs. Faber, is contributing, of course, to the possibility of panic by hoarding. Irate because her grocer refuses to sell her more than a dozen cans of sardines, Mrs. Faber does plan to can the peas in their kitchen garden, but her hoarding would eventually become illegal. In her car are "two sides of bacon, a case of sugar, bags of rice, eggs, a lot of flour" (Wells, 188). Britling, who disapproves, says to his wife, "And that, . . . is how England is going to war! Scrambling for food—at the very beginning" (188). Among the many things Britling must cope with during the early days of the war, food is never an issue. While he may be uncertain about his foreign investments, Britling still has the means to take in and feed an upper-middle-class Belgian refugee, Mr. Van der Pant, whose wife is temporarily misplaced in England. She and their children have been sent to England earlier and, because of bureaucratic bungling, cannot at the moment be found. Dining with the Britlings on the first evening, Van der Pant notices that they are serving a Moselle. Apologetically, Britling asks, "Do you care . . . to drink a German wine?" Van der Pant replies that the wine is good and "[a]fter the peace it will be Belgian" (253). We can assume the wine has come from Britling's cellar, bought before the war, but the dinner once again suggests that "usual style of living" to which Dorothy Peel alludes (Peel, 32). Only those middle-class women who perhaps need to gain status from their patriotism must make a show of conservation. These are the women at whom, as we have seen, much propaganda was aimed, and one of the places where propaganda was most effective.

In many ways, propaganda, the demand for patriotic acts, establishes a system of surveillance, one of reward for performance and punishment for noncompliance, what Michel Foucault in *Discipline and Punish: The Birth of the Prison* defines as the Panopticon, which was literally an "architectural mechanism" designed to place prisoners, patients, schoolchildren, anyone "authorities" wish to watch, under constant surveillance. According to Foucault, the Panopticon has a much broader metaphorical application as a "generalizable model of functioning; a way of defining power relations in terms of the lives of everyday men." The Panopticon is "a figure of political technology that may and must be detached from any specific use" (Foucault, 205). Pledge cards mailed to Herbert Hoover, window cards placed conspicuously in the front window for the neighbors to see, the U.S. Food Administration uniform, all assure inquiring eyes that the woman of the house is doing her patriotic duty. British matrons "did their bit" by holding recruiting meetings and young women took to the streets to present white feathers, symbols of cowardice, to any able bodied male not in uniform.

Food especially becomes important as a tool of control when it becomes a reward for desired wartime behavior, as is depicted in Helen Zenna Smith's novel *Not So Quiet . . . Stepdaughters of War*. First published in 1930, *Not So Quiet* is the grim chronicle of a V.A.D. (Voluntary Aid Detachment) ambulance driver's experiences. Smith, pseudonym for freelance writer Evadne Price, obtained the war journal of a V.A.D. by the name of Winifred Young, who had turned over the diary with the stipulation that Price remain faithful to its tone. The resulting novel depicts an insurmountable rift between home front and front lines, a rift maintained by propaganda, social pressure, and, in the case of the V.A.D.'s, food deprivation.

First, we should acknowledge that a front line position will by nature be spartan. But the conclusions of the Royal Society's food studies also apply here. William Bate Hardy's assumption that "food is fuel, and . . . the quality of fuel supplied fixes the output of work" must, and in most cases does, inform the decisions of those supplying food to troops. For much of the war, for instance, the British were able to provide the men in the trenches with a daily ration of rum for their morning tea. Not so the ambulance drivers in *Not So Quiet*. In the opening pages of the novel, as one of the drivers prepares beef broth for the drivers, Smithy remarks that they are always hungry, that in fact they survive on "Bovril, biscuits, and slab chocolate" sent from home (Smith, 10). The canteen food is "vile at best," (10) and Smithy's descriptions of the food are indeed disgusting. Not only is the food badly prepared, in Smithy's words, "one is liable to find hair-combings in the greasy gravy; bits of plate leavings from the day before and an odd hairpin" (51). On top of the bad cooking, ingredients fall into the category of mystery meat, what Smithy calls "sinister looking joints of some strange animal" that the drivers "often go outside in groups to examine" (51). Because of the immense responsibility of the drivers— ferrying wounded and dying men in the dark on icy roads often under enemy fire—logic might dictate better treatment. Indeed, Smithy comments that the "hospital orderlies say they would never stand our rations." She goes on to explain that the orderlies "have Army rations, of course" (51). The key here is the reliance on the home front for what should be treats, but what becomes sustenance. Beef broth and chocolate have never been expected to feed an army, but the unwillingness to acknowledge that these middle class women are doing work that is both essential and exhausting—they are only civilians doing their bit—keeps them hungry.

At the root of the V.A.D.'s ill treatment is not only that desire to enlist civilians in the war effort, but also the focus, also reflected in the United States, on demanding war work of middle-class women, what Smithy refers to as "refined women of decent education" (Smith, 50). Middle-class women, aware of that historical burden of moral superiority, are in fact easy targets. Eager to please, eager to exert their moral superiority on wounded soldiers, and always reluctant to complain, the drivers, Smithy argues, are "the only class that suffers in silence, that scorns to carry tales. . . . We dare not face being called 'cowards' and 'slackers,' which we certainly shall be if we complain" (50). Home, in this case, becomes a threat, not a solace, the place where they will be disgraced if they return prematurely. The Panopticon, the home front, is most definitely "a way of defining power relations" and the V.A.D.s are at the bottom of the hierarchy.

Smithy's words address another aspect of middle-class compliance— the hope that contributions to the war effort will enhance social status, will grant upward mobility to those who seek it, as Smithy's mother does. Mrs. Smith is a rabid warmonger who will do anything to out-recruit her neighbor Mrs. Evans-Mawnington. Mrs. Smith's letters to Smithy shamelessly reflect the competition between the two: at one point Mrs. Smith "has seventeen more recruits than Mrs. Evans-Mawnington up to date" (Smith, 76). That these numbers reflect potential casualties, men maimed or killed, means little to either woman. Because their money was earned in manufacturing, jam in the Smith's case, both women seek an enhanced social status through the war service of their children. Mrs. Smith has no idea, nor does she wish to, of the horrible conditions under which her daughter lives; she does not fathom the devastation Smithy lives with daily. Smithy has quickly perceived the force of the jingoism that is prevalent back home. A brave V.A.D., she is one of England's "splendid daughters," who must not write home that she does not "believe in God or them or the infallibility of England or anything but bloody war and wounds and foul smells" (Smith, 30). Smithy believes telling the truth would result in being called a "silly hysterical little girl," or ultimately being disowned, as Smithy is. The truth can never win out over jingoism when upward mobility is the prize.

Evadne Price's novel reflects the power of propaganda on a middle class desperate to be socially accepted. Propaganda and its promise of enhanced social status—the reward for good behavior—keeps the V.A.D.'s within view of the Panopticon—under constant surveillance—and at the same time, implies their complicity. The role of food then becomes one of coercion, a way for those on the home front to maintain power. Food in the form of the care package becomes a function of the Panopticon, as a way of maintaining surveillance. As a reward for "doing their bit," the packages serve as a kind of bribe, while at the same time reminding the recipients of their complicity. Bovril and biscuits become part of the system of surveillance. As the drivers drink the last of a bottle of Bovril, someone points out, "If there isn't a parcel soon with a new supply we go out empty tomorrow" (21). The new supply arrives with a letter from Smithy's aunt, who is leaving her money to Smithy because she is "so *pleased* with [Smithy's] patriotism and noble example to all girls of [her] age" (Smith, 79). If Smithy remains compliant, she will receive more than potted meat for her service, she will become an heiress.

Popular fiction published during the war bears out the idea of rewards for patriotic behavior. A striking counterpoint to *Not So Quiet*, R. W. Campbell's 1918 novel *Dorothy V.A.D. and the Doctor* clearly served as a recruitment tool designed to lure young women who were looking for husbands into war service. At the beginning of her service in a British hospital, Dorothy is clearly interested in finding a man, but the bravery and sacrifices of her "dear boys" make of Dorothy a fine nurse. Still able to quote Ella Wheeler Wilcox after nursing war wounds, Dorothy is rewarded with the attentions and finally the hand of handsome Dr. Vawhan. In spite of British food shortages, Dorothy and her doctor drive into the countryside for tea. Unaware, it would seem, of rationing, Dorothy is concerned with their "first meal," with getting "the right blend of tea, the correct cut off the cake, and the dainty effects of a pretty picnic" (Campbell, 86). Only a few pages prior to this "pretty picnic," Dorothy has assisted her doctor in the amputation of a soldier's leg, but this tragedy does not tarnish the moment for them. On the contrary, Dorothy's unquestioning devotion to nursing layered over her "femininity" makes her the perfect wife. Vawhan, as he observes Dorothy's transformation from husband hunter to "one of England's splendid daughters," serves as the eyes of the Panopticon. At the end of their tea as he outlines for Dorothy his plans for the ideal postwar society, he tells her: "I've been watching you, old girl. I know how you have developed from a careless school-girl into a conscientious nurse" (95–96). Here, the compliant girl is rewarded for her good behavior with cakes and a husband, an enticing message for young women considering service and for those hoping to marry well.

Like the food scientists who argued for ample bread for working-class families to keep them productive, civilians on the home front used food as a way of eliciting desired behavior. The occasional jar of potted meat and tin of ginger tea biscuits compelled V.A.D.'s like Smithy to continue working "under conditions no professional scullery-maid would tolerate for a day" (Smith, 50). Housewives back home, whether supervising servants or doing the cooking themselves, were unwilling to relinquish their moral grip on household and family, and thus joined the fight by using domestic science to prepare tasty, but patriotic meals. Campbell's Soup and meatless meals became a way of life for a society that had roughly twenty years before, dined in splendor. Dietary sacrifices became a specific way to "do your bit" and avoid the censure of those prying eyes that supported the mechanism of the Panopticon. Whether under the auspices of the British Ministry of Food, the U.S. Food Administration, or zealous parents, food becomes a powerful political force. Because it is a necessary commodity, food served the cause of social control as well as any other source of propaganda. Incidentally, food also served Herbert Hoover well, in 1929, rewarding him, for at least one term, with the U.S. presidency.

Notes

1. For a study of food rationing in World War II, see Amy Bentley's *Eating for Victory: Food Rationing and the Politics of Domesticity* (Urbana: University of Illinois Press, 1998). Bentley focuses on World War II propaganda and what she refers to as the "Wartime Homemaker," devoting limited space to the precedent of Hoover's World War I propaganda campaign, the U.S. Food Administration, and the National War Garden Commission which in posters asks women "Are YOU a Victory Canner?"

2. My copy of this sheet music, according to a stamp on the cover, belonged to the Thelma Leah Rose School of Dancing, which we might speculate, used it as the score for a dance number.

3. Both American and British posters appealed to women to conserve food. Often posters are class specific, not only in the food items depicted, but in the clothing and hairstyles of the women.

4. The date printed on the Hoover conservation request is July 23, 1917, roughly three weeks before Congress formally appointed Hoover head of its newly created Food Administration.

5. In his strongest antiwar poem "Dulce et Decorum Est," Owen indirectly addresses poet Jessie Pope, author of numerous children's books, as well as *War Poems* and *More War Poems*, verse of the newspaper variety, by suggesting that if she had seen the death from phosgene gas described in the poem, "My friend, you would not tell with such high zest / To children ardent for some desperate glory, / The old Lie: Dulce et decorum est / Pro patria mori." Owen had in early drafts dedicated the poem to Pope, but removed the dedication in the final draft. See *The Collected Poems of Wilfred Owen* (New York: New Directions Books, 1965), 55.

6. For a full discussion of Enid Royce, see "Squeezed into an Unnatural Shape": Bayliss Wheeler and the Element of Control in *One of Ours*, in *Cather Studies Volume 6: Willa Cather and War*, ed. Steven Trout (Lincoln: University of Nebraska Press, December, 2006).

Works Cited

Bentley, Amy. 1998. *Eating for Victory: Food Rationing and the Politics of Domesticity*. Urbana: University of Illinois Press.

Booth, Charles. *Life and Labour of the People in London*. 17 vols. London: Macmillan, 1892–1903.

Campbell, R. W. 1918. *Dorothy V.A.D. and the Doctor*. London: W. & R. Chambers, Limited.

Cather, Willa. 1922. *One of Ours*. 1922. Reprint, New York: Vintage, 1991.

Ford, Ford Madox. 1950. *Parade's End*. 1950. Reprint, New York: Vintage, 1979.

Foucault, Michel. 1955. *Discipline and Punish: The Birth of the Prison*. 1975. Trans. Alan Sheridan. New York: Vintage.

Goewey, Edwin A. "Women to the Farmer's Rescue: The Hand that Rocks the Cradle Must Be the Hand to Feed the World." *Leslie's Weekly Illustrated Newspaper* 3264 (1918): 440+.

"Ham Croquettes that Are Different." *The Saturday Evening Post*. September 21, 1918, 2.

Hoover, Herbert. "What I Would Like Women To Do." *Ladies' Home Journal*. August, 1917, 25.

Hull, Andrew J. "Food for Thought?: the Relations between the Royal Society Food Committees and Government, 1915–19," *Annals of Science* 59 (2002): 263–298.

Kingsbury, Celia M. "'Squeezed into an Unnatural Shape'": Bayliss Wheeler and the Element of Control in *One of Ours*." *Cather Studies Volume 6: Willa Cather and War*. Ed. Steven Trout. Lincoln: University of Nebraska Press, December, 2006.

Leffingwell, Elmore, and James Lucas. "Don't Forget the Salvation Army (My Doughnut Girl)." New York: Broadway Music Corporation, 1919.

Marwick, Arthur. 1970. *The Deluge: British Society and the First World War*. New York: W. W. Norton Co., Inc.

Neal, Marion Harris. "Helping Hoover on Thanksgiving ay." *The People's Home Journal* 33, No. 11 (1918): 26.

Peel, Dorothy C. 1917. *The Eat-Less-Meat Book*. Reprint, New York: Gordon Press, 1975.

Purdy, Mabel Dulon. "Into the Kitchen with Hoover!: What the Food Administration Has Accomplished in Just One Year." *McClure's Magazine*, September, 1918, 28.

Rowntree, Seebohm. 1901. *Poverty: A Study of Town Life*. London: Macmillan.

Selected Recipes for Wartimes. 1918. N.P: Calumet Baking Powder Company.

Shapiro, Laura. 1986. *Perfection Salad: Women and Cooking at the Turn of the Century*. New York: Henry Holt.

Smith, Helen Zenna. 1989. *Not So Quiet . . . Stepdaughters of War*. 1930. Reprint, with a foreword by Jane Marcus, New York: The Feminist Press at the City University of New York.

War-Time Cook and Health Book. 1917. Lynn, MA: Lydia E. Pinkham Medicine Company.

"The Weaker Sex? No, Not Woman, But Man!" *The St Louis Post-Dispatch Sunday Magazine*, October 21, 1917, 3.

Wells, H. G. 1916. *Mr. Britling Sees It Through*. Reprint, London: Hogarth Press.

CHAPTER 3

Cooking *In Memory's Kitchen*

Re-Presenting Recipes, Remembering the Holocaust

Marie I. Drews

I wasn't quite expecting her description of it: "a story of the survival of the spirit amid the horrors of the Holocaust," she wrote. Jewish chef Joan Nathan's tribute (1996) to the newly edited collection *In Memory's Kitchen: A Legacy from the Women of Terezín* (1996), the cookbook that housed recipes collected by concentration camp victims, harbored an optimism that appeared incompatible with such an atrocious historical moment. There was a degree of truthfulness to Nathan's statement. Indeed, the book suggested endurance, both the physical survival of the documents and the survival of women's experiences revealed in lists of ingredients and directions for preparation. And there was a story: the story of Wilhelmina (Mina) Pächter's *Kochbuch*, a collection of recipes Pächter gathered and contributed to during her internment in Terezín[1] that kept safe tales of foods eaten before the war. Yet, as I read her article it seemed too simplistic for Nathan to suggest that the precarious compilation many called pejoratively a "Holocaust cookbook" served only as a "story of survival." I imagined the warped and worn pages that framed Pächter's fading font and the epithet's inadequacy became only more clear.

In September 1996, food writer Cara De Silva and translator Bianca Steiner Brown published Pächter's recipes for broad distribution in both scholarly and popular markets. Provided in the text were transcriptions of Pächter's eighty-two recipes originally written in German, as well as translations from the German into English. Because De Silva's collection was the first to make available recipes collected during the Holocaust and confirmed the common yet previously undiscussed practice of cookbook writing in the camps, Nathan's interest in the manuscript as well as her desire to publicize the collection in her *New York Times* feature is hardly surprising—she had already discussed the recipes two years earlier in her own Jewish cookbook (Nathan 1994, 355). At the close of her article, Nathan provides an image of one of Pächter's original manuscript recipes: *Gesundheits Kuchen (Pächters)* or Pächter's Healthcake. Curiously, alongside this manuscript image, one De Silva also includes in her collection, Nathan includes an adapted recipe for *Gesundheits Kuchen*, now composed of store-bought ingredients, illuminated by simple baking instructions, and explained in terms of nutritional information. While the Healthcake recipe survives in Pächter's hand, for Nathan, it also persists in an adapted, bake-able form that readers are tacitly encouraged to experiment with in their own kitchens.[2]

When I first read Nathan's article, I was not sure what to make of these two recipes lying side by side on the *Times* newsprint. Because I understood the social and memorial worth of cryptic ingredient lists and batter-spattered cookbook pages, I was concerned about how the "story of survival" Nathan so forthrightly announced would change as Pächter's recipes shifted from one form to another. Certainly there existed a void between the story told by the image of Pächter's manuscript recipe, one that was transcribed during a starvation so brutal it would lead to her death in Terezín in 1944, and the story told by Nathan's modified adaptation written over fifty years later. I was uncertain as to whether the foods produced from these recipes would resemble each other, not to mention whether either the recipes or their end products would represent the experiences and meanings Pächter intended. Thus, I did not know what I should do with Nathan's recipe even as it was the one that made the most sense in my kitchen. *Can I, or should I, bake the Healthcake and eat it, too? Or, should I keep Pächter's text on my shelf and mournfully celebrate her recipes only through reading them?* These questions I asked myself are the questions with which I begin my discussion.[3]

Through focusing on the recipe for *Gesundheits Kuchen*, I examine the translation and transformation of Pächter's original *Kochbuch* into De Silva's 1996 edited collection, *In Memory's Kitchen*, and then into Joan Nathan's adapted recipe. What is at stake in the transformation of Pächter's recipe is the question of how we will remember the women who suffered Holocaust torture even as the texts they produced are translated and adapted to suit current reading—or making—conditions. Reading cookbooks as "stories" that allow for "self-representation," as Anne L. Bower suggests (1997b, 31), enables one to study collections like Pächter's in order to understand the culinary, and therefore, life experiences of those who were killed during the Holocaust. While the cookbook genre seems to ask that food goods described in recipes be produced for consumption, politics of representation, especially those surrounding volatile historical periods like the Holocaust, reinforce the essentialist questioning of whether baking from the recipes is an "ideologically sound" treatment of a protected text or whether it fosters "misrepresentative" notions of what it means to responsibly mourn and memorialize. Pächter's recipes challenge this dualistic categorization by demonstrating how the important intersections of cooking, story, history, and memory allow for an alternate genre and practice of Holocaust representation.

Given the loaded moment of cultural production from which Pächter's cookbook emerges, I situate my discussion of her text within the context of Holocaust representation debates. The accessibility and (seemingly) safe nature of the cookbook genre complicates traditional literary forms of Holocaust writing and highly contested debates over how Holocaust texts should be used by public audiences.[4] By nature, the cookbook genre facilitates what Lucy M. Long calls "culinary tourism," the practice of "exploring" differing food traditions as a traveler explores new landscapes, either abroad or from home (Long 2004b, 20). Translations and adaptations of these cookbooks which advocate the practical "use" of Holocaust recipes—namely, De Silva's and Nathan's writings—aid the culinary tourist and seem at the outset to support appropriative and exploitive tourisms that provide edible souvenirs rather than lessons about how to protect privileged documents, documents that carry with them the everyday reminiscences of those exterminated in the camps. I argue, however, that through participating in a different kind of reading (and practice) of Holocaust recipes, a reading which pays particular attention to the uniqueness of genre, the complexities of translation, and the value of the produced foodstuffs, it is possible to rework the act of baking from what is often too quickly read as the culinary tourist's disconnected "experience for experience's sake" into a more engaged form of culinary understanding. This understanding allows readers—and cooks alike—to see the ways that, through translation and transformation, the recipe collection's rendering of history must necessarily shift in order to maintain its currency and thus its practicability in the present if it is to maintain its initial goal of cultural, historical, and culinary remembrance.

Perhaps one of the most contested facets of cookbook and recipe study is the degree to which representations of food traditions, especially those presented in the form of ingredient lists and cooking directions, can reveal reputable information about a people's history and culture. Cookbook scholar Anne L. Bower remarks that both historical and formal features of the genre hinder the attention paid to food texts. Food, especially in its gendered association with women's work, has been deemed "unworthy of serious study"; the "ubiquity" of recipes and cookbooks, as well as their "formulaic" and prescriptive nature, surely leaves them as trifling subjects for investigation (Bower 1997a, 6–7, 8).[5] When these contested genres intersect with Holocaust studies, a field in which the representation of history functions to maintain the memory of a devastated people, the ideological stakes of "responsible" representation go up and are complicated further as they are associated with the difficulty of reading food texts in an environment where their study remains questioned.

Understandably, then, explicit study of food and food texts has remained largely absent from Holocaust scholarship.[6] This absence is best illustrated and explained by Gary Weissman's use of a food metaphor to describe one critique of American representations of the Holocaust. In *Fantasies of Witnessing: Postwar Efforts to Experience the Holocaust*, Weissman notes that a common fault of many American renderings is "sweetening or sugarcoating" Holocaust history and experience, a practice that "involves depicting it as a story with a happy ending, thereby denying its true horror" (Weissman 2004, 12). Because the language of food and cooking is not usually associated with trauma but rather with flavorful production, Weissman's description seems rhetorically justified. Joan Nathan's euphemism for the cookbook as a "story of survival" invokes Weissman's "sweetened" representation as it emphasizes what endures rather than what was lost. For some, the cookbook's "sweetening" elicited ardent antagonism: director of the Simon Wiesenthal Center in Jerusalem, Efraim Zuroff, called the cookbook "sick," its recipes "imaginary" (Gross 1997), and Holocaust scholar Norman Finkelstein called it "kitsch" (1997, 83n76).[7] It is true that detailed descriptions of death and devastation are missing from the recipes like *Leberknödel* (Liver Dumplings), *Zwetschken Strudel* (Plum Strudel), and *Wasserbett Teig* (Waterbed Dough); rather, the outcome of the book suggests the survival of and the survival through decadent dinners and desserts. For some, this marketing of a Holocaust text that presented recipes for the sweet and the savory rhetorically and materially trivialized a pernicious time period, easing its dreadfulness with baked goods.

Because they were worried that the importance of the cookbook as a piece of Holocaust literature might be slighted if it were used in the kitchen, several scholars who examined *In Memory's Kitchen* after its publication declared that, while the text was important, the recipes were not for the making. Michael Berenbaum, director of the United States Holocaust Memorial Museum (USHMM), endorses the recipe collection in his foreword to De Silva's book. He cautions, however, that it is not a "conventional cookbook" and thus "is not to be savored for its culinary offerings but for the insight it gives us in understanding the extraordinary capacity of the human spirit to transcend its surroundings, to defy dehumanization, and to dream of the past and of the future."[8] Berenbaum worries that readers will take the book into the kitchen in an attempt to participate in (or perhaps tour) a history that is incomprehensible, an "inner courtyard of . . . hell" that no one can imagine (Berenbaum 1996, xvi). Berenbaum's desire to protect Pächter's text was complicated by its fervent marketing and subsequent popularity. The book sold over fifty thousand copies in its first year of publication and appeared on the *New York Times* Notable Books of the Year in 1996, suggesting a high number of individuals buying and possibly cooking from the book (Innes 1997; *New York Times* 1996). It was clear from reviews of the *Kochbuch* in magazines like *People* (Green 1996, 30), *Newsweek* (Shapiro 1996, 73), and even the cooking magazine *Bon Appetit* (Steel 1997, 24) that readers outside the academy were eating it up.

The book's simultaneous academic importance and wide-ranging recognition heightened tensions between scholarly and public readers, and more importantly, Holocaust and kitchen contexts. For Tim Cole, author of *Selling the Holocaust* (1999), the popularity of De Silva's collection certainly illustrates public consumption of the Holocaust, an event which he argues has "emerged as an icon in the West." Cole suggests that this consumption takes place as individuals visit late twentieth-century *tourist* venues (Auschwitz, Ann Frank House, Yad Vashem, USHMM) whose voyeuristic exhibits and souvenirs promote the Holocaust's iconic treatment (Cole, 15–16). Cole uses the example of the availability of a Holocaust text as unconventional as a recipe collection to explain the consumption that he sees taking place through these tourist attractions. In doing so, he locates the publication of *In Memory's Kitchen* in the same arena as this souvenir-gathering tourism (15): "not only is it possible to buy a 'Holocaust' cookbook in the 1990s, but it is also possible to 'consume' the 'Holocaust' equivalents of 'kitsch or trashy literature . . . picture postcards, toys and games, and battlefield tourism,'" he writes, quoting George Mosse's 1990 discussion of trivializing objects produced after World War I.

What is most intriguing here is not Cole's abhorrence of the cookbook but rather his positioning of it within discussions of Holocaust tourism and kitsch. In his offhand reference, he suggests that Holocaust representation, which takes place in such a form as a cookbook, somehow solidifies the notion of negligent memorialization. Unlike Berenbaum who speaks from within the museum institution and argues that the text is far from trivial but that it must be handled reverently—read only—to remain respectful, Cole reads the cookbook as "kitschen" literature, an irresponsible low-brow representation for sale and selling well. For him, it seems, the recipes cannot be separated from their maligned kitchen beginnings and are bought merely for public consumption, tokens of a misguided tourist experience.

The relationship that Cole draws between kitsch and the cookbook genre in his critique explains the near absence of Holocaust scholarship that engages with food studies. Catherine A. Lugg defines kitsch as "the beautiful lie" that "comforts the receiver though the exploitation of cultural myths and readily available symbolism" with intentions to "pacify, not provoke" (Lugg 1999, 5). Her analysis of kitsch as a political strategy offering consolation and conciliation is important in relation to food studies, especially considering the many social and cultural roles food and consumption play that have little to do with the nourishment of one's body. Does talk about food production and recipes (as opposed to food scarcity and starvation) in terms of history, particularly violent history, then, inevitably lead toward Weissman's historical "sweetening," the safeguarding of a past, which for many remains too terrible for serious engagement?

In the literary marketplace, food rhetoric, images, practices, and locales—as they are employed both playfully and euphemistically—have aided in the alleviation of social, political, and cultural ills, thus trivializing literatures and products produced in the kitchen, or what becomes the "kitschen." When situated in the context of the kitsch, food talk becomes a novelty, especially as it is related to the resourcefulness and creativity associated with producing food goods. It is not surprising that David C. King's children's book *World War II Days: Discover the Past with Exciting*

Projects, Games, Activities, and Recipes (2000), a book which pacifies inter/national history for younger audiences, would include recipes. When food becomes novelty, the spaces associated with food production become safe spaces. For instance, the images on the covers of Joanne Lamb Hayes's books *Grandma's Wartime Kitchen* (2000) and *Grandma's Wartime Baking Book* (2003) suggest that while the war may have been going on outside, standing in a gleaming kitchen with Mom or Grandma, wrapped in a clean apron, was a place where one could remain untouched, at least physically, by international devastation. Set alongside popular notions of kitsch sentimentality, initial concerns about readers' response to Pächter's recipes are warranted. It is telling that when I first told my peers about my work with De Silva's collection, some looked at me confused, thinking that recipes from a "Holocaust cookbook" must necessarily explain how to make soup from shoes or how to cook vermin. Further investigation of De Silva's collection, however, demonstrates that this was indeed not the case.

Employing Lucy M. Long's discussion of culinary tourism offers a third possibility of reading the cookbook whereby readers can navigate Cole's extremism and Berenbaum's conservatism, stand-ins for essentialist critiques of "incorrect" and "correct" representations, and the cookbook can be used in ways that allow for multivalent understandings of the Holocaust experience. Long defines culinary tourism as "intentional, exploratory participation in the foodways of an other—participation including the consumption, preparation, and presentation of a food item, cuisine, meal system, or eating style considered to belong to a culinary system not one's own." This tourism is practiced not as a response to hunger but rather "for the sake of experienc[e]" (Long 2004b, 21), an experience that Barbara Kirshenblatt-Gimblett suggests locates individuals in "a space of contact and encounter, negotiation and transaction" (Kirshenblatt-Gimblett 2004, xii). What sets culinary tourism apart from the simple act of eating is the suggestion that a culinary tourist's desire for food is driven by "curiosity" and a longing to experience difference rather than by physical needs of "hunger" or satiety (Long 2004a, 6).

The foodways of the "other," Long explains, involve the historical, regional, religious, cultural, and economical facets of preparing, eating, and serving food. The culinary tourist will "negotiate" these foodways as "exotic," as "edible," and/or as "palatable" depending on the way that the specific foodway in question is framed, named or translated, explicated, selected for a menu, or adapted (Long 2004b, 37). The outcomes of the negotiation process Long outlines here pertain largely to the ingestion of an "othered" food or foodway. *Will this food be too exotic to eat? Can I eat it? Will it taste good?* It is important, too, to extend this negotiation process to cover not just the taste and edibility of a food but also its significance within the culture in question. *Will it mean something important—for me or for others—if I prepare and eat this food?* This final negotiation is of utmost importance in deciphering the several translations of Pächter's cookbook, translations that confuse tastes, stories, and histories.

Although the concept of tourism itself is almost always imbued with negative associations, analyzing the differing representations of Pächter's recipes through the lens of culinary tourism allows readers to begin to work through Joan Nathan's curious juxtaposition of the original recipe image and its modern-day adaptation. What lies in the visual space between the photograph of Pächter's manuscript recipe and Nathan's rewriting of it is what I see as a series of five translations through script, language, and form—transformations that directly address the many facets of culinary tourism. Examining these translations and their accompanying contexts demonstrates engaged reading processes that readers must practice when working with the recipe genre, especially when that genre is derived from such traumatic circumstances. Conscious application of the tenets of culinary tourism allows readers to understand the recipes' important cultural meanings. Simultaneously, it also allows them to further interrogate their own relationship with the recipes in terms of purpose, practicability, and participation, helping them to decipher the ethical advantages and consequences of their decision to bake or not to bake.

Pächter's recipe collection surfaced over two decades after her death when one of several strangers who had been keeping the book safe during those years arrived at the home of Anny Stern, Pachter's daughter. "When first I opened the copybook and saw the handwriting of my mother, I had to close it," remarked Stern who had fled to Palestine in 1939 to escape the Holocaust and eventually immigrated to the United States (De Silva 1996b, xvi, xxxviii). Stern's initial response to the cookbook, to her mother's handwriting, offers an important starting place to examine the meaning and form of recipe publication, a genre where the memorial value maintained in a handwritten manuscript cannot be overlooked. For Stern, it is the sight of her mother's script in the cookbook that allows the words to come alive, and she is able to remember her mother; the holiness of the book, therefore, can be attributed to a visual confirmation of life that appears in the manuscript pages.

For these reasons, what can be argued as the most authentic version of Pächter's recipe for *Gesundheits Kuchen* appears in Cara De Silva's text and Joan Nathan's article as a photograph of the original recipe recorded in the cookbook delivered to Stern's door. It is here where readers see the closest representation of the text as it would have looked at the time of its production. According to Miriam Meyers, handwriting plays a significant role in the reading of recipes as it signals specific memories about the writer or the recipe or the circumstances of the writing. Handwritten recipes connote the familiar and familial facets of food production and allow for the persistence of personal remembrances associated with the production. More than recipes, more than foodways, Stern saw her mother in the copybook (2001, 108).

The photograph of the original document also provides a visual link between the cookbook genre and more conventional types of writing produced in the camps (letters, diaries, poetry, stories, etc.). This link is crucial considering the exclusion of kitchen texts from canonical Holocaust literatures. Through including the photograph, De Silva privileges the authority of the manuscript recipe as a Holocaust artifact that confirms the presence of written discussions about food, about hunger as Myrna Goldberg would suggest (2003, 162). Certainly De Silva recognized the value in associating the handwritten recipes with other forms of literature; perhaps that is why she also chose to incorporate a selection of Pachter's poems and letters (which are translated by her grandson, David Stern) at the back of the recipe collection (De Silva 1996a, 81–103), even including a photographic sample of each genre in manuscript form.

While *In Memory's Kitchen* was the first widely published *Kochbuch* that came out of the camps, Pächter's text was not outstanding as a piece of Holocaust literature. In fact, recipe recording was a common practice for victims as they were moved into ghettos and then into camps. De Silva names three recipe collections in the Beit Theresienstadt in Israel, including those of Malka Zimmet, Arnostka Klein, and Jaroslav Budlovsky, and she explains that even though collections at Yad Vashem have not yet been organized in regards to food, there are "certainly" more recipe collections housed there (De Silva 1996b, xxix). Similarly, several recipe texts were produced in Ravensbrück, a women's camp north of Berlin. In her study of that camp, Rochelle G. Saidel also names four recipe writers: Rebecca Buckman Teitelbaum, Eva Hesse Ostwalt, Francesca Kwester-Stern, and Anna Maria Berensten-Droog (2004, 53–57). While De Silva's work garnered popularity and provided voice to recipe writers, unsuccessful attempts at circulation of this genre were made before De Silva's project. Edith Peer, a former prisoner at Ravensbrück, produced five hundred copies of her book *Ravensbrück 1945, Fantasy Cooking Behind Barbed Wire* (n.d.), but because the book included some recipes that were not kosher, her cookbooks were subsequently unwanted and discarded (Gilletz 2003).[9] Advancing technology and a resurging interest in food study may aid in the transmission and preservation of cookbooks; however, many have yet to be examined by scholars, and an innumerable amount remain hidden in museums and family archives. A digital copy of Andela Hrg's 1942 *Recepti* book, available online as a part of the United States Holocaust Memorial Museum's Jasenovac Collection, provides a positive example of the possibility of preservation of forgotten food texts that we can only hope to see more of in the future.

Because the manuscript offers visual confirmation of the text's rooted history, the first translation of Pächter's handwritten recipes into typescript is the initial step of the cookbook's transformation from a Holocaust artifact into a tool that supports the tourist experience. Visually, the recipes become less personal and more uniform as the blank space between them replaces the tight-knit cursive script. In the recipe for *Gesundheits Kuchen*, readers do not see the swooping hook Pächter puts on the "n" in the word *Kuchen*, nor do they see the line, the intended pause, drawn between the final preparation and baking instruction and the reference to how much batter should be put in the cake pan. Readers are also unaware that the space between *Gesundheits* and *Kuchen*, which to native speakers of German seems to be a typographical error, appears clearly in Pächter's handwriting (De Silva 1996a, 62).[10] Artfulness surrenders to the standardized Times New Roman font.

The published version of Pächter's recipes is also much clearer than the manuscript. If for De Silva "the story of the book is as much or more in the mistakes than it is in the actual recipes," as she mentioned in an interview shortly after the book's publication, readers must question how these mistakes are glossed over if not remedied in the word processing (De Silva 1996c). As Cara De Silva and translator Bianca Steiner Brown decipher the script, illegible words must be filled in; at times they are unable to acknowledge additions made in the manuscript that are not acknowledged as additions in the type. In the recipe for *Apfelknödel*, it is apparent in the manuscript that the writer of the recipe almost forgot to specify that "etwas Fett"—or "some fat"—needed to be added to make the dumpling dough (De Silva 1996a, 11). If the typed recipe is read without looking at the original manuscript, there is no suggestion that this ingredient was one the writer remembered to add after the fact (13). The transformation into type is not exact; at times it requires speculation and interpretation, especially for recipes that are "muddled or incomplete," as De Silva explains, missing ingredients, process description, or punctuation (De Silva 1996b, xli). The culinary tourist's experience, then, begins in this first translation as the universal typescript facilitates his/her ability to decipher the manuscript.

Elizabeth L. Eisenstein's work on the advancements of print culture provides an explanation of the curious and complicated ideological shift that takes place in the movement from script to print. Eisenstein argues that this change reinforces the "common" whereby a mass-produced text loses its exceptionality. In their reproduction and ready availability, texts that were once unique become "ubiquitous," she notes. Anne L. Bower's suggestion that the study of cookbooks has suffered because of their "ubiquity" reflects Eisenstein's discussion of print culture. Indeed, recipes are available everywhere—they are printed in magazines, newspapers, and even on the packaging of foods themselves. While, as Eisenstein notes, advancements in printing technology cannot be judged too harshly because they have made available texts that might disappear otherwise, she maintains that the ever-accruing numbers of printed texts allow readers to "overlook" the important texts that are available. De Silva's and Nathan's decisions to provide the manuscript recipe alongside the printed recipe encourage readers to overcome what Eisenstein calls the "current myopia" of the effects of print culture (Eisenstein 1997, 17). Ultimately, De Silva and Nathan emphasize the need for attribution to the original text, and leave an image, a script, a person to fill what appears to be unexceptional typescript.

Bianca Steiner Brown's translation of the recipes from German into English marks the second transformation of the text. This translation makes Pachter's recipes "accessible" to readers who are unable to understand the complicated language of the original, thus exhibiting a key trait of Long's definition of culinary tourism (2004b, 38). The public's post-translation embrace of *In Memory's Kitchen,* a genre otherwise ignored by the academy, signaled that readers were desirous of this kind of text, one which allowed English-speaking culinary tourists to encounter protected pre-Holocaust foodways. At issue in this transformation, however, is that translation is not a simple process of transmitting meaning to meaning through language. Rather, it is a process of recreating knowledge and meaning using alternate words that may not necessarily carry with them the exact same cultural and historical definitions and contexts. At times, Long notes, this kind of translation requires "invention" (Long 38). The life of the recipe resides not only in the handwriting, but also in the nuanced language, the detailed instructions—all part of the talking that the cook does from the page.[11] Reading Pächter's recipes as resistant to the Nazi extermination project, as De Silva and other scholars suggest, depends on the slight variation in language that is always complicated by translation.

Problems occurring in this kind of language translation are typical to most Holocaust texts, in which some words do not cross over from German into English. According to De Silva, the majority of the recipes are written in German but strict German translation is difficult, even impossible, in cases where the Czech language appears or where the German "is sometimes ungrammatical, rough-hewn, Slavicized, or misspelled." De Silva is aware of issues of translation; although there were some clarifications made, she argues, the recipes were kept "as literal as possible," and while clarifications were added in brackets, no corrections were made (De Silva 1996a, xlii). Despite the emphasis De Silva puts on keeping the recipes "authentic" even in translation, changes take place as the recipes are re-created in a new language and a new time period. Brown, a former inmate of Terezín, chooses to retain original amounts and ingredients when she translates the recipes into English (i.e., she maintains use of the measurement "decagrams"); at times, however, she does explicate cooking language for the reader using bracketed phrases. For instance, in the recipe for *Milchrahmstrudel*, Brown clarifies the meaning of the term "snow" as "[stiffly beaten egg whites]" (De Silva 1996a, 59). There is also a glossary included with the text to encourage further understanding of the translated terms.

While Brown and De Silva have the best intentions of maintaining the literal authenticity of the recipes as they translate them from one language and era to another, the bracketed explanations serve the larger purpose of making more organized and detailed recipes that were recorded during chaos. Readers inarguably use these additions to help them make sense of the recipes, but they must also read the language beyond the brackets carefully if they are to be able to understand the recipes' larger ideological importance. If recipes are indeed media through which their writers "let fantasy run free," as the most quoted recipe phrase from the cookbook purports (De Silva 1996a, 52), reading past the instructions for material production is an essential process in understanding how the victims used recipes as what De Silva calls, "an act of psychological resistance, forceful testimony to the power of food to sustain us, not just physically but spiritually" (1996b, xxvi). Close reading illustrates how hope for the possible is a common thread that runs through the recipes: the phrase "as desired" appears several times; generosity is encouraged when adding ingredients; and women are allotted the authority to make choices.[12] There is warmth. Provisions are plenty. Recipe writers make use of active verbs suggesting that readers can follow the instructions of those who once cooked rather than the inflammatory and dehumanizing commands of Nazi officials and the *Sonderkommando*, interned Jewish prisoners who were made to violently commandeer fellow prisoners. Reading beyond the instructional purpose of the recipes cognizant of the complexity of translation adds richness and possibility to the cookbook genre as a whole.

Accordingly, however, one cannot assess the purpose of Brown's bracketed clarifications without considering the debate over the appropriateness of baking from the book. Brown's inclusions aid readers in understanding how a dish is put together—she often identifies when recipe writers have omitted a step, making sure that current readers are able to follow the process (De Silva 1996a, 12).[13] For Brown, a previous editor of *Good Housekeeping* and *Gourmet* magazines, the recipes cannot be translated into English without being set up in a way that allows readers to best understand *how* they might go about preparing the foods listed. Creative, close reading of the recipes does not preclude the fact that the recipe genre is set within kitchen space. The "Practical Notes" that read as a glossary of terms help present-day readers to determine amounts: a "coffeespoon," for instance is "smaller than a teaspoon"; a "decagram" is equal to 0.35 ounces (De Silva 1996a, 79). Measurement tables that infer the same kind of information appear in "conventional cookbooks"; they not only suggest, but also intend that its recipes will be reproduced. The recipes become real only as they are written in relationship to a real kitchen, and yet they maintain their larger social and historical meaning when they are examined as writing that cannot be contained within that kitchen.

Reading the recipe genre on these two planes encourages inquiry: does translating and making Pächter's text, or using it as what could be called an "agent of culinary tourism," co-opt the original and create for it a new representation that is not memorial but appropriative? Can one read or use the recipe on one plane and not the other? In the case of Brown's and De

Silva's and even Nathan's translations, the recipes call for both careful, creative reading, and production; they are translated in ways that responsibly
facilitate both. In his essay, "The Task of the Translator," Walter Benjamin
provides a helpful explanation of the key facets of the practice and the
problems of translation that allow for us to move away from the idea that
translation—in both language and practice—must inevitably entail
appropriation. Benjamin writes, "While content and language form a certain unity in the original, like a fruit and its skin, the language of the
translation envelops its content like a royal robe with ample folds. For it
signifies a more exalted language than its own and thus remains unsuited
to its content, overpowering and alien" (Benjamin 1968, 75). Benjamin's
reading of translation is powerful in that it suggests that translation is a
celebration of the original, "a royal robe with ample folds," not a trivial-
ization of the initial language which cannot be reinscribed as it was in its
lifetime (for Benjamin, "a translation issues from the original—not so
much from its life as from its afterlife" [71]). When De Silva includes
both the image of Pächter's manuscript recipe and the German typescript,
she demands that readers be aware of the "exalted" original, which will
remain "overpowering and alien" because of the moment and circumstances of its inscription. The original is not lost, but it cannot be re-created. It must be dressed anew, in a different language, a different reading,
and a different practice.

The reworking of Pachter's recipe to fit modern-day kitchen know-
how is a challenging task, however, one that leaves much power in the
hands of both the translator *and* the reader. The ramifications of such a
revisioning, if inappropriate, can be quite dangerous. They can mean the
difference between a solemn, memorial experience and a comfort-bearing
or novelizing encounter that serves the purpose of experimentation. The
translator is responsible for providing significant contextual and historical information as well as valid interpretation, and thus she or he has a
bearing on how readers see and understand the worth of a text in the
world. At the same time, the ideological responsibility of a specific translation must also evolve out of the way that it is read and interpreted.
Readers need be aware of what they are reading, and they, too, need be
cautious of their motivations and expectations, grappling with the
recipes on both literal and figurative planes. In the case of work with
Pächter's recipes and others recorded during the Holocaust, the absence
of translator/reader engagement enables the further deterioration of food
and kitchen studies as a viable and valuable field of historical study.

What engaged culinary tourism asks is that as both translators and readers transform a recipe that what "once was" into a food good that is "possible now" is that they do so sensitive to the multiple meanings that also inevitably shift in the making.

When Joan Nathan chooses to feature Pächter's cookbook in her *New York Times* article (1996) and then adapt the recipe for *Gesundheits Kuchen,* she moves another step beyond Cara De Silva's work in meeting the readers' desires to pursue culinary tourism, to experience the food goods Pächter chronicles in her recipes. Readers will remember that, for Lucy M. Long, "adaptation" is one of the last "strategies of negotiation" of an othered foodway (Long 2004b, 43). Nathan does not signal that the recipe she includes is a translation; rather she simply marks it as "adapted" from *In Memory's Kitchen.* There are significant changes in this adaptation including the substitution of certain ingredients (milk for cream) and the substitution of current kitchen implements used for baking (Pächter's recipe calls for the cake to cook for forty-five minutes in a conventional oven set to 350 degrees). One of the most striking visual changes is the breaking down of the instructions into an orderly list of steps that readers should follow rather than a list of phrases that cite action. Nathan's tailoring of the Healthcake recipe caters to readers' use even more so than De Silva's text in that the language Nathan uses suits contemporary kitchen-speak; in fact, it even benefits readers' curiosity regarding nutritional information—Nathan's Healthcake has a whopping 545 calories and 30 grams of fat per slice.

The inclusion of nutritional information with a recipe that was produced out of fatal starvation is an act that readers need hold up for ethical consideration, an act that would certainly fuel Tim Cole and Norman Finkelstein in their labeling of the cookbook as "kitsch." Does Nathan remain a conscientious translator by providing this information? I admit it was the inclusion of this nutritional information that originally instigated my questioning of the use of Pächter's recipes. I was disgusted. My response mirrored Rona Kaufman's response to reading about the use of Pachter's recipe: "I felt a little sick to my stomach," she writes (Kaufman 2004, 427). It was too audacious of an inclusion to merit my respect, especially in the context of the minimal calorie intake of those suffering in the camps. Norbert Troller, also a victim of Terezín internment, writes of the hunger he experienced and parenthetically notes that food rations were "approximately one-third of the customary calories in their most unappetizing form" (Troller 1991, 94).[14] Following Troller, De Silva remarks that in Terezín, "the fewest calories . . . would have to go to those least likely to survive" (De Silva 1996b, xxxviii).

Continued interrogation of the nutritional information, however, does prompt an analysis of the beneficial meanings its inclusion might create for the Healthcake, meanings that might not be created in any other way. As time moves forward, so too must representations of a text like Pächter's, and in the case of recipes, perpetuation necessitates the use of shifting kitchen discourses. Ingredients must change. Methods of cooking and preparation must be altered. Here, the included nutritional information provides another example of this rhetorical shifting, one that happens to be more striking yet perhaps useful, nonetheless. Today, readers know that one slice of cake would use up 46 percent of their daily recommended value of fat and 27 percent of their caloric intake (based on a 2,000 calorie diet). The reader as translator must take that knowledge and situate its meaning in dialectical relationship to its past meaning, its meaning within the context of starvation.

In a contemporary culinary culture that fears fat, readers might not make the cake, but knowing the nutritional information does allow them a new language to develop an understanding of Holocaust hunger. What does it mean when those without food, those forced to endure a death diet, those who, as Troller explained, were allowed access to one-third of the calories they needed to survive, think of and write a recipe for a piece of such decadent cake, a piece of cake with such a high caloric content? Their recipes become spaces, albeit rhetorical, where they are able to have *more* than enough, more than what is necessary, more than even a starving body could handle. They are able to have what they dream, what they deserve. They are able to resist, as De Silva argues. The nutrition information, while alarming, becomes a tool that aids the comparative understanding of subsistence and starvation. And while there will always be fear of what might be lost in shifting kitchen discourse in this way, cultural practices must progress so that their texts do not disappear—translation and, here, adaptation (both in linguistic and sociocultural forms) become a necessary part of preservation and continuation, making meanings in the present that allow for a more convincing understanding of the past.

The fifth translation that completes the process of culinary tourism calls for the recipe to take shape as an edible good. Recipe texts, I argue, must be transferable from time period to time period so that they can be reproduced within a changing culture. The word "reproduced" here in relation to the first four transformations signals readers' ability to best understand the food product Pächter might have had in mind when she wrote down the recipe. In this last translation, it is necessary to get out the flour and the eggs and produce, for recipes call to be interpreted and reinterpreted, set and reset. Like drama, they need to be *performed* if they are to enable remembrance, resistance, and persistence in the present. The recipes written by Pächter and the women who contributed to the *Kochbuch* were never merely "imaginary" as Holocaust scholar Efraim Zuroff suggests (Gross 1997); rather, they arose out of real memories of foods once eaten. Performing the recipes—cooking in memory's kitchen—then, ensures the preservation of these women's dishes materially, edibly, so that they are not lost as elusive fantasies, so that, as Janet Theophano suggests, readers in the present are able to "preserve a vanishing way of life" (Theophano 2002, 51).

It is important, however, that those who proceed to this fifth transformation have done so conscious of the inherent alteration of meanings that takes place when the recipe for *Gesundheits Kuchen* is read, translated, adapted, and produced in the present. This acknowledgement and consideration is what sets the sociocultural and memorial worth of engaged culinary tourism apart from more appropriative food tourisms that serve the interests of economics and entertainment and the benefits of public experience rather than the possibility of personal development through informed performance. The food tourism that C. Michael Hall and Liz Sharples define in the collection *Food Tourism Around the World: Development, Management and Markets* privileges consumption ("food tourism is quite literally the consumption of the local and the consumption and production of place" [2003, 10]). Engaging oneself in the practice of reading, translating, and producing, on the other hand, devalues the act of consumption and instead privileges the process of understanding the value of the end food good, a value which need not be validated through taste, edibility, or digestion. This engaged culinary practice allows for time and takes much time, elevating process, not product.

The performance or the making of Pächter's recipes by an engaged reader-cook is one that can and does arise respectful of the past, aware of the historiocultural implications of Holocaust inscription. Chuck Martin of the *Cincinnati Enquirer* provides an obscure but beautiful discussion of how a group of Holocaust survivors put Pächter's *Kochbuch* into practice, orchestrating a kitchen performance that was at once memorial and mournful. In May 2003, De Silva visited the Max Kade German Cultural Center at the University of Cincinnati. Martin chronicles the story of

Trudy Coppel, Hanna Lewin, Dina Bure, and Zell Schulman, Holocaust survivors who prepare two recipes from the book, Mina Pächter's Cake (*Pächter Torte*) and Poppy Seed Slices (*Makové Řezy*), to eat after De Silva's lecture.[15] "The women believe this is their best contribution to the cause," Martin writes (2003). "Baking and feeding people is their way of ensuring that no one forgets the horrors. *Others*, they say, are better at public speaking." Using a recipe recorded by someone who shared a similar experience allows these women who are not so comfortable speaking publicly the opportunity to do the work of cultural "rememory" (Morrison 1987, 36). Their baked goods are served, tangible and tasteful—the kitchen toil of "hands that reached out for morsels of food" years earlier. "This is important. The memories. Even though it is difficult to talk about, it's important," Hanna Lewin comments (Martin 2003). The food, in its preparation and creation, helps these women speak.

Cooking Pächter's recipes allows these survivors to share *their* "story of the survival of the spirit amid the horrors of the Holocaust." These women's stories and personal experiences make baking a method of return, return to the unspeakable, but also return to times before the war's silencing. Through experiencing the foods of the women who died in Terezín, those who have no other way of relating to the Holocaust may also be able to develop a consciousness of the atrocity in ways that they had not been able to before because it has been for them an incomprehensible event. Barbara Kirshenblatt-Gimblett's suggestion that "food experiences . . . form edible chronotypes," or what she also calls "space-time convergences," provides a helpful way of deciphering the possibilities of baking from Pächter's *Kochbuch* (2004, xiii). Not only does engaged culinary tourism provide the opportunity for involved, memorial practice which, as Long explains, is anchored in "our own bodies and physicality," it does so within a familiar context, a familiar place in the home, a familiar space in one's memory where, "utilizing the senses of taste, smell, touch, and vision," individuals are provided with "a deeper, more integrated level of experience" (Long 2004b, 21, 47n5).

While critics might argue that Pächter's recipes are kitsch or "ubiquitous" and thus have little to offer Holocaust scholarship, following Michel de Certeau, the "everyday" nature of cooking and kitchen work is the medium through which the women in the camps, otherwise silenced, are allowed to speak, their recipes "tactical ruses" that serve as "immemorial links," locating them within a larger humanity, a larger history, a larger story (de Certeau 1984, xvii, 40). Using the recipes allows readers and cooks to listen to those whose lives were ended without explanation, to figuratively join them in the kitchen as individuals, persons who went about their daily lives preparing foods that they enjoyed eating with their families, preparing foods whose eating brought about pleasure. To make the recipes, to cook for memory, is to represent, to re-present, those who suffered—tangibly—keeping their memories alive in kitchens and at dinner tables, encouraging the survival of their reminiscences, of their baking, in an ever-changing present where transformation does not signify loss of cultural and historical significance but rather a cloaking of the original meaning in a "royal robe with ample folds."

Epilogue

I'm sure you're wondering: did I make the *Gesundheits Kuchen*? Certainly, it is a possibility that I have thought much about. I have asked myself many questions, necessary questions for anyone who might bake from the book. If I were to take my copy of *In Memory's Kitchen* home to my own kitchen and plan to make the Healthcake, the conditions of my production of the cake would differ unimaginably from the original conditions of its making. What would my motives be for making the Healthcake? A big part of me is curious about what the cake would taste like. I wonder if I would be able to decipher the recipe in my own kitchen. Would the cake turn out? To at least some extent, I would make the cake for the experience of the making—to try it out. As a Colorado girl who grew up in the Lutheran church, I am an outsider to Jewish cultural traditions. I don't think it would happen, but there is the wondering: in the making, would I forget where the recipe came from? Would the cake lose its social significance given my present-day awareness of the nutritional information that Joan Nathan points out? With a flowered apron tied round my waist and potholders in hand, would I stray too far from a conscious application of informed culinary tourist practices?

I wish I could describe the cake to you, its texture, my baking experience, what I felt as I ate it. But, no, I haven't made the cake yet. It is not yet the right time. Despite my research and reading, despite my argument that, yes, Pächter's recipes should be used in the kitchen, for me the decision to bake her cake remains complicated. I haven't reached the moment in my life for the making of the Healthcake, the moment when I know I will be able to most consciously, most responsibly, most attentively understand the meaning of making and eating her cake. But perhaps that is part of the process of becoming engaged with the culinary: knowing when and why, understanding the implications, struggling with the complications, preparing oneself for how to digest the history, the memory, the suffering that surrounds what seems a simple piece of cake. Knowing when one is ready requires more than pulling the pans out of the cabinet and preheating the oven. It must.

Pächter's recipes sit on my kitchen shelf next to a few other cookbooks, next to jars of flour and sugar. That is where they belong. And I know that years from now when I have children I will make the cake. My children will help me read the recipe. We will talk about what it means to make the Healthcake together. I will teach them what I know about the people who wrote the recipes, as much as I can about who they were and what they did before World War II. Through their questions, my children will continue to teach me about the incomprehensibility of why those who wrote the recipes had to die. And we will break the eggs, and we will add the cream. Ours will be a making that means something more than just the process, more than just the eating.

Notes

1. In his foreword to *In Memory's Kitchen,* Michael Berenbaum (1996, ix–xiv) provides helpful information about Terezín, the camp located a forty mile distance north of Prague that for many served as the "anteroom to Auschwitz." Terezín, the camp that would later be renamed Thereisenstadt by the Germans, was an atypical camp run as a "model ghetto, a place that purported to demonstrate the Führer's decency to the Jews" and later used for the production of a Nazi propaganda film. Nazi *Kultur* was reinforced in the camp as Czech, and later German, Austrian, Dutch, and Danish Jews, were provided with books and education as well as the opportunity to participate in arts including music, theater, and painting.

2. Joan Nathan is not the only writer to publish adapted recipes from the *Kochbuch* for a contemporary audience. See also: Charlotte Innes (1997) and Mary MacVean (1996).

3. To date, Rona Kaufman (2004) provides the most substantial interrogation of *In Memory's Kitchen,* which unfortunately was published after I completed final drafts of my chapter. She begins her discussion with a question similar to the one that I ask—are the recipes to be used or should

they be treated as a protected historical document, even a "sacred text" (428)?—thus, affirming that the complicated nature of not only Holocaust writing, but also kitchen literature is central to a discussion of Cara De Silva's collection. Kaufman's point of departure is not an adapted recipe, however, but rather writer Laura Shapiro's suggestion of baking from one of the translated recipes (2004). Like myself, Kaufman goes through the similar ideological battles about the purpose of De Silva's text and the ways that it is translated and read in the present. Kaufman concludes that if readers desire to bake from *In Memory's Kitchen*, they must "seek more and more translation," but she ends there (443). I consider my discussion to provide a methodology for continued translation.

4. For a helpful discussion of trends in Holocaust representation, see Michael Rothberg's *Traumatic Realism: The Demands of Holocaust Representation* (Minneapolis, MN: University of Minnesota Press, 2000).

5. See also Janet Floyd and Laurel Forster, eds. *The Recipe Reader: Narratives—Contexts—Traditions* (Burlington, VT: Ashgate, 2003).

6. Explicit scholarly investigations of food studies and the Holocaust are limited. Myrna Goldberg (2003) provides an excellent discussion about recipe recording in her larger discussion of food and gender. Similarly, there has been relatively little scholarship done on *In Memory's Kitchen* or other recipe collections coming out of the camps. In addition to Kaufman's article, Sara Lewis Dunn (2004) compares *In Memory's Kitchen* to other war-time cookbook collections in her article "Kitchen Wars and Memoirs." Janet Theophano's *Eat My Words: Reading Women's Lives through the Cookbooks They Wrote* (2002), and Miriam Meyers' *A Bite Off Mama's Plate: Mothers' and Daughters' Connections through Food* (2001) also include discussions of De Silva's book.

7. Finkelstein's comment was brought to my attention in Tim Cole's *Selling the Holocaust: From Auschwitz to Schindler: How History is Bought, Packaged, and Sold,* (1999, 15).

8. Similarly, Sara Lewis Dunn chooses to "label [*In Memory's Kitchen*] a memoir rather than a cookbook simply because its recipes were produced out of memories of better times rather than a desire to impart instruction" (2002, 6).

9. Thanks to Ms. Tinny Lenthen, librarian at the Sydney Jewish Museum, for sending me a copy of Edith Peer's introduction, a picture of the cookbook, and several recipes. In regards to Norere Gilletz's information that Peer's book did not succeed because its recipes were not kosher, Rona Kaufman points out that not all recipes in De Silva's collection are

kosher, which may confirm the chaotic time of the recipes' recording (Kaufman 2004, 430).

10. Because of the complicated authorship and translation of the text, cited recipes are organized using De Silva's name and refer to the 1996a item in the reference list.

11. Myrna Goldberg focuses her examination of gender and hunger on what she refers to as "food-talk," or discussions about cooking that took place in the camp, discussions that reappear in literature, memoirs, interviews, and recipes (2003, 163).

12. See the following recipes in De Silva 1996a: *Gries {sic} Auflauf* (36); *Mazeloksch* (38); *Eiswurfel* (58), *Nuss Zopf* (31), *Schussel Pastete* (21–22).

13. In the recipe for *Leberknödel*, bracketed inclusions explain that the step where the dumplings should be boiled has been left out.

14. Also quoted in De Silva (Introduction 1996b, xxxviii).

15. The recipes for the goods that these women make can be found in De Silva 1996a, 53, 72.

Works Cited

Benjamin, Walter. 1968. "The Task of the Translator: An Introduction to the Translation of Baudelaire's *Tableaux Parisiens*." In *Illuminations*. Trans. Harry Zohn, 69–82. New York: Harcourt, Brace, & World.

Berenbaum, Michael. 1996. Foreword to *In Memory's Kitchen: A Legacy from the Women of Terezín*. Ed. Cara De Silva and trans. Bianca Steiner Brown, ix–xvi. Northvale, NJ: Aronson.

Bower, Anne L. 1997a. "Bound Together: Recipes, Lives, Stories, and Readings." In *Recipes for Reading: Community Cookbooks, Stories, Histories*. Ed. Anne L. Bower, 1–14. Amherst, MA: University of Massachusetts Press.

———. 1997b. "Cooking Up Stories: Narrative Elements in Community Cookbooks. In *Recipes for Reading: Community Cookbooks, Stories, Histories*. Ed. Anne L. Bower, 29–50. Amherst, MA: University of Massachusetts Press.

de Certeau, Michel. 1984. *The Practice of Everyday Life*. Trans. Steven Rendall. Berkeley, CA: University of California Press.

Cole, Tim. 1999. *Selling the Holocaust: From Auschwitz to Schindler: How History is Bought, Packaged, and Sold.* New York: Routledge and Kegan Paul.

De Silva, Cara, ed. 1996a. *In Memory's Kitchen: A Legacy from the Women of Terezín.* Trans. Bianca Steiner Brown and David Stern. Northvale, NJ: Aronson.

———. 1996b. Introd. to *In Memory's Kitchen: A Legacy from the Women of Terezín.* Ed. Cara De Silva and Trans. Bianca Steiner Brown and David Stern, xxv–xliii. Northvale, NJ: Aronson.

———. 1996c. In Memory's Kitchen. Interview by Elizabeth Farnsworth. *PBS Online Newshour* December 17. http://www.pbs.org/newshour/bb/europe/december96/cook_12–17.html (accessed October 16, 2006).

Dunn, Sara Lewis. 2002. "Kitchen Wars and Memoirs." *Tennessee Philological Bulletin: Proceedings of the Annual Meeting of the Tennessee Philological Association* 39: 6–14.

Eisenstein, Elizabeth L. 1997. *The Printing Press as an Agent of Change: Communications and Cultural Transformations in Early-Modern Europe.* vols. I and II. New York: Cambridge University Press.

Finkelstein, Norman. 1997. "Daniel Jonah Goldberg's 'Crazy' Thesis: A Critique of Hitler's Willing Executioners." *New Left Review* 1 No. 224 (July–Aug): 39–87.

Floyd, Janet, and Laurel Forster, eds. 2003. *The Recipe Reader: Narratives—Contexts—Traditions.* Burlington, VT: Ashgate.

Gilletz, Norene. 2003. "Sharing food with friends." *Gourmania* (November 12). http://www.gourmania.com/articles/sharing_food.htm (accessed October 16, 2006).

Goldberg, Myrna. 2003. "Food Talk: Gendered Responses to Hunger in the Concentration Camps." In *Experience and Expression: Women, the Nazis, and the Holocaust.* Eds. Elizabeth R. Baer and Myrna Goldberg, 161–179. Detroit: Wayne State University Press.

Green, Michelle. 1996. "In Memory's Kitchen: A Legacy from the Women of Terezín." *People Weekly* (December 2): 30.

Gross, Tom. 1997. "Outrage Over 'Holocaust cookbook.'" *Jerusalem Post*, February 14.

Hall, C. Michael and Liz Sharples. 2003. "The Consumption of Experiences or the Experience of Consumption? An Introduction to the Tourism of Taste." In *Food Tourism Around the World: Development,*

Management and Markets. Eds. C. Michael Hall et al., 1–24. Burlington: Butterworth Heinemann.

Hayes, Joanne Lamb. 2000. *Grandma's Wartime Kitchen: World War II and the Way We Cooked.* New York: St. Martin's Press.

———. 2003. *Grandma's Wartime Baking Book: World War II and the Way We Baked.* New York: St. Martin's Press.

Hrg, Andela. 1942. *Recepti.* Trans. unknown. Logor Stara Gradiska-Veljaca. *Jasenovac Collection* [Online]. United States Holocaust Memorial Museum. http://www.ushmm.org/museum/exhibit/online/jasenovac/collection/jasenovac/ wj0010–1.html (accessed October 16, 2006).

Innes, Charlotte. 1997. "The Food of Memory." *Los Angeles Times*, July 23, sec. H.

Kaufman, Rona. 2004. "Testifying, Silencing, Monumentalizing, Swallowing: Coming to Terms with *In Memory's Kitchen.*" *JAC* 24 No. 2: 427–445.

King, David C. 2000. *World War II Days: Discover the Past with Exciting Projects, Games, Activities, and Recipes.* New York: Wiley.

Kirshenblatt-Gimblett, Barbara. 2004. Foreword to *Culinary Tourism.* Ed. Lucy M. Long, xi–xiv. Lexington: University Press of Kentucky.

Long, Lucy M. 2004a. Introd. to *Culinary Tourism.* Ed. Lucy M. Long, 1–19. Lexington: University Press of Kentucky.

———. 2004b. "Culinary Tourism: A Folkloristic Perspective on Eating and Otherness." In *Culinary Tourism.* Ed. Lucy M. Long, 20–50. Lexington: University Press of Kentucky.

Lugg, Catherine A. 1999. *Kitsch: From Education to Public Policy.* New York: Falmer.

MacVean, Mary. 1996. "'In memory's kitchen': Recipes that Survived the Holocaust." *Columbian* (WA) (November 19).

Martin, Chuck. 2003. "Holocaust Survivors Bake for a Special Cause." *Cincinnati Enquirer*, May 5, 2003. http://www.enquirer.com/editions/2003/05/05/tem_monlede05.html (accessed October 16, 2006).

Meyers, Miriam. 2001. *A Bite Off Mama's Plate: Mothers' and Daughters' Connections Through Food.* Westport: Bergin & Garvey.

Morrison, Toni. 1987. *Beloved.* New York: Plume.

Nathan, Joan. 1996. "At Rosh ha-Shanah, Poignant Memories of Holidays Past." *New York Times*, September 11, sec. C.

———. 1994. *Jewish Cooking in America.* New York: Knopf.

New York Times. 1996. "Notable Books of the Year 1996." December 8, sec. 7.

Peer, Edith. [n.d.]. *Ravensbrück 1945, Fantasy Cooking Behind Barbed Wire.* Sydney Jewish Museum, Sydney, Australia.

Rothberg, Michael. 2000. *Traumatic Realism: The Demands of Holocaust Representation.* Minneapolis, MN: University of Minnesota Press.

Saidel, Rochelle G. 2004. *The Jewish Women of Ravensbrück Concentration Camp.* Madison, WI: University of Wisconsin Press.

Shapiro, Laura. 1996. "Hope from Recipes of Resistance." *Newsweek*, September 9.

Steel, Tanya Wenman. 1997. "Books for Cooks." *Bon Appetit*, February.

Theophano, Janet. 2002. *Eat My Words: Reading Women's Lives Through the Cookbooks They Wrote.* New York: Palgrave.

Troller, Norbert. 1991. *Thereisenstadt: Hitler's Gift to the Jews.* Trans. Susan E. Cernyak-Spatz and Ed. Joel Shatzky. Chapel Hill, NC: University of North Carolina Press.

Weissman, Gary. 2004. *Fantasies of Witnessing: Postwar Efforts to Experience the Holocaust.* Ithaca: Cornell University Press.

CHAPTER 4

"More Than One Million Mothers Know It's the *REAL* Thing"

The Rosenbergs, Jell-O, Old-Fashioned Gefilte Fish, and 1950s America

Nathan Abrams

On June 20, 1953, Julius and Ethel Rosenberg were executed for the crime of espionage. They had been tried and found guilty of passing atomic secrets to the Soviet Union. Their execution had not only led to an intensification of the domestic Cold War in America, but also greatly increased Jewish fears of anti-Semitism and charges of disloyalty. The spectacle of the Rosenbergs served as a jolting reminder to Americans of the long history of Jewish radicalism in the United States. In the new Cold War climate, which was hostile towards any form of leftism, this history could serve to undermine the position of the American Jewish community as loyal, patriotic American citizens. The oldest Jewish defense agency in the United States, the American Jewish Committee (AJC), for example, expressed "considerable concern" that "the non-Jewish public may generalize" from "public disclosures of spy activities by Jews and people with Jewish sounding names" and "impute to the Jews as a group treasonable motives and activities (Flowerman 1950). David Suchoff observed that the "Popular Front, Moscow-tinged rhetoric of the Rosenbergs" presented "a nightmare scenario" because it "foregrounded Jewish names in connection with popular fears of conspiracy and thus built on the mass-cultural fantasies of Jewish subversion that the Jewish investigation of Hollywood had already prominently produced in 1947" (Suchoff 1995, 157). Consequently, the Rosenberg case soon developed into a nodal point for the construction of Jewish-American identities as either loyal or subversive. The trial built up into what Deborah Dash Moore called "a definitional ceremony in which opposing versions of American Jewish identity competed for ascendancy" (Moore 1998, 21–22). At stake was the loyalty of the entire American Jewish community. The defendants, the prosecution (Irving Saypol and Roy Cohn), and the judge (Irving Kaufman) were Jewish. The key piece of evidence in the conviction of the Rosenbergs was a box of Jell-O. As a result, by examining the symbolic importance of food within the American Jewish community during the 1950s, in particular its relationship to the Rosenbergs and the wider Cold War context, I will argue that food took on a new, politicized significance for American Jews that has not been extensively examined hitherto. Taking Marjorie Garber's essay "Jell-O" as my starting point, I aim to examine the cultural values attached to specific food products at a precise moment in American history of the 1950s and how these were reconciled with concepts of Jewishness and Americanness (Garber 1995, 11–22).

"Food, we know," sociologist Herbert Gans observed, "plays a significant role in Jewish society, recreational, and religious life in America" (Gans 1956, 428). Isaac Rosenfeld put it more humorously: "The simple act of eating has become for us [Jews] a complicated ceremonial . . ." (Rosenfeld 1949, 386). During the 1950s, the role and nature of food in American Jewish life shifted. Suburbanization and a move away from the observance of previous generations increasingly threatened traditional Jewish culinary practices. In his famous study of a Jewish suburban community, Marshall Sklare observed a decline in maintaining kosher homes. While approximately 46 percent of an earlier generation had bought kosher meat, surveys of their children estimated that only 5–10 percent continued to do so (Sklare 1972, 204). Anxious about the continued observance of their children, Orthodox and traditional Jews often took them to holiday resorts where not only could they eat kosher, but they could also meet other, kosher Jews. Perhaps the most famous of these was the Grossinger hotel whose advertising consciously associated its kosher cuisine with Jewish traditions of matchmaking. According to Donna Gabaccia, "Under their guidance, food not only provided an opportunity for sociability, but the means to endogamous marriage and reproduction within American Judaism" (Gabaccia 1998, 83).

Kashrut (the body of Jewish dietary laws) came under further threat from a series of postwar developments in the food industry: food technology, particularly in the areas of refrigeration, canning, freezing, and transportation; the new consumer products available for both storing and cooking food; a new level of disposable income; an increased amount of leisure time; and the opening of the first McDonalds restaurant in 1954, the establishment of the McDonalds Corporation the following year and the advent of standardized, production line, nonkosher hamburgers. The consumption of Chinese food, particularly amongst New York Jews, was also growing in popularity during the 1950s to the effect that Gaye Tuchman and Harry Levine remarked: "Cantonese Chinese restaurants had become a New York Jewish family tradition" (Tuchman and Levine 1996, 30). One woman reminisced that her aunt had three sets of dishes at that time: the traditional dairy and meat sets as required by *kashrut* for the separation of dairy and meat products and a disposable set exclusively for takeout Chinese meals. Another man recalled that in his small town outside Seattle, eating Chinese food was regarded as sophisticated in the same way as going to an art house movie (Tuchman and Levine 1996, 28, 29). Traditional Jewish food practices had become a sensitive issue in 1950s America.

The sensitivity surrounding kosher food at this time was demonstrated by the uproar caused by Isaac Rosenfeld's controversial Freudian interpretation of the laws of *kashrut* that appeared in *Commentary* in 1949. Rosenfeld suggested that the dietary laws echoed the injunctions in sexual behavior and that the desire to eat *trayf* (nonkosher) mirrored the urge to participate in the world of forbidden sexuality. Rosenfeld pointed out in his article, "When the Lord forbade Adam and Eve to eat of the Tree, He started something which has persisted throughout our history: the attachment of all sorts of forbidden meanings to food, and the use of food in a system of taboos . . ." (Rosenfeld 1949, 385). The article created a furor, spawning pages of letters. It had upset so many readers that it was the only article that *Commentary*'s editor, Elliot Cohen, ever publicly apologized for publishing. The apology itself then produced further correspondence. The uproar over Rosenfeld's article indicated that the issues of *kashrut* were extremely touchy during the 1950s.

Similarly, during the early Cold War, the Jewish community felt its position become unsettled. Following the Holocaust, many Jews still feared the continuation of anti-Semitism. The onset, development, and intensification of the Cold War exacerbated this. The arrests of Judith Coplon, Robert Soblen, Jack Soble, Morton Sobell, and the Rosenbergs compounded these anxieties. It was feared that the public would increasingly equate Communism with Judaism and American Jews feared the cementing of this link. Arnold Foster, general counsel of the Anti-Defamation League recalled: "There was an evident quotient of anti-Semitism in the McCarthy wave of hysteria. Jews in that period were automatically suspect. Our evaluation of the general mood was that people felt if you scratch a Jew, you can find a Communist" (Navasky 1980, 112). Many Jews felt doubly sensitive at this time as Jews were disproportionately represented within the Communist Party and the establishment of the State of Israel had opened them up to charges of dual loyalties.

Consequently, elements within the American Jewish community devoted a great deal of effort and resources in an attempt to construct the concept of loyal American Jews that contained the subversive elements of Jewish radicalism. Thus, once the Rosenbergs had been arrested these elements sought to contain the fallout. The organization that took the primary role in assisting the public prosecution of the Rosenbergs was the AJC. The AJC (American Jewish Committee) had been founded in 1906 in response to the pogroms and the worsening condition of Jews in Eastern Europe and was dedicated to protecting the civil and religious rights of the global Jewish community. For most of its early existence it was an elite organization of middle- and upper-class American German-Jewish philanthropic and community leaders who had largely emigrated to America during the nineteenth century. Rabbi Andhil Fineberg, who had been Chairman of its Staff Committee on Communism since 1950, was appointed to coordinate the AJC's response to the Rosenbergs. As a result, a specific subcommittee on the Rosenbergs was set up and instigated a propaganda campaign. In an attempt to protect the entire Jewish community, the AJC aimed to dissociate the mass of American Jewry from the activities of the Rosenbergs. The AJC did not lend any support to the Rosenbergs; indeed it repeatedly and publicly upheld their guilt, advocating their execution. In doing so, it sought to reconstruct Jewish-American memory by writing out the recent history of Jewish radicalism in the United States. As a result, the AJC's magazine, *Commentary*, was criticized for "obscuring the actual political traditions" that Jews held in America (Avishai 1981, 254).

To this end the AJC collaborated with the State Department to produce and distribute a book for mass circulation. Entitled *The Rosenberg*

Case: Fact and Fiction, the text was the product of extensive contact between the two agencies. For the AJC the book represented an attempt to deny any "efforts to mislead the people of this country by unsupported charges that the religious ancestry of the defendants was a factor in this case" (Fineberg 1953, 69). On the part of the State Department, it was "an adequate presentation of the American side of the case for dissemination among Europeans" (Slawson 1953). The collaborative efforts of elements of the Jewish community, including the AJC, Judge Kaufman, and prosecutors Saypol and Cohn, together with the Administration, directed towards the execution of the Rosenbergs was a clear assertion of their determination to eradicate subversion. In the Administration's view, the Rosenbergs were subversive because they were communist spies; to the Jewish community they were subversive because they represented the history of Jewish-American radicalism. Together, they hoped to bury two decades of American and Jewish Marxism along with the Rosenbergs (Dickstein 1977, 45).

As mentioned at the outset, the key piece of evidence in the conviction of the Rosenbergs was a box of Jell-O. The prosecution argued that a Jell-O packet was cut in half and used as a password between Julius Rosenberg and Ruth Greenglass. According to prosecutor Saypol, the Jell-O box "forged the necessary link in the chain that points indisputably to the guilt of the Rosenbergs" (Schneir and Schneir 1968, 374). In their detailed study of the case, Ronald Radosh and Joyce Milton describe the alleged scene:

> Later, after the kitchen table had been cleared, Julius asked Ruth to step into the kitchen so that he could give her a recognition signal, to be used in case another courier had to take Ann's place. Julius took a Jell-O box from the kitchen cabinet, removed the contents, and cut the side panel of the box into two irregularly shaped pieces. One he kept, the other he gave to Ruth, who took it into the living room to show her husband. David would later testify that he remarked on what a clever idea the Jell-O box was and Julius, obviously pleased, replied, "The simplest things are the cleverest." (Radosh and Milton 1997, 69)

Judge Kaufman stated to the jury: "the Government contends that you have a right to infer that there existed a link between Julius Rosenberg and Yakovlev [the Soviet agent] in that Julius Rosenberg in some way transmitted . . . the Jell-O box-side to Yakovlev" (Garber 1995, 11). Roy

Cohn even went out and bought a box of Jell-O to show to the jury in order to strengthen the government's case. During his summation, Saypol held up the (alleged) Jell-O box. It worked: the prosecution won and the Rosenbergs were found guilty.

Jell-O to the jury in the Rosenberg case signified guilt. To Orthodox American Jews it signified *trayf*—a nonkosher food product forbidden for consumption by *halacha* (Jewish law). The word *trayf* derives from the Hebrew for "torn." *Trayf* is the opposite of "kosher," which is one of Judaism's contributions to an international language denoting that which is proper and meets accepted rules and standards. In Judaism the term does not only refer to acceptable food. *Tefillin* (phylacteries) and Torah scrolls are "kosher" in that they meet all *halachic* (Jewish legal) requirements. The expression is also applied to individuals: acceptable witnesses are called *edim k'sherim*; an upright, proper, observant Torah Jew is referred to as an *adam kasher* (kosher man). Jell-O was *trayf* because it contained the ingredient gelatin. Gelatin was then typically derived from the skin and bones of nonkosher animals, in particular pigs; hence it was a prohibited substance. When gelatin appeared in the 1920s and 1930s it caused a stir within the Jewish community. According to Garber, "gelatin as a product, and Jell-O as a brand, was much in debate among Jewish leaders in the period from 1933 to 1952" (Garber 1995, 15). The 1936 *Kosher Food Guide* included an entry entitled, "Jell-O—is it Kosher or Trefa?":

> Jell-O was absolutely trefa as the gelatine contained in the product is derived from trefa bones and parts of skins, as for instance the skins of hams, etc. As there is unfortunately no kosher animal gelatine produced, we naturally answered to various enquiries about the permissibility of Jell-O or similar products for consumption by Jews that these articles are trefa. (Nathan 1994, 364)

Until certified kosher synthetic gelatins came on the market Orthodox Jews would be wary of using any gelatin in their cooking. As comedian Lenny Bruce put it: "Jello is goyish [non-Jewish]." This did not deter Cecil B. De Mille, though, when he used a quivering strawberry Jell-O mold to simulate the parting of the Red Sea in his 1923 production of *The Ten Commandments*.

Among nonorthodox American Jews, however, it was probably Jell-O's very un-kosherness that made it so enticing. Its packets proudly proclaimed its *trayf*ness clearly stating "Jell-O Brand, Gelatin dessert." As Gaye Tuchman and Harry Levine point out, "Jewish immigrants, and especially their children and grandchildren, were open to new secular and cultural experiences. Many were eager to prove that they could behave in 'un-Jewish' ways" (Tuchman and Levine 1996, 27). For them, Jell-O symbolized cosmopolitanism and was a remedy for what was perceived as Jewish parochialism. As good, Popular Front, atheist Stalinists, the Rosenbergs would have actively embraced universalism during the 1930s and rejected, albeit not completely, the particularism and religion of Judaism. Jell-O also opened up a world of forbiddenness: it was ripe for rebellion against the norms of *kashrut*; it was gentile, potentially exotic, and taboo; its appearance did not automatically provoke repugnance or require any expertise to eat (unlike say, shellfish). At the same time, it didn't *look* nonkosher so that there wasn't such a leap against deeply entrenched *kashrut* practices for those who were not ready to take it. Garber admits in her article that

> as a young Jewish girl growing up on Long Island in the fifties in a secularized family and eating Jell-O brand gelatin dessert on the average of three times a week, in all of its six delicious flavors, it never occurred to me to worry about whether what I was eating was kosher, much less whether it was a highly disguised kind of meat. (Garber 1995, 17)

In this way, it was appropriate for those Jews who wanted to assert their freedom from the traditional orthodoxy of their ancestors. It was what Tuchman and Levine called "safe treyf" (Tuchman and Levine 1996, 29).

Added to this was Jell-O's Americanness. Jell-O was a quintessentially *American* product that had originated in 1897. As Joan Nathan has written:

> What American in the 1920s and 30s could resist the appetizing photographs of gently rippling Jell-O salads in the *Ladies Home Journal*? The majority of Jews, wanting to embrace everything American, to be part of this new age of science and technology, were open to new products that would shorten their time in the kitchen and these included the new Jell-O deserts. (Nathan 1994, 364)

American Jews may have perceived eating Jell-O as "cosmopolitan, urbane, and sophisticated" (Tuchman and Levine 1996, 25). Jell-O was advertised in Jewish publications, it was eaten in Jewish homes, and its popularity amongst Jews was undeniable. Indeed, once Julius had removed the contents of the Jell-O box, Ethel undoubtedly used them to make the dessert. Recipes for Jell-O desserts began to appear in Jewish cookbooks. Jell-O's translucence possibly endeared it to its consumers since ethnic dreams of assimilating into the American mainstream could be read into its very substance. Anything could be added to it (indeed Jell-O salads were very popular dishes at the time), producing a union between the quintessential American product and other (possibly ethnic) ingredients. Not only was the *trayf*ness of Jell-O hidden or submerged (such that one could pretend it wasn't there, and in many ways it resembled the jelly that congeals around cooked gefilte fish), the addition of acceptable ingredients within it clearly made it safe and even kosher-looking. Thus, the forbidden substance was so well disguised that it did not instinctively repulse and hence impair the capacity to assimilate. To appropriate an observation of Tuchman and Levine's (made in regards to Chinese food) Jell-O provided a "flexible open-ended symbol, a kind of blank screen upon which they [Jews] projected a series of themes relating to their identity as modern Jews . . ." (Tuchman and Levine 1996, 25).

From the 1930s to the 1950s, therefore, despite a certain amount of consternation amongst Orthodox Jews, the majority of nonpracticing American Jewry considered Jell-O to be safe in as much as it was American yet simultaneously and subconsciously attractive, taboo, and possibly exotic. Yet, in the paranoid era of the 1950s, Jell-O became a sign of guilt. It marked the differences between kosher and *trayf* as well as marked the boundaries between loyalty and subversion, pro-American and Communist. The Rosenbergs were convicted by a box of Jell-O; thus, since the Rosenbergs were guilty of passing atomic secrets to the Soviet Union, Jell-O became a signifier of subversion, disloyalty, and un-American activity. Indeed, Jell-O's manufacturer General Foods had already been connected with such activity through its sponsorship of actress Jean Muir in the television role of Mother Aldrich, who, it was alleged, had belonged to fellow-traveling organizations; fearing a possible decline in Jell-O consumption, General Foods withdrew its sponsorship. What is more, because Jell-O was nonkosher, these labels could become subsumed under the umbrella term, *trayf*—the antithesis of kosher. Leo Rosten's *The Joys of Yiddish* describes a *trayf* person as "someone untrustworthy, malicious, tricky, of whom you should be aware" (Rosten 1968, 417). These practices as a result were then marked as un-Jewish. Arthur Miller summed up the linkage of *trayf* with subversion and of *kashrut* with loyalty when, in 1964 following his ordeal with the House Un-American Activities Committee (HUAC), he wrote the words: "I wanted out, to be a good American again, kosher again" (Miller 1994, 184). Perhaps it is no coincidence that in November 1951, two Orthodox rabbis (Samuel Baskin and Simeon Winograd) reversed the kosher certification of Jell-O having previously endorsed it. The desire of an incidental coalition of liberal anticommunist Jews and the rabbinic authorities to outlaw Jell-O also mirrored the larger Cold War project to outlaw and contain deviancy, particularly in the realms of political activity. By forbidding Jell-O, therefore, sections of the American Jewish community attempted to contain the desire to participate in the world of forbidden activities. As Garber noted: "Jell-O itself both marked and crossed the borderline between Jewish and Christian, American and foreign, kosher and *trafe*" (Garber 1995, 21).

Jell-O was *trayf* because it was a signifier for the Rosenbergs' poor parenting and a key strand of the prosecution's case against the Rosenbergs was the denigration of them as inadequate parents. Ethel and Julius's son, Robert Meeropol, observed how: "It was particularly important to cast my parents in a bad light, because the public might otherwise come to feel sympathy for a young married couple with small children and recoil at the government's act of killing them" (Meeropol 1995, 239). Thus, the Rosenbergs, in particular Ethel, were demonized as bad parents. In sentencing them to death Judge Kaufman stated:

> Indeed the defendants Julius and Ethel Rosenberg placed their devotion to their cause above their own personal safety and were conscious that they were sacrificing their own children, should their misdeeds be detected—all of which did not deter them from pursuing their course. Love for their course dominated their lives—it was even greater than their love for their children. (Meeropol 1995, 239)

Robert added that he felt Kaufmann "believed that by sentencing them to death he was doing my brother and me a favor by making sure that we did not grow up in the household." What is more, he felt that the Judge "sought to absolve himself and the government for orphaning Michael and me by blaming my parents for what happened to us" (Meeropol 1995,

240). The government's chief ally within the American Jewish community, the AJC, was also very concerned with the status of the Rosenberg boys devoting a great deal of energy to ensuring that they were not used as the focus of an anti-American, pro-Rosenberg propaganda campaign. A prominent attorney and member of the AJC, Morris Ernst, for example, volunteered to offer his analysis of the dynamics of the Rosenbergs' relationship to the FBI as well as to become the Rosenbergs' attorney so that he could assist the FBI better.

Ethel, in particular, was personally targeted and she soon became the "moral and emotional focus" of the trial (Carmichael 1993, 102). Ethel was projected as a bad mother in contrast to the traditional stereotype of the Jewish mother—an overcaring ("hysterical" according to Rosenfeld), matriarchal figure who stuffs her children with far more than they can possibly digest. Ethel was presented as a cold, heartless woman who willfully chose to orphan her children while prohibiting them from visiting her during her first year of imprisonment. One juror explained that "I had two daughters at the time, and it bothered me how they would subject their children to such a thing. I just couldn't understand it" (Antler 1995, 206). One FBI report stated that "Ethel was not a good mother after all" (Antler 1995, 206). She was characterized as the dominant partner in the marriage. When sentencing them, Judge Kaufman may have described Julius as the "prime mover in this conspiracy," but he warned:

> let no mistake be made about the role which his wife, Ethel Rosenberg, played in this conspiracy. Instead of deterring him from pursuing his ignoble cause, she encouraged and assisted the cause. She was a mature woman,—almost three years older than her husband almost seven years older than her younger brother. She was a full-fledged partner in this crime. (Philipson 1993, 306)

Ernst observed that: "Julius is the slave and his wife, Ethel, is the master" (Meeropol 1995, 230). President Eisenhower, in his wisdom, felt "in this instance it is the woman who is the strong and recalcitrant character, the man is the weak one. She has obviously been the leader in everything they did in the spy ring" (Meeropol 1995, 230).

These images were picked up and conveyed by the press. In contrast to the *baleboosteh* (a Yiddish term meaning a praiseworthy mother), Ethel was presented as a poor mother to her children. Her refusal to be victimized and likewise break down under the pressure of her arrest and trial was taken as evidence that she lacked maternal feeling, that she cared more for communism than her own children. In her study of Ethel, Ilene Philipson explains that this image was carefully constructed by the Rosenbergs as part of their defense strategy: "they would show no fear or undue concern over what had occurred, for to do so would demonstrate guilty consciences. If they acted calm and unruffled, they seemed to have reasoned, their behavior would reflect their innocence" (Philipson 1993, 243). Ethel, it was noted, "entered into her role [of aloof indifference] with a certain amount of zeal" by not revealing anything through facial expression, gesture, or language (Philipson 1993, 243). However, her tactic backfired. The public was perplexed by her indifferent public persona and she was perceived as a "cold, virtually emotionless" (Philipson 1993, 2), hard-hearted Soviet operative who "thought and felt whatever [her] political commitment required [her] to think and to feel" (Warshow 1953, 413–418). *Commentary* associate editor, Irving Kristol, described her as a "grim tricoteuse," as opposed to "the glamorous and gay Mata Hari" (Kristol 1954, 609). As Philipson has pointed out, "Her stoicism on the witness stand, and when she heard the verdict of guilt and sentence of death shocked people at the time. It was so unlike a woman, and so peculiarly unlike a woman of her background" (Philipson 1993, 2). Ethel was variously described as "cold," "lacking 'normal' feminine characteristics," "unnatural," "steely, stony, tight-lipped" (Antler 1995, 206). Ethel was publicly demonized as "silent and mysterious, conspiratorial and political, dominating and evil" (Antler 1995, 207).

The construction of Ethel as a bad mother and housewife jarred with postwar representations of women as homemakers. The early Cold War period was one where women were simultaneously pedestalized and contained within carefully prescribed gender roles. Ethel attempted to invoke such representations and assume "the role of a typical nineteen-fifties American housewife—uninformed about politics and current events, focused on hearth and home, unaware of her husband's activities outside the family" (Philipson 1993, 6–7). But her apparent unconcern over the fate of herself, her husband, and her children undermined this role, and the jury refused to believe that she fit the stereotype of a typical 1950s housewife. What is more, the prosecution had successfully alleged that Ethel had confined Julius to the kitchen (cutting up Jell-O boxes), while she was in the other room plotting atomic espionage. By her inversion of Cold War gendered roles (man as breadwinner/woman as homemaker),

Ethel stood in contrast to such representations and therein possibly laid her danger. Significantly, only one jury member was female and she was a housewife. Ethel thus had to be executed because she had undermined carefully prescribed gender roles and in doing so "unnaturally" contradicted the "natural" Cold War order of domestic and sexual containment. The publication of the Rosenbergs' prison correspondence after the death further exacerbated the public perception of them as heartless spies. The carefully selected collection letters clearly demonstrated their willingness to sacrifice the personal for the political, to replace the warmth of human relationships with the coldness of Communist ideology. As Irene Philipson explained: "The fact that a wife and mother, particularly in the midst of the postwar celebration of family and motherhood, could speak as frequently about world issues as about her children, confirmed the worst anti-Communist assumptions" (Philipson 1993, 244).

These characterizations of the Rosenbergs were also propagated by elements of the Jewish community. The AJC was keen to distance American Jewry from the Rosenbergs hence it cooperated in the fashioning of them as a dysfunctional family in contrast to the tight-knit family units that were so important to Jewish tradition and Judaism. Good Jewish mothers did not abandon their children for secular, atheist causes; good Jewish mothers fed their children wholesome Jewish, kosher, cooking. Not Jell-O. Ethel was a bad Jewish mother because not only did she feed her children nonkosher, *trayf* food products, but she also neglected them for a secular, atheistic ideology. The AJC, together with other elements of the American Jewish community, struggled with the Rosenbergs for the right to assert an authentic Jewish–American identity, some of which was played out over food and motherhood.

The AJC attempted to discredit and marginalize the Rosenbergs in order to privilege the loyalty of American Jewry. Writing in *Commentary*, Leslie A. Fiedler observed: "These were not, after all, common criminals who plead innocent mechanically on the advice of counsel; these were believers in a new society, for whose sake they had already deceived their closest friends and endangered the security of their country" (Fiedler 1951, 110). The most vigorous attack, however, was framed in terms of the Rosenbergs' inscribed memories of Jewishness. These struck at the very heart of the AJC's attempt to prove the loyalty of Jews as a group and consequently the link between the Rosenbergs' subversion and Jewishness had to be broken. During their trial and the letters written while they were in prison, the Rosenbergs repeatedly linked their Jewishness with their commitment to Communism. Even after their deaths the Rosenbergs continued to speak, for their prison letters were published posthumously. These served as further textual reminders of the sensitive indices of politics and ethnicity at a time when the AJC and others had hoped the issue was literally dead and buried. In their correspondence, the Rosenbergs perceived their predicament in terms of their own Jewish memories. Julius believed that the "heritage of our Hebrew culture has served our people throughout the ages and we have learned its lesson well." During Passover he felt that "this cultural heritage has added meaning for us, who are imprisoned . . . by the modern Pharaohs." Chanukah represented "the victory of our forefathers in a struggle for freedom from oppression and tyranny, [and] is a firm part of our heritage and buttresses our will to win our own freedom." Furthermore, the Rosenbergs fused their Jewish memories with notions of American democracy: "Our upbringing, the full meaning of our lives, based on a true amalgamation of our American and Jewish heritage which means to us freedom, culture and human decency, has made us the people we are." To this it was added: "At Hebrew school . . . I absorbed quite naturally the culture of my people, their struggle for freedom from slavery in Egypt. I found the same great traditions in American history." These statements explicitly signified an interweaving of discourses of Jewishness and crucially, in the Cultural Cold War, of freedom. In a most subversive manner, Julius declared that "I take second place to no other American in my loyalty to my country" (Rosenberg 1953, 67, 112, 27). His expression of loyalty to America threatened to single-handedly undermine the Committee's careful construction of Jewish patriotism. What is more, it was done in exactly the same discursive terms. This link had to be broken and thus S. Andhil Fineberg wrote in the *American Legion Magazine*: "the Rosenbergs had long neglected any contact or connection with Jewish religious, educational, or social organizations . . . they were renegades who had abandoned their religion." He then contrasted them to Judge Kaufman and Irving Saypol—"loyal, religious Jews" (Fineberg 1953, 44).

As a result, a renewed attack against the Rosenbergs, but this time aimed at their posthumous correspondence, was initiated. *Commentary* staffer Robert Warshow denigrated their discourse of Jewishness as "crudely calculated" and "patently disingenuous," repeating "the worn platitudes of a thousand sermons about the Jewish tradition." Their Jewishness was the product of adopting the role required of them; they commodified it, and had it been necessary they would have used any other tradition or heritage made available to them. They were mere "catch-words" mobilized to assert their identity: "The Rosenbergs thought and felt whatever their political commitment required them to think and feel" (Warshow 1953, 78–79, 80). Leslie A. Fiedler's article echoed almost exactly the same sentiments. He asked rhetorically: "but in what sense were the Rosenbergs Jews?" Their Jewishness, he answered, was "the exploitation of a vocabulary" which was "played on tearfully by" communist activists. Fiedler continued: "they neither know nor care what Judaism actually is about; they will use as much of it as they need, defining it as they go." They use their Jewish memories because of the "accident" of their birth, "any other tradition would have done as well—and does." The scene after his death whereby Julius Rosenberg was draped in the Jewish ritual prayer shawl and the Psalms were sung was denigrated as an "absurd masquerade" of "fake piety" (Fiedler 1950, 28, 31, 36, 42, 43, 37).

The Rosenbergs had to be proven to be false, fake, and inauthentic in order to break the link between Jewishness and communism. Consequently, the Rosenbergs were attacked in a remarkably vicious manner, particularly considering that it was done posthumously. Morris Dickstein located the vehemence of these attacks in "a burning memory of the thirties" (Dickstein 1977, 41). It was a common critique of the intellectual life of the 1930s and the culture that grew out of it that it had distorted and destroyed "the emotional and moral content of experience, putting in its place a system of conventionalized 'responses'" (Warshow 1947, 540). Furthermore, the Rosenbergs reminded liberal anticommunist Jewish intellectuals of their earlier Marxism and they were keen to use the Rosenbergs not only to discredit their former radicalism, but also to distance themselves from it while simultaneously attacking the Soviet Union. In this way, these intellectuals attempted to rewrite the history of Jewish radicalism in America. Jews in America had long been participants in all shades of the radical movement from labor organizations to the Communist Party and many Jewish intellectuals were heavily involved in radical activities during the 1930s. The attack on the Rosenbergs allowed these intellectuals either to downplay their previous Marxism or to erase it altogether. As Jewish intellectuals Leslie A. Fiedler and Robert Warshow betrayed the scars of inscribed memories. They demonstrated a marked fear for their position. As youths these individuals not only denied their own communities, but also were denied access to the resources of the privileged and hence they sought out communities of their own. The postwar world, however, seemed to signify the end of this search as these young intellectuals adopted the twin communities of America and its Jews. Yet, the advent of the Rosenbergs and the revelation of their Jewishness once again threatened to remove these intellectuals from their newly discovered communities and the loss of their newly won privileged status that they had spent so long attaining.

The AJC then promoted counterproducts to Jell-O. Through its magazine, *Commentary*, the AJC promoted a Jewish cuisine that was ethnically sound (kosher) but at the same time was loyal and American. It is to the food products advertised in this journal that I shall now turn. *Commentary* was established by the AJC in 1945 as "a journal of significant thought and opinion on Jewish affairs and contemporary issues." The magazine had no religious affiliation and hence did not promote any particular sectarian agenda. Many of its writers took a secular, liberal, anticommunist view of most subjects. Its editorial board was composed of ex-radicals who had abandoned Trotskyism in the 1930s and 1940s. They sought to produce a journal of highbrow thought that distinguished itself from both the masses and the more mediocre elements of the middle-class American Jewry. Food played a part in this process, as *Commentary*'s writers linked food to social status at this time. This attitude was summed up in an article entitled, "Highbrow, Lowbrow, Middlebrow," in which Russell Lynes attempted to describe 1950s American urban social system in terms of food consumption practices, so the tossed salad, for example, became a sign of a highbrow individual who could also be discerned by his/her taste in cars, clothes, and posture (Lynes 1949, 14).

Commentary did not advertise Jell-O products. Jell-O was ersatz: it benefited from the huge increase in newly developed and sophisticated flavorings and food colorings during the 1950s, which led to a concomitant decrease in reliance on natural fruit and flavors. In defense of this a General Foods researcher claimed that: "There are not sufficient strawberries grown in the world to supply the demand for strawberry flavor" (Levenstein 1988, 109). Similarly, the authenticity of the Rosenbergs was questioned, as if they too were an ersatz product. As if to reinforce the notion that the Rosenbergs were somehow not "real," but artificial constructions of mass culture, the editor at *Commentary* responsible for producing critiques of that very culture (movies, comics, etc.), Robert Warshow, was selected to write the critique of the Rosenbergs' prison correspondence. Indulging in what Irving Howe called "perverse overkill" (Howe 1982, 215), Warshow wondered if "the literal truth had not in some way ceased to exist for these people." He went on to further question their very nature as humans, as if they were mere representations who have "no internal sense of their own being." He deplored the "falsity of the Rosenbergs' relations to culture, to sports, and to themselves." Thus, with no essential being, "they filled their lives with the second-hand" (Warshow 1953, 73, 74, 76). In this way, Warshow presented them as commodified products of mass culture. Indeed, Andrew Ross has pointed out that Warshow's argument here practically replicated his critique of mass culture (Ross 1989, 33). Leslie A. Fiedler added that "the Rosenbergs were not able to think of themselves as real people" for they were "replaceable." They did not have "selves realer than those official clichés" and "they could not hit upon any note that rang true." Since the Rosenbergs were not "real" their identities were fabrications, mere simulated constructions of Communist Party propaganda. Fiedler concluded: "they failed in the end to become martyrs or heroes, or even men. What was there left to die?" (Fiedler 1950, 38, 26). In the words of Morris Dickstein, the Rosenbergs had been thoroughly dehumanized (Dickstein 1977, 44). With no basis in reality, therefore, the Rosenbergs could be ignored. Like mass culture, they were worthless, meaningless, empty, and hence disposable.

Like the Rosenbergs, Jell-O was a commodified product of mass-produced culture. It was linked to the Rosenbergs and thus subversive, disloyal, and communistic. Jell-O thus represented the worst excesses of Stalinism. Reading the pages of *Commentary* and similar intellectual publications, a clear distaste for mass culture can be discerned. Mass culture was linked to Stalinism and the Popular Front period of history of which the Rosenbergs were the paradigm. Lionel Trilling, for example, wrote, "Stalinism becomes endemic in the middle class as soon as that class begins to think; it is a cultural Stalinism, independent of any political belief: the cultural ideas of the ADA will not, I venture to say, be found materially different from those of the PAC [Stalinist Political Action Committee of the CIO]" (qtd in Berman 1982, 80). Through the Rosenbergs, Jell-O came to symbolize the middlebrow, mass commodifed culture of the Popular Front era. Contributor Agnes McCrea Davis wrote of "unfortunate excursions into the Jello Belt." She described Jell-O as "commercial trash," which "cheapen[ed]" Jewish cuisine: "There seems to me no excuse for associating these nasty concoctions with Jewish food . . ." (Davis 1950, 491–492). Thus, the excision of Jell-O from the pages of *Commentary* stood for an attempt to circumscribe that culture and write it out of the history of American Jewry.

In its place *Commentary* promoted and advertised traditional Jewish food products. These were represented as being quintessentially authentic foods that contained real, natural, and kosher ingredients unlike the ersatz and *trayf* Jell-O. One advert in 1952 described *The Complete American Jewish Cook Book*, edited by Anne London and Bertha K. Bishov, as "The greatest Jewish cook book ever published—3500 recipes for delicious food with rare Jewish flavor—prepared in strict accordance with dietary rules." In other articles, M. Tsanin extolled the virtues of the traditional Jewish food *cholent* (Tsanin 1951, 270–272), while Irving Pfefferblit contrasted mass-produced American bread—"that tasteless, flavorless, bodiless miracle of modern science"—to the skilled craft of handmade bagel-making which had defied the age of machine techniques: "the Jewish *bagel* stands out like a golden vision of the bygone days when life was better, when things had substance, staying power, and an honest flavor of their own" (Pfefferblit 1951, 475).

But perhaps the most prominent foodstuff was *gefilte fish*. Gefilte fish means "stuffed fish" and is a poached fishball made from whitefish, pike, or carp with filler (bread crumbs or *matzo* meal) served on the Sabbath and holy days among German and Eastern European Jews in particular. Gefilte fish carried the mark of Jewish authenticity. *The Jewish Home Beautiful*, the guide for aspiring Jewish mothers, stated: "If there is any one particular food that might lay claim to being the Jewish national dish, gefilte fish is that food" (Greenberg and Silverman 1958, 126). Unlike Jell-O, the preparation of gefilte fish required skill and patience (as did the bagel). One company, Mother's, advertised its product by connecting it to history and tradition. Its gefilte fish was "old-fashioned" and "homestyle" unlike the newly developed Jell-O. It was the "real" thing (underlined for emphasis) unlike the ersatz Jell-O. It was made in the "finest tradition" and carried with it all of the symbols of *kashrut* and Jewish authenticity including Hebrew writing. And unlike Jell-O the *trayf*ness of which was hidden and submerged, gefilte fish was clearly and visibly kosher and safe. Had Ethel read her *Jewish Home Beautiful*, she would have learned that the good Jewish mother serves her children gefilte fish and should not be filling them with *trayf* products. In contrast to Ethel's stand "one million" Jewish mothers know better. One million Jewish mothers are not subversive or disloyal. They are loyal Americans who give their kids loyal, kosher foods.

Gefilte fish took its place as the centerpiece of Jewish cooking. The importance of gefilte fish to Jewish cuisine was demonstrated in September

1954, which marked the tercentenary of the arrival of Jews in America. Banquets were held to mark the event as an important date in Jewish-American memory. The most important of these banquets was the National Tercentenary Dinner held on October 20 in New York City at which President Eisenhower was the guest of honor. Gefilte fish was good enough to be served to the President! During the 1950s, gefilte fish was further popularized for a mass audience by *The Goldbergs*, an immensely popular television program which attracted some 40 million viewers per week, when in one episode ("Molly's Fish") its eponymous heroine, Molly Goldberg, was invited by a leading food manufacturer to produce some of her own recipe gefilte fish in his test kitchen. On the more everyday level, ready-made gefilte fish entered Jewish food consciousness to such an extent that by the 1970s a jar of Manischewitz gefilte fish was considered essential to celebrating Jewish holy days. Furthermore, gefilte fish was upheld as a method of prevention against assimilation as represented by the consumption of Chinese food: "Down with chop suey! Long live gefilte fish!" Thus, as Donald Weber has pointed out, ethnic food became an "agent of social incorporation: how, that is, the offering of (say) gefilte fish enacts a ritual of integration, of conformity, above all of reassurance" (Weber 1997, 158).

Other advertisements included those for Manischewitz and Streit's *matzo* as well as Pepsi-Cola. To link these foods produced under the most modern conditions ("inner-wrapped" and "oven-fresh") with their heritage, traditional Jewish symbols were invoked such as the menorah and Hebrew lettering. Pepsi-Cola, another quintessentially American product, was reinvented to connect Americanness (loyalty) with tradition as it also obtained the Jewish ritual seal of approval during the 1950s (the *hechsher*). Pepsi, Manischewitz *matzo*, and gefilte fish were all linked by what Jell-O is not: the symbols of *kashrut*. Jell-O can never be kosher because it contains nonkosher gelatin—to remove it would irrevocably alter the product. These other products, however, were kosher, safe, and loyal. It must be stated here that these products had also benefited from the remarkable transformations in production, preservation, and distribution within the food industry that occurred in the postwar period in America. Thus, Mother's proudly proclaimed that their gefilte fish was originated from their "spotless kitchens." Yet, as food technology improved, the need to authenticate certain products as traditional and kosher became even more imperative. New methods and techniques might detract from the authenticity of the product itself hence Mother's pronounced emphasis on tradition in an attempt to elide to an extent the modernity of the condition of its product's production. Furthermore, the 1950s witnessed the age of processed food and TV dinners backed up by bold, colorful advertisements, which proclaimed their benefits and, as mentioned above, *kashrut* had been under attack for some time as a result of a decline in traditional observance, suburbanization, and the widespread advent of both Chinese and fast food.

To counteract these trends or to exploit a niche in the market, manufacturers began a twin process of mass production of traditional Jewish foods and the *kosherization* of American products. *Matzo*, gefilte fish, and borscht all became available in prepared form. This had the effect of promoting the celebration of Jewish life while decreasing the time and energy expended in such celebrations. Mother's explicitly played upon such concerns: "Make Passover Memorable! Mother's Old-Fashioned Gefilte Fish. Time, work and money-saving. Ready-to-serve, in vacuum-packed glass jars with easy-open Steriseal caps." Pepsi-Cola, Maxwell House coffee, jelly, soups, sweets, cakes, noodles, ketchup, and hundreds of other products were sanctioned for use in kosher homes and on holidays thus enabling Jews to celebrate their festivals with American products. Jenna Weissman Joselit remarked that "thus almost every American diet staple is now available in kosher or Passover form" (Joselit 1995, 195). In advertising these products, manufacturers highlighted a commitment to family and domestic life in contrast to the dysfunctional Rosenberg family. Advertising encouraged a desire for these new kosher products whilst simultaneously diminishing misgivings about packaged, mass-produced foods. Kosher products emerged with the double marking of the traditional rabbinical imprimatur and of modern science's approval. Companies such as Manischewitz and Streit employed the latest techniques to guarantee the utmost hygiene and freshness.

Joselit believes that "it is not too far-fetched to say that these advertisements, together with the food products themselves, became new, typically twentieth century resources in the preservation and affirmation of Jewish identity" (Joselit 1990, 57). Marshall McLuhan observed that "any acceptable ad is a vigorous dramatization of communal experience" (McLuhan 1974, 243). And T. J. Jackson Lears pointed out how advertising folk icons such as Aunt Jemima, Aunt Belle, Betty Crocker, and in this case, the Jewish Mother, "epitomized a whole constellation of nuturant values associated with the preindustrial household and community life" for an uprooted suburban bourgeoisie that felt unconnected with their communities of origin (Jackson Lears 1994, 348). "Traditional foods and ways of eating," it has been stated, "form a link with the past and help ease the shock of entering a new culture" (Kalcik 1984, 37). As a consequence, the consumption of kosher foods became a way of affirming and celebrating tradition, Jewish identity, and cultural continuity. "In America," Tuchman and Levine observed, "the food of one's ethnic group symbolizes tradition and community" (Tuchman and Levine 1996, 25). A new category of Jewishness emerged—the "gastronomic Jew"—who derived his/her identity from digestion of ethnic foodstuffs rather than from scrupulous observance of the dietary laws (Joselit 1990, 25). Leslie A. Fiedler wrote: "It is well known that the last nostalgia of the assimilating Jew is for—hot pastrami and gefilte fish. 'Kugel Jews' the scornful phrase calls them; and yet there is in the last trivial loyalty, as there is in the Jewish conviction that 'goyim don't know how to eat right,' and in the incredible portion of their income that even the poorest Jews spend on food, a scarcely conscious memory of the sacramental nature of the Jewish meal . . ." (Fiedler 1949, 197). Nathan Glazer and William H. Whyte, Jr. both noted a "Jewish revival" (Glazer 1955, 493) and "a revival among Jews of religious and cultural practices which intensify one's sense of Jewishness . . . such as the dietary laws" (Whyte, Jr. 1957, 414–415). Kosher-style foods suddenly enjoyed a new popularity in postwar American Jewish life leading Ruth Glazer to write that "the egg beater is today the most effective weapon for propagating the faith" (Glazer 1956, 294). New cookbooks were produced in the 1950s both to meet and encourage the "kosher revival": *The Molly Goldberg Cookbook*; *The Art of Jewish Cooking*; *The Jewish Holidays and Their Favorite Foods*; *The Jewish Holiday Cookbook*; and *Aunt Fanny's Junior Jewish Cookbook*.

In a further attempt to enable Jews to be American in a traditionally Jewish fashion kosher gelatin substitutes and hence acceptable Jell-O's were developed. The patent abuse and misuse of a quintessentially American product undoubtedly caused part of the furor over the use of a Jell-O box in passing atomic secrets to the Soviet Union. How dare such people misappropriate a pillar of American cuisine in order to destroy the very country that produced it? Or, as Garber wrote:

> Considered in the context of the Rosenberg case, there is a sense in which the use of a Jell-O box as the supposed clue to a Communist conspiracy to deliver America and its free enterprise system into the hands of the Soviet Union ranks as the ultimate if trivial outrage. A Communist Jewish man is in the kitchen, cutting up Jell-O boxes, while his neglected children listen to the radio

("Jell-O Again"), and his wife, who *should* be in the kitchen making kosher Jell-O molds, is masterminding the theft of atomic secrets. Is this any way to rebuild America? (Garber 1995, 19)

So that Jews could continue to be both traditionally Jewish and loyal Americans at one and the same time, a range of conspicuously kosher alternatives to Jell-O began to appear, such as Kojel. Just as American gelatin products were being kosherized, there was also an attempt to recover Jell-O as a quintessentially American product. It is possible that the brand suffered by its high-profile linkage with the Rosenbergs. As a consequence, subsequent advertising campaigns attempted to reassert Jell-O's Americanness. Yet, Jell-O continued to occupy an ambiguous space in which its *kashrut* is still the subject of some debate. According to the only full-length scholarly treatise on Jell-O, Rosemarie Bria's 1991 Columbia University dissertation, "How Jell-O Molds Society and How Society Molds Jell-O: A Case Study of an American Food Industry Creation," Jell-O is currently certified as kosher by a recognized Orthodox rabbi as a result of the collagen having been taken apart by the chemical digestion to produce a new substance that is no longer fish/meat-based in origin. Consequently, Kraft Foods puts the kosher symbol of the plain letter K on its packets of Jell-O. However, this certification is controversial: because a letter of the alphabet cannot be trademarked for any manufacturer can put a K on its product. The upshot is many reliable Orthodox authorities would not agree that Jell-O is kosher.

The history of American Jewish cuisine in the 1950s demonstrates Donna R. Gabaccia's observation of "the symbolic power of food to reflect cultural or social affinities in moments of change or transformation" (Gabaccia 1998, 9). Food was one of the ways in which American Jews in the 1950s attempted to move into the American mainstream, but on their own terms. They sought simultaneously to articulate their loyalty to America (kosher) while distancing themselves from subversive elements such as the Rosenbergs (*trayf*). At the same time, an underlying trend of attempting to contain Jewish deviancy can be detected—the desire to prevent American Jews from participating in forbidden political and religious activities. Similarly, the manner in which Ethel Rosenberg was personally targeted as a bad mother and housewife demonstrated that elements of the American Jewish community were keen to uphold the larger bounds of gender roles. Through food and motherhood this was achieved by the promotion of traditional Jewish products that fitted into the

American way of life as well as the incorporation of American products into the traditional Jewish way of life.

Notes

I would like to thank the New Voices in Jewish Thought Seminar, and in particular, Cynthia Port, for their useful comments and suggestions.

Works Cited

Antler, Joyce. 1995. "A Bond of Sisterhood: Ethel Rosenberg, Molly Goldberg, and Radical Jewish Women of the 1950s." In *Secret Agents: The Rosenberg Case, McCarthyism, and Fifties America*. Ed. Marjorie Garber and Rebecca L. Walkowitz. New York and London: Routledge and Kegan Paul.

Avishai, Bernard. 1981. "Breaking Faith: *Commentary* and the American Jews." *Dissent* 28 (Spring): 236–256.

Berman, Ronald. 1982. "The 50's." *Commentary* 74, No. 5 (November): 79–80.

Bria, R. D. 1991. How Jell-O Molds Society and How Society Molds Jell-O: A Case Study of an American Food Industry Creation. Ed.D. diss., Columbia University.

Carmichael, Virginia. 1993. *Framing History: The Rosenberg Story and the Cold War*. Minneapolis and London: University of Minnesota Press.

Davis, Agnes McCrea. 1950. "Cookery Without Frippery." *Commentary* 9, No. 5 (May): 491–492.

Dickstein, Morris. 1977. *Gates of Eden: American Culture in the Sixties*. New York: Basic Books.

Fiedler, Leslie A. 1951. "Hiss, Chambers, and the Age of Innocence: Who Was Guilty—And of What?" *Commentary* 12, No. 2 (1951): 109–119.

———. 1950. "Afterthoughts on the Rosenbergs." In his *The End of Innocence*. Boston: Beacon.

———. 1949. "Hasidism and the Modern Jew." *Commentary* 7, No. 2 (February): 195–198.

Fineberg, S. Andhil. 1953. *The Rosenberg Case: Fact and Fiction*. New York: Oceana.

———. 1953. "They Screamed for Justice." *American Legion Magazine* 55 (July).

Flowerman, Samuel H. 1950. Confidential memorandum to John Slawson, Re: Public Relations Effects of Activities of Jewish Atom Spies, July 31, AJC Records RG 347, GEN–12, Box 139, France: Rosenberg Case Reaction FO-EUR, 52–54, AJC Records, YIVO.

Gabaccia, Donna R. 1998. *We Are What We Eat: Ethnic Food and the Making of Americans*. Cambridge, MA: Harvard University Press.

Gans, Herbert J. 1956. "American Jewry: Present and Future." *Commentary* 21, No. 5 (May): 422–430.

Garber, Marjorie. 1995. "Jell-O." In *Secret Agents: The Rosenberg Case, McCarthyism, and Fifties America*. Ed. Marjorie Garber and Rebecca L. Walkowitz. New York and London: Routledge and Kegan Paul.

Howe, Irving. 1982. *A Margin of Hope: An Intellectual Autobiography*. London: Secker & Warburg.

Glazer, Nathan. 1955. "The Jewish Revival in America." *Commentary* 20, No. 6 (December): 493–499.

Glazer, Ruth. 1956. "Holiday Cook." *Commentary* 21, No. 3 (March): 294–295.

Greenberg, Betty D., and Silverman, Althea O. 1958. *The Jewish Home Beautiful*, 9th ed New York: The National Women's League of the United Synagogue of America.

Joselit, Jenna Weissman. 1995. *The Wonders of America: Reinventing Jewish Culture 1880–1950*. New York: Hill & Wang.

———. 1990. "'A Set Table': Jewish Domestic Culture in the New World." In *Getting Comfortable in New York: The American Jewish Home, 1880–1950*. Ed. Susan L. Braunstein and Jenna Weissman Joselit. New York: The Jewish Museum.

Kalcik, Susan. 1984. "Ethnic Foodways in America: Symbol and the Performance of Identity." In *Ethnic and Regional Foodways in the United States: The Performance of Group Identity*. Ed. L. K. Brown and K. Mussell. Knoxville: University of Tennessee Press.

Kristol, Irving. 1954. "The Web of Realism." *Commentary* 17, No. 6 (June): 609–610.

Lears, T. J. Jackson. 1994. *Fables of Abundance: A Cultural History of Advertising in America*. New York: Basic Books.

Levenstein, Harvey. 1988. *Paradox of Plenty: A Social History of Eating in Modern America*. Oxford: Oxford University Press.

Lynes, Russell. 1949. "Highbrow, Lowbrow, Middlebrow." *Harper's* 198.

McLuhan, Marshall. 1974. *Understanding Media: The Extensions of Man*. London: Abacus.

Meeropol, Robert. 1995. "Rosenberg Realities." In *Secret Agents: The Rosenberg Case, McCarthyism, and Fifties America*. Ed. Marjorie Garber and Rebecca L. Walkowitz. New York and London: Routledge and Kegan Paul.

Miller, Arthur. 1994. *After the Fall.* In his *Plays: Two*. London: Methuen.

Moore, Deborah Dash. 1988. "Reconsidering the Rosenbergs: Symbol and Substance in Second Generation American Jewish Consciousness." *Journal of American Ethnic History* 8.

Nathan, Joan. 1994. *Jewish Cooking in America*. New York: Knopf.

Navasky, Victor S. 1980. *Naming Names*. New York: Viking.

Pfefferblit, Irving. 1951. "The Bagel: On This Rock . . ." *Commentary* 11, No. 5 (April): 475–479.

Philipson, Ilene. 1993. *Ethel Rosenberg: Beyond the Myths*. New Brunswick, NJ: Rutgers University Press.

Radosh, Ronald and Joyce Milton. 1997. *The Rosenberg File*, 2d ed. New Haven and London: Yale University Press.

Rosenberg, Julius and Ethel. 1953. *The Death House Letters of Ethel and Julius Rosenberg*. New York: Jero.

Rosenfeld, Isaac. 1949. "Adam and Eve on Delancey Street." *Commentary* 8, No. 4 (October), 385–387.

Ross, Andrew. 1989. *No Respect: Intellectuals and Popular Culture*. New York and London: Routledge and Kegan Paul.

Rosten, Leo. 1968. *The Joys of Yiddish*. London: Penguin.

Schneir, Walter and Miriam Schneir. 1968. *Invitation to an Inquest: A New Look at the Rosenberg-Sobell Case*. New York: Dell.

Sklare, Marshall. 1972. *Conservative Judaism: An American Religious Movement*. New York.

Slawson, John. 1953. Internal memorandum to Morris Fine, October 22, AJC Records, RG 347 GEN–12, Box 139, France: Rosenberg Case Reaction FO-EUR, 52–54, YIVO.

Suchoff, David. 1995. "The Rosenberg Case and the New York Intellectuals." In *Secret Agents: The Rosenberg Case, McCarthyism, and Fifties America*. Ed. Marjorie Garber and Rebecca L. Walkowitz. New York and London: Routledge and Kegan Paul.

Tsanin, M. 1951. "Tcholent to the Rescue." *Commentary* 11, No. 3 (March): 270–272.

Tuchman, Gaye and Harry Levine. 1996. "Safe Treyf." *Brandeis Review* (Summer): 29–30.

Warshow, Robert. 1953. "The 'Idealism' of Julius and Ethel Rosenberg." *Commentary* 16, No. 5 (November): 413–418.

———. 1947. "The Legacy of the 30's: Midde-Class Culture and the Intellectuals' Problem." *Commentary* 4, No. 6 (December), 540.

Weber, Donald. 1997. "Memory and Repression in Early Ethnic Television: The Example of Gertrude Berg and *The Goldbergs*." In *The Other Fifties: Interrogating Midcentury American Icons*. Ed. Joel Foreman. Urbana and Chicago: University of Illinois Press.

Whyte, William H. Jr. 1957. *The Organization Man*. Garden City, NY: Doubleday Anchor Books.

CHAPTER 5

Cooking the Books

Jewish Cuisine and the Commodification of Difference

Eric Mason

It is easy to miss the small encircled "U" often printed on modern food items to signify that a food has been prepared in accordance with kosher (*kashrut*) practice. It is hard to be completely unaware, however, of Jewish culinary practices since, as anthropologist Joelle Balhoul writes, they are the "most quotidian and obvious form of sociocultural distinction in the Jewish tradition" (1995, 485). In some cases, these culinary traditions become the targets of what Edward Said calls "ideologies of difference," ideologies which use difference as a way to ascribe negative characteristics or qualities to an Other (1986, 41). In the repressive forms of these ideologies, "a particular cultural trait or tradition—the smell of somebody's food, the color of their skin, the accent that they speak with, their particular history, be it Irish or Indian or Jewish—becomes the site of contestation, abuse, insult, or discrimination" (Bhabha 1999, 16). For example, according to the Anti-Defamation League, the encircled "U" symbol has been singled out by certain racist groups as evidence that consumers are subjected to a "'kosher tax' to make rabbis rich" (1991).

Ideologies of difference often underlie such assertions of repressive power regarding marginalized groups. But although it is most often considered repressive, power is productive as well: power "produces things, it induces pleasure, forms knowledge, produces discourse. It needs to be considered as a productive network that runs through the whole social body, much more than as a negative instance whose function is repression" (Foucault 1980, 120). Because culinary tradition is a network of production (of discourse, knowledge, and, without question, pleasure) with ideological investments that should not be taken lightly, this chapter seeks to engage a genre that is conspicuously about production and pleasure: the cookbook. Admittedly, production is always tied to consumption, just as recipes are normally included in cookbooks under the auspices that following them will result in a consumable product. But cookbooks directly engage not only the particularities of Jewish cooking, but also the ideologies of difference through which Jewish culinary tradition and Jewish identity are produced.

Specifically, this chapter seeks to understand how difference is implicated in the modern interest in Sephardic cuisine, the cooking of the descendants of the large Jewish community that lived in Spain and Portugal during the Middle Ages. Sephardic cuisine emerged generally from the Diaspora, and specifically from the intolerance of the Spanish Inquisition. Despite this heritage, or, perhaps, because of it, Sephardic-themed cookbooks have recently become "the top-selling Jewish cookbooks on Amazon.com," consumer interest having grown steadily following the five hundredth anniversary of Ferdinand and Isabella's edict of expulsion, which in 1492 gave Jews only a few months in which to leave the country or convert to Catholicism (Keys 2003). The current success of these cookbooks, I argue below, is based on a commodification of difference that positions Sephardic cooking as the exotic Other of Jewish cuisine, a process that in many ways reproduces within Jewish culture the same types of ideological discourses of difference to which Jews and many other marginalized groups have historically been subjected.

It is not the cookbook genre itself that is at issue. After all, locally produced cookbooks appear in the liberatory literacy education advocated by Paulo Freire. And cookbooks need not submit to the dominant discourse that evaluates them according to their use-value as instruction manuals. Other models exist, such as "the cookbook as inheritance. As memoir. As resistance. As life force. As testimony" (Kaufman 2004, 431). My goal is neither to vilify individual cookbook authors nor the genre as a whole, but to suggest ways in which the production and reception of cookbooks often participate in a cultural politics of difference, a politics in which cookbooks are signs of an ongoing struggle over the meaning and valuation of difference. Cookbooks (and their televisual equivalent, the cooking show) often promise consumers encounters with the Other that are "marked as more exciting, more intense, and more threatening" than ordinary life while simultaneously denying the "significance of that Other's history through a process of decontextualization" (hooks 1999, 183, 186). The successful conversion of difference into a commodity depends on this simultaneous marking and erasure.

Below, the role of difference will be considered within several cookbooks, primarily Faye Levy's *Jewish Cooking for Dummies*, Claudia Roden's *The Book of Jewish Food*, Time-Life's *The Cooking of Spain and Portugal*, and Linda Kay Davidson and David M. Gitlitz's *A Drizzle of Honey: The Lives and Recipes of Spain's Secret Jews*. This last book reconstructs the recipes of Jews living (and cooking) secretly in medieval Spain under the disciplinary gaze of the Inquisition, and, out of all of the cookbooks above, most challenges the discourse of commodity culture by situating its recipes in a historical context in which difference matters.[1] There may seem to be more consequential venues than cookbooks in which to analyze the production of difference, venues in which "dehumanization" and "violent extremism" are clearly instigated by "processes of cultural differentiation that demonize difference" (West 2002, 2). But it should be recognized that a similar logic found in the demonization of difference can motivate the excessive celebration of difference as well. If not equally troubling, they are at least equally suitable subjects for ideological critique. As Louis Althusser notes, the "material existence" of ideology is constituted through the practices and rituals of everyday life, and thus it is likely that it is in everyday practices such as cooking that one can witness the production of individuals as subjects within ideology (2001, 112). Cookbooks thus reveal to us that the work of ideology is always, literally, in the making.

Eating Ideology: Jewish Culinary Tradition

". . . in any particular society, cooking is a language through which that society unconsciously reveals its structure, unless—just as unconsciously—it resigns itself to using the medium to express its contradictions."
> —Claude Lévi-Strauss, *The Origins of Table Manners*

"There's no such thing as Jewish cooking, per se."
> —Jeffrey Nathan, host of APB's "New Jewish Cuisine"

Before analyzing the ways in which cookbooks construct Jewish difference, it is useful to understand the ideological formations that inform
Jewish culinary traditions. Jewish cooking is subject to a host of restrictions both gastronomic and culinary (i.e., regarding both what food is
acceptable for consumption and how that food should be prepared). These
dietary laws are enforced by *mashgiah* (inspectors who prevent violations of
Jewish dietary laws) and authorized by religious texts such as the Torah
and the Talmud, the latter being highly concerned with food and cooking,
covering what is and is not permissible in the kitchen, market, and
slaughterhouse in "extreme minutiae" (Roden 1996, 24). One gastronomic law states that the hindquarters of animals from which the nerve
and tendons have not been removed is forbidden (*terefah*), and is based on
a biblical story in which Jacob's thigh was injured by a stranger, leaving
him with a limp (according to some interpretations, all hindquarter meat
is forbidden, regardless of the removal of nerves or tendons, a process
known as "porging" [Roden 1996, 19]). One culinary law is the injunction against storing, cooking, or eating dairy (*milshig*) and meat (*fleyshig*)
together. In some observant households, entirely separate sets of utensils,
dishes, and linens are used for each type of meal.

In light of such elaborate rituals, it is tempting to agree with Lévi-
Strauss's statement above that cooking is a language that reveals the structure of Jewish culture. The notion that culinary traditions reveal a
preexisting unconscious social structure is undercut, however, by the
extensive rabbinic literature which has advanced a host of competing
explanations for this culinary "language," including "moral, philosophi-
cal, mystical, and metaphysical" explanations (Roden 1996, 21). Rather
than claim, as Lévi-Strauss does, that culinary traditions reveal the structure of a society, attention should be drawn to how these traditions are
represented, for it is in these representations that one can begin to see how
structure is not an essence revealed in practices, but how practices and discourse dialectically construct each other, engaging in acts of marking and
erasure that constitute culture rather than reveal it.

The opening page of Faye Levy's popular cookbook *Jewish Cooking for
Dummies*, for instance, promises the reader that the recipes contained in
the cookbook are a "pleasure to prepare and to eat," that the cuisine is
"simple to prepare," and that even the "shopping is easy" (2001, 1). Such
enticements reveal less about the structure of traditional Jewish culture
than they do about the desires of modern homemakers. In a society
devoted to the "ideology of ease," the promise of simplicity and swift grat-

ification is a powerful ideological force (Dilger 2000). Descriptions attuned to modern sensibilities, sometimes in opposition to conventional understandings of Jewish tradition, appear throughout *Jewish Cooking for Dummies*. The section titled "Meat: Slow Cooking is a Virtual Mandate" seems to fulfill the promise made in the cookbook's introduction that it will explain to the unenlightened reader "why cholent for Shabbat (Sabbath) cooks all night" (Levy 2001, 2). But the slow cooking section invites the reader to "discover the advantage, ease, and pleasure of the gentle, relaxed cooking methods for meat," stating that "the key to these techniques' appeal is the *flavor exchange principle*" (Levy 2001, 211).

Admittedly, the text does make passing mention that the "ultimate slow-cooked dish is the overnight Sabbath stew," but the "flavor exchange principle" offered as the key to why meat is slow cooked is not a rabbinical teaching, but a symptom of an ideology which calls upon cooks to create, first and foremost, main courses "full of flavor" (Levy 2001, 211). How such a principle could conflict with less consumer-oriented traditions is revealed when Claudia Roden tells a story in which a friend of hers, eating the slow-cooked Sabbath meal with a family in Jerusalem, complains that the meal was not very tasty. The family's (ideological) reply: "It's not supposed to be" (Roden 1996, 148). Representations of Sabbath meals that emphasize taste or ease in the slow cooking of the meal often downplay the role that religious laws have in promoting this cooking method. These laws explicitly prohibit any work, including lighting fires and cooking food, from Friday sunset to Saturday evening.

According to Roden, these religious laws have "given rise to a very wide range of meals-in-a-pot to be prepared on Friday afternoon and left to cook overnight for Saturday lunch" (1996, 10). The mandate to slow cook meat overnight is not represented in Levy's text primarily as an issue of religious observance, but as an expression of the properties of the ingredients themselves, which, according to the flavor exchange principle, "contribute good taste to each other," allowing the dish to become "more than a simple sum of its ingredients" (Levy 2001, 211). By focusing on such qualities, Levy's *Jewish Cooking for Dummies* distances itself from the representation of dietary laws as having religious origins, adopting instead the discourses of taste and of convenience, discourses held sacred primarily by commercial food interests.

Although some cookbooks intentionally obscure the religious origins of culinary traditions, it would be wrong to assume that all references to food in Jewish tradition have these origins. In fact, the attribution of culinary traditions to religious sources can at times itself be primarily ide-ological. The Bible recounts how the exodus of the Jews from Egypt had as its end the Promised Land, the "most familiar and most cherished" description of which is specifically food-based: the land "flowing with milk and honey" (Levine 1986, 43). Milk and honey are often presented in biblical texts as luxury items used in trade and as gifts. In modern Judaism, honey especially is associated with pleasure and good health. At Rosh Hashanah, the Jewish New Year, it is customary to avoid bitter foods and to "eat a piece of apple dipped in honey while a prayer is said asking God for a sweet year" (Roden 1996, 28). The Book of Exodus reports that even the "divinely bestowed-mannah in the wilderness has the taste of honey" (Levine 1986, 43).

Although people have been "virtually unanimous in understanding the phrase 'flowing with milk and honey,' as an Eden-like hyperbole stressing the abundant fertility and lushness" of the Promised Land, this is not necessarily an understanding in accord with biblical text or based on rabbinical interpretation (Levine 1986, 43). As in *Jewish Cooking for Dummies*, the popular understanding locates the meaning of this phrase in the essences of the ingredients—the sweetness of the honey, the richness of the milk—rather than in the sociohistorical context of the Jews. Étan Levine writes that "biblical diction paired 'milk and honey' not simply because of their gastronomical or culinary affinity, but because both milk and honey are products of the very same topographical-economic condi-tions. And these are the conditions of bare survival: almost the very oppo-site of a Garden of Eden, Paradise or the like" (1986, 44). Milk and honey are both "products not of rich, cultivated farmlands, but of poor, uncul-tivated grazing areas . . . it is there, amidst the wild thickets, rocks and bushes, that the wild honey is also found" (Levine 1986, 44). So, milk and honey do not define a landscape of abundance but, rather, one unsuit-able for agriculture.

It is significant that the popular understanding of these foods is cen-tered on what it is like to consume them rather than what it is like to pro-duce them. The desire to talk about milk and honey as items for consumption, and therefore to associate the land "flowing with milk and honey" with a state of luxury, might be considered an identification based on class, a desire to speak from the position of one who has the leisure to consume these items, rather than one who provides the labor to produce them. In other words, this desire is ideological. There is no religious origin revealed in this food-related phrase, only ideological discourse shaped by, among other things, class-based identifications and topography.[2] In fact, there is only one place in the Bible, in the Book of Numbers, where a "'land flowing with milk and honey' may well signify lushness and fertility *par excellence* . . . [and it is in] nostalgic allusion to Egypt, not to the land of Israel!" (Levine 1986, 46). So when Roden writes that Exodus recalls the "wistful longings of the Jews for the foods that they had left behind in Egypt" (1996, 8), it seems possible that these longings have more in common with nostalgia prompted by the fact that the "nomadism or semi-nomadism [of exile] was not an *ideal*" life, or perhaps even with stereotypes of Jewish people that associate them with a hunger for wealth, than they do with any religious doctrine (Levine 1986, 50). The association of the Jews with a superabundant Promised Land may even signal the presence of an "imperialist nostalgia" in which the "contemporary longing for the 'primitive' is expressed by the projection onto the Other of a sense of plenty, bounty, a field of dreams" (hooks 1999, 182).

It is important, despite the ideological nature of assigning origins, to recognize the many Jewish practices that do integrate culinary and religious traditions. At the family level, the relation between food and religion is continuously underscored by the "contrast between the sobriety of weekday food and the opulence of Sabbath and holiday food" (Roden 1996, 25). At the cultural level, food sustains identity because all Jews can be said to "share a few special foods that are fundamentally Jewish" (Sokolov 1988, 88). Since these foods are what Raymond Sokolov calls "liturgical foods," this identity is particularly a religious one, and the most important religious celebration is "Passover, the only traditional holiday that revolves around food."[3] The foods of the Seder supper are integral to the celebration of Passover. In deference to the "memory of the Jews who fled [Egypt] in such a hurry that their dough did not have time to rise," leavened foods are forbidden, including all grains and grain products that may ferment naturally when exposed to moisture (Roden 1996, 34). Unleavened bread is allowed, such as *matzos*, as long as the flour has been specially prepared to protect it from fermentation. Other ritual foods include the following:

- Karpas, a green vegetable representing new growth, dipped in salt water symbolizing the tears of slaves
- Bitter herbs, reminiscent of the bitter times of slavery
- A roasted egg, representing a sacrificial offering to God in the Temple

- A lamb-shank bone, representing the lamb sacrificed on the eve of the Exodus
- A fruit and nut paste called *haroset* that recalls the color of mortar made from Nile silt which the Jews used to build pyramids for the pharaohs (Roden 1996, 36).

The significance of these emblematic foods is the role they play in the ritual reassertion of a traditional Jewish identity. For Jews, cooking and consuming these dishes serves as a "link with the past, a celebration of roots, a symbol of continuity" (Roden 1996, 11). Especially through these foods' association with slavery, their consumption becomes a remembrance of (forced) production. Also, in the more general case of remembering Diaspora, nomadism, and struggle, these meals defy the nostalgic associations that motivate the interpretation of the land "flowing with milk and honey" as a site of luxury.

Although the Jewish holidays are more extravagant than the weekly Sabbath, the Sabbath meal is more regularly experienced, and so the traditions surrounding this meal should be considered as well for their role in forming Jewish identity. The injunction against lighting fires on the Sabbath might lead one to believe that the Sabbath meal would typically be a cold kosher dish. But, although work is prohibited on the Sabbath, the Sabbath is "not meant as a day of suffering, so special efforts are made to serve hot food that does not involve cooking or lighting fires" (Sokolov 1988, 89–90). The *matzo* eaten at Passover may be a "principal example of a universal Jewish food, always and everywhere basically the same. There is, however, another, more elusive category of Jewish food found throughout the world wherever there are practicing Jews" (Sokolov 1988, 88). This category of Jewish food includes all those hot dishes served midday on Saturday after the Sabbath morning service.

For Ashkenazi Jews (those Jews with roots in Germany and, more generally, Eastern Europe), this Sabbath meal was traditionally a slow-cooked stew of beef and beans known as *cholent*, which Jewish-American poet John Hollander has called the "cassoulet of the Jews" (Qtd. in Sokolov 1988, 88). This dish is so central to Jewish identity that one even hears that "A test of 'who is a Jew' is supposed to be whether you like cholent" (Roden 1996, 148). But while every Jewish cookbook will have a recipe for *cholent* (sometimes noting multiple variations), Sokolov writes that it is a "mistake . . . to think of cholent as a dish" (Sokolov 1988, 88). Rather, *cholent* is "any hot food that satisfies the religious definition of a dish kosher for *Shabbat* (Sabbath)" (1988, 89). The "worldwide diaspora of [*cholent* as] a culinary concept" is a function of its religious significance, not its gastronomic appeal (Sokolov 1988, 88).

Rabbi Marc Wilson, also known as "Rabbi Ribeye," also thinks of *cholent* as an "ingenious, robust, aromatic answer" to religious admonitions, and as a dish that shows what can happen "when form is allowed to follow function" (Wilson 2004). In truth, although what Sokolov calls the "cholent concept" may indeed be universal, the term "*cholent*" is not (1988, 90). Similar stews (similar in function, but not identical in ingredients) in other Jewish communities are given the following names: in Calcutta, *hameen* or *khamin*; in the Middle East, *tfina, dfina, adafina,* or *adefina*; in Spain, *cocido* or *adafina*; in Yemen, *gillah*; and, in Morocco, *sefrina* or *skhina* (Sokolov 1988, 90–91). As Sokolov quips, "a cholent was not always a cholent" (1988, 88).

What all of the above dishes do have in common is that "all of them [are] hot and buried, cooked while you sleep and pray" (Sokolov 1988, 91). By "hot and buried" Sokolov is referring to the tradition in which cooks prepare the Sabbath meal on Friday before dark, cook it in a covered dish, and only uncover it on Saturday. The dish remains "hidden" or "buried" this entire time, a tradition that is traceable to rabbinical commentaries on the Talmud that contain the phrase "*taman at hakhamin*," which translates literally as "'hide or bury the hot things,' meaning cover the hot food" (Sokolov 1988, 90). So, the Sabbath meal really does not require specific ingredients (although there are ingredients that are, by religious decree, not allowed). But it is exactly the content of *cholent* which cookbooks promise to reveal, transforming a religious mandate into a culinary formula.

In a poem entitled "Princess Sabbath," the German poet Heinrich Heine addresses *cholent* with hyperbolic praise, calling it "kosher ambrosia," a comparison that Sokolov acknowledges is "bombastic" yet "apt in one way at least: neither ambrosia nor cholent is a definable food in the ordinary sense" (Sokolov 1988, 89). The reason that *cholent* is not a "definable food" is that "*cholent*" is an empty signifier, a "signifier without a signified" (Laclau 1996, 36). Since *cholent* is defined not by what you put in it, but by what you can not put in it, its meaning is purely relational, defined within a "system of differences" that reveals the "structural impossibility in signification" (Laclau 1996, 37). The impossibility of signification is not unrelated to Roden's statement (as well as Jeffrey Nathan's statement at the beginning of this section) that "There is really no such thing as Jewish food" (Roden 1996, 9). Cookbooks, while attempting to overcome this impossibility by assigning a positive content to each dish, nevertheless rely on a system of differences, a system that positions Sephardic cuisine as the exotic Other of Jewish culinary tradition.

Sephardic Supplements: On the Diversity of Jewish Cuisine

In an article in the Jewish newspaper, *Forward*, titled "Ashkenazim Embrace Sephardic Fare in Latest Cooking Craze," the author characterizes the allure of Sephardic food:

> Now is the moment of Sephardic food. In the never-ending search for the "latest" thing, Ashkenazi Jews are embracing Sephardic cooking by the multitudes, attending Sephardic cooking courses, buying up cookbooks . . . , liberally using olive oil (how *very* Mediterranean) and consuming ubiquitous tubs of hummus, now found everywhere from small-town supermarkets to kosher pizzerias. (Keys 2003)

The popularity of Sephardic cuisine is directly tied here to the differences that mark it as fashionable and adventurous. Questioned by the article's author, kosher chef Jeffrey Nathan openly admits that, in his cookbook, *Adventures in Jewish Cooking*, "80 percent or more [recipes] are Sephardi— even though I'm Ashkenazi" (Qtd. in Keys 2003). Claudia Roden voices a similar confession about her cookbook, stating that "It may seem to you, on looking at the book, that I have chosen a disproportionately large number of Sephardi recipes" (1996, 14). She assures the reader that the "criterion of [recipe] selection throughout was to include only the most delicious" (Roden 1996, 14). While this may satisfy the consumer concerned primarily with flavor and for whom difference "becomes spice, seasoning that can liven up the dull dish," it does little justice to the numerous Jewish communities who are "classed as Sephardi, although many of the communities share little of the heritage of Spain or the Mediterranean and have never thought of themselves as Sephardi" (Roden 1996, 15). Furthermore, although she admits the groups she collects under the rubric "Sephardi" are very diverse, Roden justifies their "unity" by claiming that what is important is that "their dishes go well together in a meal" (1996, 15). For Roden, the discourse of taste becomes a way of avoiding "socially responsible versions of difference" (West 2002, 12).[4]

Roden is at least partially aware of the ethics involved here, stating that the "alternative—to call the Sephardi recipe section as belonging to 'the *other* Jews'—would not do either" (1996, 15). But even though she begins her research planning to produce a "grand comprehensive project" that would catalog the culinary traditions of all Jewish communities, she finds herself only able to focus on those communities in "important Jewish centers and whose cooking is most widespread, and most particularly on those whose cooking is prestigious" (Roden 1996, 11, 12). This approach is troublingly similar to Arjun Appadurai's description of surviving cookbooks from the preindustrial world, which were mainly the projects of native royalty or aristocrats, whose wealth and station both enabled and necessitated the consumption of sumptuous meals aspiring to "high cuisine" (Appadurai 1988, 4). One modern cookbook boasts that great dishes are often "a poor man's food that has become the rich man's treat" (Feibleman 1969, 76–77). In such cases, cookbook authors draw upon "regional, provincial, and folk materials" and supplement these materials with luxury and spectacle in order to "distance themselves from their local sources" (Appadurai 1988, 4). Such decontextualizations serve the needs of classes that have access to the time, space, ingredients, and other resources needed for culinary experimentation. In view of the tendency for cookbooks to exploit some classes in order to benefit other classes, we should ask a question inspired by Gayatri Spivak: Can the subaltern cook?

As the title of Nathan's *Adventures in Jewish Cooking* does, many cookbooks evoke narratives of exploration to describe the process of learning about a cuisine. The first chapter of *Jewish Cooking for Dummies* promises readers they will soon be "discovering what lies behind Jewish cooking" (Levy 2001, 9). Roden's *The Book of Jewish Food* is subtitled "An Odyssey from Samarkand to New York," and working on it, she notes, has been "for me a voyage of discovery" (1996, iii, 14). Time-Life's *The Cooking of Spain and Portugal* (which includes Sephardic cooking, "*sepharad*" being the Hebrew word for Spain) is structured as a "gastronomic tour through the galaxy of Iberian cuisine" (Feibleman 1969, 12). Such statements position the cookbook reader as a culinary tourist, if not a pioneer or explorer conquering a new world. Roden argues that Jewish cooking has always been shaped by "a touch of cosmopolitanism which broke through even the ghetto walls. Jewish culinary interests were always wider than those of their immediate environment" (1996, 10). In ancient times, these interests were satisfied by the many itinerant "merchants and peddlers, traveling rabbis, preachers and teachers, students and cantors, professional letter carriers, beggars (who were legion), and pilgrims on their way to the Holy Land" (Roden 1996, 10).

But the seminomadism of ancient Jewish cooks is not the same as the culinary tourism of the modern consumer. If it was, the history of Diaspora would be apparent in cookbook authors' appraisals of the significance of Sephardic cuisine. Instead, Sephardic cuisine is presented as being worthy of attention because it is "not only more healthy, but also more tasty" (Keys 2003). Hence, the popularity of Sephardic-themed cookbooks with titles promising to deliver recipes for the "Healthful Food" of "Exotic Sephardic Kitchens" (Sternberg 1996; Marks 1992). This transforms Diaspora into a positive yet depthless commodity. The desire for depth can lead to what Charles Taylor calls the "politics of difference"—the commitment to the flourishing of cultural difference rather than to its exploitation, a call "to recognize and even foster particularity" through intercultural dialogue (Taylor 1992, 38, 43). But cookbooks rarely provide opportunities for such dialogue. Rather, they construct difference as an "unexplored terrain, a symbolic frontier that will be fertile ground for [the] reconstruction" of the consumer's hegemonic identity (hooks 1999, 180). What they offer is the commodification of difference.

In her provocatively titled essay, "Eating the Other," bell hooks writes that commodity culture "perpetuates the idea that there is pleasure to be found in the acknowledgment and enjoyment" of difference, offering encounters with an exoticized Other that are a "new delight, more intense, more satisfying than normal ways of doing and feeling" (hooks 1999, 179). By making difference into a commodity available to anyone, cookbooks promote "paradigms of consumption wherein whatever difference the Other inhabits is eradicated" (hooks 1999, 186). This eradication is achieved by not only making difference available for appropriation, but also by the denial and decontextualization of the specific history of that difference. This decontextualization can occur in many ways, most obviously when the recipe is presented as simply a set of ingredients and instructions.[5] Other techniques contribute as well, such as the artificial grouping of recipes into categories by main ingredient, difficulty, or meal type. Often, little room is apportioned for the historical context of the recipe, although sometimes the contributing author of the recipe is named. Even this practice is slightly misleading in that few recipes are owned by a single person or original in any meaningful sense. Gazing over the recipes in her cookbook, Roden writes that "Each recipe has a name. There is 'kobeba Latifa,' 'fromage blanc Adèle,' 'hamud Sophie,' 'pasteles Iris,' 'blehat Rahel,' and so on. Most of the people are dead now. They were my parents' generation. But their recipes keep their memory very much alive, at least for me" (1996, 4). Roden's qualification, "at least for me," is telling. Although these names evoke memories in Roden, they are for cookbook consumers mainly signifiers of a nonspecific Other, memories of whom have been "commodified as resources for pleasure" (hooks 1999, 180).

Names are, unsurprisingly, one of the signifiers through which difference is most commonly constructed. The first way listed in Ruth K. Setton's article "Ten Ways to Recognize a Sephardic 'Jew-ess'" is by her name (1997, 80). She writes that Sephardic names, like her own middle name, Knafo, are "often unpronounceable, unmanageable, redolent of incense and cumin"; they conjure images of "arches and Alhambra, dusty streets and brown hoods" (Setton 1997, 80). The second way to recognize a Sephardic Jew-ess, she claims, is by her cooking. Setton describes a detailed scene from her childhood, remembering her mother's salads of "oranges and black olives, the colors alone nearly sending me on another voyage; purple beets and celery; cooked peppers red, yellow and green, drizzled with olive oil and seasoned with preserved lemon, chili peppers, and cumin" (Setton 1997, 80). Setton's colorful description of her mother's food underscores the role of the visual in the construction of difference. The visual is especially important to commodity culture and a key site in the struggle over the value and meaning of difference. The subject of the full-color photograph in the modern cookbook is most often the dish itself, which, having been prepared especially for photography in the studio, yields little historical information.

Two images in Peter S. Feibleman's *The Cooking of Spain and Portugal* make visible hooks' claim that commodity culture at once accentuates and eradicates difference, ensuring the viewer that "one's familiar world will remain intact" (hooks 1969, 182).[6] The first picture dominates the book's cover and is of a pan of *paella*, the dish that the cookbook's author claims is the "Spanish culinary triumph best known outside the country" (Feibleman 1969, 72). The dish's bright yellow rice is dotted with colorful vegetables, chicken, and shellfish. Placing this dish on the cover, then, eradicates difference by reassuring the reader of the familiarity of the book's content (by displaying the most recognizable dish in Spanish culture) and accentuates difference by providing a visual synecdoche for the exotic diversity of the Iberian Peninsula (by displaying a colorful dish made up of a complex blend of ingredients). The cookbook encourages this latter interpretation when it states:

> Like the people of the Iberian Peninsula, the cooking of this region is a blend of many ingredients. The blend is complex at times, but the ingredients are not disguised and never spiced to alter basically simple tastes. The strength of Iberian cooking is natural, and its subtlety is derived from the combination of ingredients, the fundamental mixture itself. . . . it is always purely Iberian, and once you come to know it, you will not be likely to mistake it for anything else. (Feibleman 1969, 10)

The image drawn of a "purely Iberian" identity is a view of culture that Stuart Hall calls an "essentialized notion of ethnicity" (1999, 226). The characterization of Iberian cuisine, despite its complexity, as knowable and manageable, works to neutralize the "metaphorical Other that threatens to take over, consume, transform via the experience of pleasure" (hooks 1999, 180).

The background on which the *paella* pan rests on the cover of *The Cooking of Spain and Portugal* is noteworthy as well. The tessellated cobalt-blue tiles behind the *paella* on the cover are single-hued, drawing little attention to the background. A second *paella* image, the one accompanying the recipe within the book, however, shows a *paella* pan resting on a field of tiles that are clearly in an Islamic pattern, the *khatem sulemani*, the eight-pointed star that is the "most frequently occurring pattern in Islamic culture" (Abas and Salman 1995, 14). This image better captures the "mixed mongrelized world" in which Hall says that we live and the historical reality of the Moorish presence in Spain (1999, 213). This presence is evident not only in the cookbook's recipes, but in the many examples of Moorish architecture and design elements such as the tiles that make this history visible, if only in the background. The two images of *paella* are strikingly similar, so much so that the choice to place the image with nondescript blue tile on the cover of the cookbook rather than the one showing the complex Islamic tile might be seen as a move to satisfy the reader's need for a safe encounter with the Other, and to downplay the historic context of the dish's and the region's history, which include the histories of oppressed groups within Spain such as the Sephardic Jews.

Claudia Roden writes in her introduction to *The Book of Jewish Food* that "Every cuisine tells a story. Jewish food tells the story of an uprooted, migrating people and their vanished worlds" (1996, 3). The Jewish diasporas, beginning with the destruction of the Second Temple in the first century AD, undoubtedly contributed much to the current diversity of Jewish cuisine. According to Stuart Hall, the field of cooking is an "incredibly diverse field *because* it is a diasporic field" (1999, 212; emphasis in original). But the texts through which most readers come into contact with traditional Jewish cuisine—cookbooks—are predominantly texts whose primary goal is functional. In most cases, Rona Kaufman claims, the meaning-making potential of cookbooks "never goes beyond the boundaries of its accumulated ingredients" (Kaufman 2004, 433).

Despite their underdeveloped potential, cookbooks have been studied as historical documents due to their capacity to "reflect shifts in the boundaries of edibility, the proprieties of the culinary process, the logic of meals, the exigency of the household budget, the vagaries of the market, and the structure of domestic ideologies" (Appadurai 1988, 3). But we cannot be satisfied with the language Arjun Appadurai uses here that suggests that cookbooks merely "reflect" historical and ideological forces. Cookbooks are active sites of the production of difference. The otherness of Sephardic cooking in Jewish cuisine, in many cases, is built on the same logic of difference that justified the Jewish diasporas. To deny the productive power of these representations is to participate in what Thomas R. West calls "historical amnesia," forgetting that "processes of cultural differentiation have always involved wrangles over real stakes that affect people's lives and the power to constitute reality" (West 2002, 12).

The Alternative Origins of Recipes

Between 1478, when the Spanish Inquisition was authorized by Pope Sixtus IV, and 1492, when Jews in Spain were forcibly expelled by the threat of forced conversion, the central provinces of Spain became the stronghold of Christianity under Isabella of Castile and Ferdinand of Aragon. It was during this time that the traditional recipe for *adafina*, an ancient Jewish dish based on chicken or beef, vegetables and hard-boiled eggs, was radically transformed. The hard-boiled eggs were replaced with "large quantities of pork and pork fat" (Feibleman 1969, 23), resulting in a situation where

> a "pure" Christian, converted or otherwise, was a man who not only could, but did, eat pork once a day, preferably in public. Even at home he could never be caught off his guard, for anyone who came unexpectedly to share his *cocido* could see clearly that this was not the house of the infidel but of a "pure believer in the True Faith." (Feibleman 1969, 23)[7]

At a time when "Judaizers" were persecuted for their continuation of Jewish customs, and Franciscan friars "incited mobs to despoil the Jewish neighborhoods," cooking became an intensely political and perilous act (Davidson and Gitlitz 1999, 2). Peter S. Feibleman states that "Ironically, this new *cocido*, which was adapted from the cooking of the Jews, became the dish by which a man could quickly prove that he was a Christian" (1969, 24). The irony is perhaps deepened by the fact that the name of the original dish, *adafina*, is derived from the Arabic word for "hidden," presaging the "hidden" (or "crypto") Jews who remained in Spain following the edict of expulsion despite the possibility of persecution. The *conversos*, those Jews who chose to stay in Spain and convert to Christianity, were under perpetual scrutiny. Although these Jews had seemingly accepted the invitation to become Christians, records kept by the Inquisition convey considerable doubts regarding their devotion. Although some of the difficulties faced by *conversos* and crypto-Jews are referenced by *The Cooking of Spain and Portugal*, the recipes it presents are still examples of the official culinary discourse to which these groups had to submit. In short, it includes a recipe for *cocido* but not for *adafina*.

On the other hand, *A Drizzle of Honey* is a cookbook that foregrounds the experiences of the crypto-Jews and, thus, the historical context that shaped their cooking. Its recipes were recovered primarily from Inquisition testimonials intended to doom Jews to banishment or worse (and often just to deprive them of property or standing in the community). Its introduction reveals the fates of the individual crypto-Jews whose recipes were "unwillingly contributed . . . via the pens of the Inquisition scribes who recorded their confessions and the allegations of the servants and neighbors and family members who testified against them" (Davidson and

Gitlitz 1999, 11). Some of these individuals were burned at the stake, forced into labor on the royal warships, or suffered a lesser punishment such as a fine, temporary banishment, or public humiliation (Davidson and Gitlitz 1999, 12). Unlike *The Cooking of Spain and Portugal* (and most other cookbooks), *A Drizzle of Honey* selects recipes in order to make visible "the effaced itinerary of the subaltern subject," exposing the ideologies of difference that made Jewish culinary traditions available for detection and punishment (Spivak 1988, 287).

A Drizzle of Honey differs visually from *The Cooking of Spain and Portugal* as well. Its cover, for instance, shows an array of ingredients rather than a fully formed dish. While this still might be considered, like the *paella*, an image of idealized diversity due to the variety of ingredients shown, the biggest difference is in the inclusion of religious objects. The inclusion of these items justifies the cookbook's subtitle, "The Lives and Recipes of Spain's Secret Jews," by highlighting the religious origins of the crypto-Jewish food practices (Davidson and Gitlitz 1999, v). The same image appears on the back cover, but superimposed upon the image is the text of a letter written by a Jewish prisoner asking for "two dishes of honey" with which to break a fast (Davidson and Gitlitz 1999, vi). Without the demonization of difference by the Inquisition, there is no cookbook of the crypto-Jews. But, just as importantly, without the experiences of the crypto-Jews brought forth in *A Drizzle of Honey*, there is no recovery of "the 'other' suppressed and concealed by dominant modes of knowing" (Ebert 1991, 888).

The commodification of difference discourages an interrogation of its construction of an exotic Other through which it promises "sensual and spiritual renewal" while neutralizing imagined threats to hegemonic identities (hooks 1999, 183). But texts such as *A Drizzle of Honey* show us that respecting difference requires us to read cultures "on their own terms," and not to conceive of recipes as merely a detailed set of instructions assembled for our own pleasure (Kaufman 2004, 437). To do so would be to reduce difference to a commodity that caters to the anxieties of the consumer, and to silence the voice and the history of the Other. Teresa L. Ebert claims that, in contexts of struggle, "voicing this silenced 'other' displaces the dominant logic . . . and unleashes alternative potential" (Ebert 1991, 888). Unleashing this potential may involve substituting ingredients, adjusting serving sizes, and, every once in a while, refusing to follow the detailed instructions we've been given.

Notes

1. Cara De Silva's *In Memory's Kitchen: A Legacy from the Women of Terezín* is another cookbook that succeeds in situating its recipes within their historical context in ways that preserve the role of difference. Since this book is addressed in-depth by another essay in this collection, I will not include it in my discussion.

2. In some cases, the topographical reality of an area may be used to discourage inquiry into other explanations of the origins of recipes. Such discouragement can be the effect of a cookbook's claim, for instance, that ingredients for dishes are based on as what is "easily found nearby" and "whatever happens to be fresh and cheap at the market" (Feibleman 1969, 76–77). This same cookbook again treats topography as determinant when, in referring to the politically and culturally segregated landscape of Spain, it states that "Iberia *divides itself* into several zones of cooking" (Feibleman 1969, 12; emphasis added).

3. Although Raymond Sokolov claims that Passover is the "the only traditional holiday that revolves around food," food is a significant element in all Jewish holidays (1988, 88). There are special foods eaten during most holidays, as in the apple dipped in honey eaten at Rosh Hashanah (and this is just one of many dishes associated with this holiday; in Sephardic tradition, a baked sheep's head was eaten). At Hanukah, some Jews eat dairy foods as a tribute to Judith, who saved her city through a plot that began with feeding her enemy some salty cheese. Sukkot involves the use of figs, dates, grapes, and wheat to symbolize God's protection during the Jewish exodus. Purim involves the exchange of edible gifts such as pastries. Even Shavuot, the celebration of the giving of the Torah to the Jews at Mount Sinai, is celebrated with dairy and fruit-based dishes.

4. Claudia Roden contributes to another irresponsible version of difference by suggesting a structured binary difference between the "cold [provincial] world" of Ashkenazic cooking and the "warm [urban] world" of Sephardic cooking (1996, 16).

5. When cookbooks diverge from the decontextualizing conventions of the cookbook genre, they often find themselves consigned to other sections of the library or bookstore. The cookbook, *In Memory's Kitchen*, for instance, is often placed in the Judaica section, rather than with other cookbooks. Such placement is justified by statements like that from Lore Dickstein who wrote in the *New York Times Book Review* that *In Memory's*

Kitchen "is not a cookbook. It is a Holocaust document" (Dickstein 1997, 7). The claim prompts a question: Is *A Drizzle of Honey* an Inquisition document?

6. In the 1960s, Time-Life books published a twenty-seven-volume "Foods of the World" series, including *The Cooking of Spain and Portugal* volume. Time-Life gave authors an unprecedented amount of financial and material support to research the food of the countries selected. In some cases, these volumes reproduced the high and low distinctions of a country's culinary traditions, as in the two volumes dedicated to France, *Classic French Cooking* and *The Cooking of Provincial France*. At other times, the cuisines of discrete countries were grouped together, as in *Recipes from Africa* or *A Quintet of Cuisines*, which groups the cooking of Switzerland, Poland, Bulgaria, Romania, and North Africa. Each volume included a hardcover book that integrated recipes, history, and travelogue. This series has been described by New York food critic Jim Leff as the "semi-miraculous Time Life Foods of the World series—legendary tomes penned by top reporters pampered with uncommon time, budget, and editing" (Leff 2000).

7. *Adafina* and *cocido* are related by their shared heritage. The *cocido* is the descendant of the heavy stew known as *olla podrida* (the "rotten pot") which is itself a descendant of *adafina*.

Works Cited

Abas, Syed Jan and Amer Shaker Salman. 1995. *Symmetries of Islamic Geometrical Patterns*. Singapore: World Scientific Publishing.

Althusser, Louis. 2001. *Lenin and Philosophy and Other Essays*, trans. Ben Brewster. New York: Monthly Review Press.

Anti-Defamation League. 1991. "The 'kosher tax' Hoax: Anti-Semitic Recipe for Hate." http://www.adl.org/special_reports/kosher_tax/print.asp (accessed October 25, 2005).

Appadurai, Arjun. 1988. "How to Make a National Cuisine: Cookbooks in Contemporary India." *Comparative Studies in Society and History* 30 No. 1: 3–24.

Balhoul, Joelle. 1995. "Food Practices Among Sephardic Immigrants in Contemporary France: Dietary Laws in Urban Society." *Journal of the American Academy of Religion* 63, No. 3: 485–496.

Bhabha, Homi. 1999. "Staging the Cultural Politics of Difference." Interview with Homi Bhabha. By Gary A. Olson and Lynn Worsham. In *Race, rhetoric, and the postcolonial.* Eds. Gary A. Olson and Lynn Worsham, 3–39. Albany: State University of New York Press.

Davidson, Linda Kay and David M. Gitlitz. 1999. *A Drizzle of Honey: The Lives and Recipes of Spain's Secret Jews.* New York: St. Martin's Press.

De Silva, Cara. 1996. "Introduction." In *In Memory's Kitchen: A Legacy of the Women of Terezín.* Ed. Cara De Silva, trans. Bianca Steiner Brown, xxv–xliii. Northvale: Jason Aronson.

Dickstein, Lore. 1997. "Hell's Own Kitchen." Review of *In Memory's Kitchen: A Legacy of the Women of Terezín.* ed. Cara De Silva, 7. *New York Times Book Review,* November 17.

Dilger, Bradley. 2000. "The Ideology of Ease." *Journal of Electronic Publishing* 6, No. 1. http://www.press.umich.edu/jep/06–01/dilger.html (accessed September 12, 2005).

Ebert, Teresa L. 1991. "The 'Difference' of Postmodern Feminism." *College English* 53: 886–904.

Feibleman, Peter S. 1969. *The Cooking of Spain and Portugal.* Foods of the world series. New York: Time-Life.

Foucault, Michel. 1980. *Power/Knowledge: Selected Interviews and Other Writings, 1972–1977.* Ed. Colin Gordon. New York: Pantheon Books.

Hall, Stuart. 1999. "Cultural Composition: Stuart Hall on Ethnicity and the Discursive Turn." Interview with Stuart Hall. By Julie Drew. In *Race, Rhetoric, and the Postcolonial.* Eds. Gary A. Olson and Lynn Worsham, 205–239. Albany: State University of New York Press.

hooks, bell. 1999. "Eating the Other: Desire and Resistance." In *Feminist Approaches to Theory and Methodology: An International Reader.* Eds. Sharlene Hesse-Biber, Christina Gilmartin, and Robin Lydenberg, 179–194. New York: Oxford University Press.

Kaufman, Rona. 2004. "Testifying, Silencing, Monumentalizing, Swallowing: Coming to Terms with *In Memory's Kitchen.*" *JAC* 24, No. 2: 427–445.

Keys, Lisa. 2003. "Ashkenazim Embrace Sephardic Fare in Latest Cooking Craze." *Forward,* March 7. http://www.forward.com/issues/2003/03.03.07/fast1.html (accessed April 28, 2005).

Laclau, Ernesto. 1996. *Emancipation(s).* London: Verso.

Leff, Jim. 2000. "Lonely Planet's World Food Series." Chowhound.com. http://www.chowhound.com/writing/lp-world-food.html (accessed October 2, 2005).

Levine, Étan. 1986. "The Land of Milk and Honey." In *Diaspora: Exile and the Contemporary Jewish Condition*. Ed. Étan Levine, 36–48. New York: Steimatzky/Shapolsky.

Lévi-Strauss, Claude. 1990. *The Origins of Table Manners*. Chicago: University of Chicago Press.

Levy, Faye. 2001. *Jewish Cooking for Dummies*. New York: Hungry Minds.

Marks, Copeland. 1992. *Sephardic Cooking: 600 Recipes Created in Exotic Sephardic Kitchens from Morocco to India*. New York: Dutton.

Roden, Claudia. 1996. *The Book of Jewish Food: An Odyssey from Samarkand to New York*. New York: Knopf.

Said, Edward. 1992. "An Ideology of Difference." In *"Race," Writing, and Difference*. Ed. Henry Louis Gates Jr., 38–58. Chicago: University of Chicago Press.

Setton, Ruth K. 1997. "Ten Ways to Recognize a Sephardic 'Jew-ess.'" *Tikkun* 12, No. 6: 78–80.

Sokolov, Raymond. 1988. "A Simmering Sabbath Day Stew: The Worldwide Diaspora of a Culinary Concept. *Natural History* 97: 88–91.

Spivak, Gayatri Chakravorty. 1988. "Can the Subaltern Speak?" In *Marxism and the Interpretation of Culture*. Eds. Cary Nelson and Lawrence Grossberg, 271–316. Chicago: University of Illinois Press.

Sternberg, Robert. 1996. *The Sephardic Kitchen: The Healthy Food and Rich Culture of the Mediterranean Jews*. New York: Harper Collins.

Taylor, Charles. 1992. *Multiculturalism and "the Politics of Recognition."* Ed. Amy Guttmann. Princeton, NJ: Princeton University Press.

West, Thomas R. 2002. *Signs of Struggle: The Rhetorical Politics of Cultural Difference*. Albany: State University of New York Press.

Wilson, Marc. March 17, 2004. "Kosher Ambrosia, Spark Struck of G-d." *The Daily Gullet*. http://www.egullet.org/tdg.cgi?pg=ARTICLE-ribeye031704 (accessed September 12, 2005).

CHAPTER 6

Typisch Deutsch

Culinary Tourism and the Presentation of German Food in English-Language Travel Guides

Lynne Fallwell

German cuisine gets bad press. Although it is neither as sophisticated as French cooking nor as sultry as Italian or Hungarian food, *Deutsche Küche* has a robust charm. Meat-and-potatoes lovers especially will find the food in Germany hearty and satisfying. And if the local food is not to your taste, Germany's larger cities offer a wide variety of good ethnic restaurants. Be careful when ordering from a German menu if you don't speak the language; ingredients such as *Aal* (eel), *Blutwurst* (blood sausage), and *Gehirn* (brains) are not uncommon, and may represent an acquired taste. Don't let this deter you from taking risks—brains are probably a lot tastier than you think. (Muller 1999, 80)

With these words, a popular American guidebook introduces readers of its 1999 edition to the food and drink awaiting them in Germany. Its culinary message is a study in contrasts. The paragraph opens by referring to the lack of respect commonly granted German cuisine, implying that this review will somehow be different. Instead, the next sentence describes how German food pales in comparison to that of other nations. True, the text concedes, the available ample, if basic, fare does possess "charm." But this word, much like its patronizing cousin "quaint," is not necessarily positive. Instead, it contributes to an overall sense of a lack of sophistication in the German dining experience, a void in which quantity substitutes for quality. According to the paragraph, those seeking a more nuanced culinary experience need not necessarily despair. Refuge is offered, at least in the larger metropolitan areas, via an array of ethnic restaurants. This alternative raises its own questions. Whose definition of "ethnic" is at play? Is it according to the writer's frame of reference, or according to some other, German, context? Likewise, what makes "ethnic food" more palatable than German offerings? This question is particularly significant given the paragraph's next section. While readers are encouraged not to be deterred from taking culinary risks, at the same time linguistically limited travelers are warned away from experimenting unless they are amicable to consuming the unexpected. Brains, blood sausage, and eel represent three of the potential culinary landmines awaiting the uninitiated. Furthermore, the use of the word "probably" leaves one wondering: Did the writers take their own advice regarding dining in Germany? Did they extend themselves beyond their own cultural definitions of edibility to find out for sure if brains really are tasty? Finally, this whole entry prompts one last question: Why does it simultaneously set up its readers to visit Germany but reject German cuisine?

As Sydney Mintz, Anna Miegs, Lucy M. Long, and others have shown, an intricate relationship exists between food, travel, tourism, and cultural perceptions—both of one's own culture and the culture of others (Mintz 2003; Long 2004; Meigs 1997). Food is more than simply about sustenance. Adding the elements of choice and preference to that of food consumption transforms a biological necessity into a social and cultural construction. In his essay "Eating and Being," Mintz points out the unique capacity of human beings "to create a symbolic world, and then both to call it a reality and to treat it as real"(Mintz 1994,105). Food and food choices play a major part in the construction of this symbolic world. Studying foodways (treating food as an information conduit connecting networks, structures, and systems) reveals the formation and operations of group identities both internally and externally (Long 2004; Camp 1982). Internally, shared food rituals help define and reinforce familial, communal, regional, and national bonds. Externally, food taboos, what is not eaten, help to further demarcate the boundary between such groups (Douglas 1966).

In addition to facilitating perceptions of unique group identity, food can also promote intergroup connectivity. It does this by serving in an ambassadorial role, functioning as a representative symbol for a particular collective (Bell and Valentine 1997; Counihan 1999). New York Bagels, Bavarian Beer, English Fish and Chips are all examples of this cultural shorthand. Mention one part of the pair and you evoke the other half. Intergroup connectivity is further possible when the lines of distinction between groups are blurred through the processes of food indigenization ("new foods finding new homes"), cultural hybridization (as evidenced in part by the growing popularity of fusion cuisine restaurants), and globalization (Goody 1997). This last point refers both to the imperialistic nature of certain foods (Coca-Colonialism, McDonaldization) and to the growing awareness of food distribution and shortages as a global problem (Mintz 2003, 21; Bell and Valentine 1997, 190, see also essays in part one; Goody 1997). Lastly, food related intergroup connectivity is expressed through culinary tourism.

Lucy M. Long defines culinary tourism as the "intentional exploratory participation in the foodways of another" (Long 2004, 21). The culinary tourist becomes an active agent in this pursuit of the unfamiliar, seeking out opportunities to push beyond regular norms and conventions in order to come in contact with new foods and their related structures (preparation, presentation, consumption, etc.). How the culinary tourist chooses to engage in this process of exploration can occur in one of two ways. The tourist can remain geographically static. This involves staying at, or relatively near, home and searching for "the Other" by trying new recipes and foodstuffs from different cultures or by dining at a local neighborhood "ethnic" restaurant (Molz 2004). The second way is geographically dynamic and requires one to engage with "the Other" by traveling to unfamiliar territory such as a foreign country. This element of travel has the further effect of transforming any act of tourism into some form of culinary tourism. Unless travelers seek to take all necessary foods with them, they will eventually have to eat local offerings. As a result, "where to eat" becomes a standard entry in tourist guidebooks, whether the guidebooks are designated for culinary-specific travel or not. In fact, studying representations of food in more broadly focused guidebooks can reveal as much, or even more, about the perceptions of foreign foodways as looking at those books which deal specifically with culinary culture. This occurs because food descriptions in general interest travel guides are one element among many (where to eat, where to sleep, what to see . . .) and as such become contextualized within a larger array of broadly based social and cultural frameworks.

Constructing frameworks is a key component of guidebooks (Koshar 1998). The function of guidebooks is to help the tourist decipher unfamiliar landscapes and the unfamiliar is made relatable by giving the visit structure. However, at the same time guidebooks serve to clarify the process for the traveler, the presence of frameworks complicates the tourist's search for the authentic. Authenticity, the search for the "real deal," is the driving aim behind the touristic experience. As Arjun Appadurai describes, this drive is rooted in doubt and is the preoccupation of the outsider, not of those who already belong to the tradition (Appadurai 1986, 25). Tourists seek to break through barriers. They want to be certain that when they claim ownership of a new experience that experience is a genuine reflection of the original. Yet, by its very design tourism is a staged undertaking (MacCannell 1973). Space and time are artificially constructed (Rojek and Urry 1997). Tourists have only a finite amount of time in which to experience the new setting and as a result only see certain spaces. Guidebooks contribute to the manipulation of authenticity by constructing frameworks based on these time and space limitations.

In this sense guidebooks are like menus, setting out for the consumer (traveler) the fare available. Just as menus influence a diner's meal choice (one most commonly makes a selection from among what is offered rather than creating a wholly new dish), guidebooks similarly shape a traveler's consumption of a new site. In terms of food, guidebooks direct readers about what kind of cuisine to expect, where to find it, when to eat it, and even how to feel about it. This last point occurs because guidebooks frame the new indigenous fare for the reader according to familiar rituals and taboos—be on the lookout for brains and eels! At the same time, guidebooks are themselves products of their environment. Where and when a guide is produced influences how it frames something. This brings us back to the example at the opening of this paper: Why does German cuisine get such bad press in English-language guidebooks and was this always the case?[1]

Answering that question rests in recognizing the relationship between foodways, guidebooks, and politics. There is fairly widespread cross-cultural acceptance of the notion that sharing a meal (accepting the food of an "Other") means accepting, at least in part, that "Other." Because eating is literally a process of internalization and therefore requires one to surrender a certain degree of autonomy, it is also an act based in trust and the formation of bonds (Curtain 1992; Counihan 1999). As Mintz states, the act of breaking bread together is "the great equalizer"

(Mintz 1994, 105). The same applies in reverse. Refusing food is a rejection of the "Other." While on the personal level the acceptance or rejection of another's food is motivated by differences in taste, those differences in taste are often grounded in larger nonfood related issues. Rejecting a nation's foodways can, for example, function as an act of censure for a perceived moral, ethical, or political transgression. This commentary need not be administered by one formal political entity toward the other. Instead, it can come from within the populace, which is the case with English-language guidebooks written about Germany.

For much of the twentieth century, Germany and the English-speaking world, led by Britain and the United States of America, shared an antagonistic political relationship. World War I and II, the rise of the Third Reich and ensuing Holocaust, and even Germany's division throughout the Cold War were all contributing factors. Not altogether unexpectedly, these political references often carried over onto the pages of travel guidebooks influencing, among other things, cultural perceptions of food. In terms of food, there is a correlation between the amount of evaluative commentary on Germany's past actions and reservations about its cuisine. Put simply, the more a guidebook talks politics, the less likely it is to showcase traditional German cuisine in a positive light. This is particularly true for books written since the country's reunification in 1989, although examples are evident throughout the century.

Of course, no guidebook offers a complete rejection of the country's food. In a business designed around promoting travel this would be counterproductive. Instead, presentation of the food-politics relationship falls across a spectrum. Where a particular book fits on that spectrum depends largely on its format and place of publication. All guidebooks start with the same basic format presenting technical information. This includes information on how to get to the country, how to travel inside the country, followed by lists indicating places to eat, sleep, and see. These rudimentary lists simply supply addresses and, if applicable, hours of operation. They contain no additional descriptive or evaluative commentary. In terms of where to eat, lists are often divided according to price and type of cuisine. Type of cuisine is then separated into "international" (French, Greek, Turkish, Balkan, Indian, Italian . . .) and "local" (German). Sometimes "local" is further subdivided into regional specialties (Prussian, Bavarian . . .) and sometimes, particularly in guides published in the last decades, there is a differentiation made between "traditional" and "new" local cuisine. "New" refers to *neue deutsche Küche*, the German version of *nouvelle cuisine*. "Traditional," as we will see, has multiple meanings but generally refers to standard fare based around the formula of "meat/potato/vegetable."

Beyond this basic format, guides differ in terms of the degree to which they seek to situate these lists within broader frameworks of history, culture, and politics, as well as food practices and other aspects of local life. This situating is done through the inclusion of evaluative and descriptive commentary. At one end of the spectrum are the fact-focused guides, those books seeking to avoid discussions of politics, current affairs, or any possibly inflammatory historical events by omitting or severely curtailing evaluative commentary. At the other end of the spectrum are the social critique guides, those books seeking to provoke an emotional response in the reader, both in terms of the country's history and its traditional cuisine.

The fact-focused approach is most common among German travel guides published during the first decades of the twentieth century. While written in English, these books are often produced by German travel companies, English-speaking enterprises based in Germany, or, as in the case of the big shipping lines, businesses sharing an obvious transnational economic connection (*Register's Guide* 1899/1900; *Northern Germany* 1910; Finke and Heymann 1930). Whatever historical information is included shows up as a very brief, very broad overview often focusing on shifts in art and architecture, or tracing some humanistic trend in leadership (*Register's Guide* 1899/1900, 17–21; *Northern Germany* 1910, xviii–xxxvii). In terms of food, the books do not evaluate one type of cuisine as superior or inferior to any other. Instead the guides concentrate primarily on providing information about local dining etiquette and customs. For example, books published up through the 1930s, in addition to supplying basic restaurant lists, would often indicate the places most suitable for ladies-only dining, men's-only establishments (indicating the presence of female escorts) and locals where gender mixing was permissible but perhaps somewhat uncomfortable for women as the establishments allowed smoking (*Register's Guide* 1899/1900, 39–44; *Northern Germany* 1910, 4, 17; Finke and Heymann 1930, 21). As these guides are either produced by German firms (the most well known being Baedekers) or a product of transnational collaboration, they focus more on helping the visitor fit into the local culture than on critiquing it.

As the century progresses, mass tourism grows, and air travel replaces transatlantic ship voyages, the field of travel publications undergoes a rapid expansion. Official transnational collaborations are overtaken by independent publications with stronger national interests. In addition, following the outcome of the two world wars, later guides begin presenting a more visible culturally and politically evaluative message. Sometimes this message is clearly articulated and sometimes it is the lack of commentary that reveals attitudes toward the larger sociopolitical climate. Let me present five different examples of guides.

The first attempts to minimize the impact of recent political history. Produced by both German and non-German sources, these books appear most frequently in the decades following World War II and deal specifically with West Germany. While they tend to contain more historical information than earlier versions, they seek to either separate the past and present (Germans today are not Germans "back then," usually referring to Nazis) or downplay the more controversial periods of German history, in particular the Third Reich and Holocaust. The tone is often conciliatory and reflects a larger Cold War agenda that seeks generally to build bonds between West Germany and the Western industrialized world. Descriptors such as "hospitable," "helpful," "kind," and "hardworking" categorize the German people, who are further portrayed largely as victims of an unfortunate history (Bransby 1962; Cooper 1954; Engel 1973). Preempting any discussion of blame, one British guide from 1962 provides the following statement: "If for any reason you happen to be a person who 'doesn't like the Germans,' then I suggest you do not visit the country. Incidentally, I give this piece of advice about all countries. In any case, I think you should steer clear of political discussions" (Bransby 1962, 26). Another book published seven years earlier, this time in Germany, also argues for the separation of tourism and politics: "You need not, of course, know much or anything of Berlin's history to enjoy the animation, attractiveness and brisk tempo of the city" (Schall 1958, 17).

Such guides are most common up through the 1970s, at which point a greater abundance of guides interested in social and political commentary emerge. These new guides reflect the ascendancy of West Germany's postwar "1968 generation," the emergence of youth-culture travel more generally, and an increasing criticism of Cold War politics. However, these more critical guides do not completely replace those seeking to limit political commentary. One modern example of the conciliatory guide is *Fodor's Germany 2003*. In a brief two-and-a-half page section titled "Relax, It's Not as Serious as You Think," the book seeks to illuminate the German national character. References to the violent past are curtailed as evidenced by the sentence summary covering events of both world wars and the Holocaust. Instead, focus is placed on postwar achievements and the country's current international leadership role (Knight 2003, 2–4. An additional chronology is included 669–674, as well as a close-up on "Coping with the German Past," 577).

In terms of presenting food, conciliatory guides seek to maintain a neutral tone. There is little by way of cuisine-related commentary in the introductory chapter. Where references do appear the focus is usually on translating necessary words like *Gaststätten* (inns), *Weinstuben* (wine taverns), *Imbiss* (fast/street cart food); giving German terms for breakfast, lunch, and dinner; clarifying dining etiquette; and listing regional specialties. Entries under individual cities simply supply restaurant listings showing only location, price, type of cuisine, and house specialty. In keeping with the books' overall tone of moving beyond the past and focusing on (re)building connections, there is little attempt to rank cuisines or draw a value judgment between "traditional German" and "international" styles of cooking.

The second category contains English-language guides written for and published in East Germany from the 1960s through the early 1980s. Here, political commentary is included in the general text but does not extend to specific discussions of cuisine. Introductory chapters commonly focus on history as class conflict, the rise of Socialism, and the social, cultural, and economic achievements of the German Democratic Republic. Within this overview, the books are not recalcitrant about their comments regarding the capitalist West or promoting the heroism of the Russian army during the war. However, this discourse does not carry over into later sections on food. Instead, information is usually confined to restaurant lists and a description of the basic composition of German meals, for example, what one eats for breakfast (*Travel Guide GDR* 1962, 1970, 1983). In cases where non-German offerings are mentioned, they come, not surprising, from other Socialist countries like Romania, Czechoslovakia, Poland (*Travel Guide* 1962, 74–75). However, reflecting the broader aims of collective Socialist solidarity, there is no evaluative commentary ranking one cuisine above another.

While East German guides do not focus on cuisine hierarchies, such rankings are a large part of guides about West Germany. The third category refers to English-language translations of existing German-language guides. These guides adopt a defensive position on food, arguing that West Germany both recognizes and can compete with cuisines from other nations. The diversity of food offerings becomes a vehicle to support a larger argument regarding the nation's validity as a tourist destination (Boehle 1954; Weimert 1973). For example, one guide from 1954 aims to correct perceived misconceptions about the German diet by revealing Germany's embrace of international cuisine:

> Many foreigners have the impression that the German is a Sauerkraut-eater and that German cooking is barbaric. And how astonished they are when they take up a menu card the first time! If you can afford it, you can eat as well as you can in Paris, Vienna, Rome or Istanbul. The menu card in our great hotels is international in character and contains all the delicacies of Europe.

At the same time it defends "traditional" fare:

> Admittedly, the German cooking is not so hyper-refined as that of other peoples—it is more solid and wholesome. But at the same time, it is very healthy and it is the source from which the Germans draw the strength for the hard work they do. And in any case, German cooking is decidedly civilized in that it is extremely varied and is able to satisfy the most fastidious taste. (Boehle 1954, 77)

I will return to these issues of "solid" and "healthy" in a moment. First I want to outline the two remaining categories of guidebooks, both of which are most prevalent in decades following reunification. They are also published outside Germany. The penultimate category encompasses those guides seeking to strike a balance, both in terms of portraying the country's history and in comparing traditional German with new German cooking and international cuisine (McLachlan 2004). For example, Gordon McLachlan's *Berlin* devotes thirty pages to the city's history. The pages are evenly distributed across time from the early years, through the rise of the metropolis, decline and revival, imperial years, Weimar, Third Reich, division and reunification (McLachlan 2000, 13–45). Unlike some examples mentioned earlier, McLachlan does not try to ignore or downplay the significance of twentieth-century events, nor does he make them his exclusive focus. Instead, there is a sense of trying to weave a balanced portrayal of the country's past. This aim of objectivity carries over into the chapter on food and drink. Traditional cuisine, *Gutbürgerliche Küche,* is presented on par with international offerings, and updated German *nouvelle cuisine*. While traditional cuisine is described as admittedly "hearty," there is no implied negative connotation and its offerings are described as both diverse and appetizing.

The final category, in contrast with the category above, consists of those guidebooks that take issue with traditional German cooking. They tend to be aimed at the younger budget traveler, as well as those looking to explore "off the beaten track." In these books there is a visible parallel between criticism of Germany's recent, violent history and criticism of its cuisine. As with the previous category, the overwhelming majority of these books originate outside Germany. The examples cited come from sources published post-reunification and focus their critique on both Germany's Nazi past and conditions in East Germany. However, this criticism is not necessarily restricted to contemporary guides. There are examples of criticism stemming from the interwar period. For instance, one guide from 1930 expresses reluctance in embracing German culture and cuisine as a result of personal reactions triggered by the First World War. In the book's introduction the author admits to having had to work through "no small amount of rancor left over from those dreadful years when most of us measured the intensity of our righteousness by the degree of our hatred for everything German" (Lauglin 1930, vii). Later, residual resentment bubbles up in the form of criticizing the country's drinking water:

In spite of all that is said about Americans going abroad to escape water drinking, there are many of us who drink water in Europe—if not habitually, at least frequently. German cities have good, wholesome water supplies. But there are travelers who do not like to drink many kinds of water. And there are the small towns whose water supply may not be all the stranger would like to have it. In Italy we drink the delicious *Fiuggi*. In France, Switzerland, England we drink *Evian* or *Vittal*. In Germany and Austria there is *no* native bottled water that is still and tasteless; few places have *Evian*, and those that do charge exorbitantly for it. Waiters will tell you that *Fachingerwasser* is like *Evian*. It is gaseous and saline. We actually suffered from thirst in Central Europe. The only thing we could do, in many places, was drink lemonade. If Germany has no spring amongst all her spas that provides clear, tasteless drinking-water that can be bottled, then I strongly recommend that she takes all tax off French and Italian bottled water and forces all hotels and restaurants to keep it in stock. (Lauglin 1930, xv)

While more recent books are not necessarily as transparent with their rancor, they are nevertheless working through mixed feelings about the country. Take the example of the guidebook mentioned at the beginning of this article. Its conflicting messages about food reflect similar sentiments about the country generally. This connection is made stronger by combining both topics into a single introductory chapter on German history, culture, food and drink, media, and social life. A selection of the chapter's introductory comments reveals its ambivalence:

Ten years after the fall of the Berlin Wall, the story of Germany still stands as a parable for the story of life in the modern era. Germany's experience encapsulates all of the promises and betrayals of life in the twentieth century and exposes the fracture line of Western civilization. It has proven a volatile political arena in the recent past. . . . But despite its long history of reactionary politics, Germany has been a perennial wellspring of revolutionaries and innovators — for better or worse. . . . These days Germans are busy trying to come to terms with this schizophrenic history and identity. (Muller 1999, 57)

While Germany's visual arts, architecture, literature, music, and film are largely praised it is the country's violent history, particularly the events of the last century, which receive first and greatest attention. Twelve of the chapter's total twenty-eight pages trace German history from "Neanderthal Man" to "This Year (1999) in Germany." Ten of those twelve focus exclusively on the twentieth century (Muller 1999, 58–70). Whatever the historic period, bloodshed, militarism, and loss of life remain constant themes—from the Roman Republic's struggles with "barbaric" Germans, through the Thirty Years' War (described as "the longest and bloodiest conflict ever to embroil Europe"), to Frederick the Great and Brandenburg-Prussia, the "blood and iron" of Bismarck, the treachery of World War I, failure of Weimar democracy, subsequent rise of the Third Reich, the Holocaust and World War II, occupation, division, and reunification, to current problems with neo-Nazis, and the derailment disaster of ICE train 884.

This sense of aggressiveness carries over into depictions of the country's diet. In a separate section on "Dietary Concerns" the nation becomes personified as "unapologetically carnivorous" (Muller 1999, 260). Furthermore, the consumption of meat becomes linked with traditional German cooking, which is then connected to the violence of the past. In contrast, contemporary Germany is seen as having reinvented itself. First, by moving away from eating animal-based protein toward an embracing of vegetarianism; second, by shifting from traditional German to international cuisine.

Vegetarianism is not a new phenomenon in Germany, nor is guidebooks' recognition of meatless cuisine. One Berlin guide from 1899 lists eleven vegetarian restaurants (*Register's Guide* 1899/1900, 41). However, the difference between these two guides is that while the earlier one only lists restaurants by address, the 1999 guide tries to explain the motivations behind these dietary choices. It gives Germans' concerns over outbreaks of mad cow disease and a growing health consciousness as factors in the increasing popularity of vegetarianism in recent years. Not all reasons for the shift are health-related. The guide also links vegetarianism to the presence of a "blooming alternative scene" (Muller 1999, 26). The connected shift in food preference and societal thinking is echoed in this quote from the section on history and culture: "With no direct link to the gruesome past of their parents and grandparents, many younger Germans have *abandoned most things 'German'* and *eagerly embraced* the global culture of techno-fueled nightlife, *international cuisines*, and fast-paced business culture" (Muller 1999, 57; emphasis mine). What emerges from such pairings is the following pattern: "traditional German cuisine = heavy and unhealthy = meat = link to violent past" versus "rejection of violent past = rejection of meat in favor of vegetarianism and/or international cuisine = new Germans." Of course, the irony of this pattern is that most guides overlook Hitler's support for both vegetarianism and violent pursuit of a thousand year Reich!

Such inconsistency aside, versions of this meat = violence pattern are repeated in other books. One Berlin guide from 2000 prepares its readers for the challenges of the German culinary experience with the statement: "It's Germany, a land whose cuisine conjures images of heavy, pork-laden, fat-saturated, salty, under-seasoned, starchy . . . well, you get the picture" (Rimmer 2000, 150). According to the book, Berlin is saved only by its abundance of foreign fare, but even here the author warns readers to be careful of imported dishes "warped to please the conservative local palate" (Rimmer 2000, 150). Sentiments regarding the oppressiveness of traditional fare are echoed in recounting the oppressiveness of Germany's history. A twenty-page chapter covers the city's past from "medieval bog," through reunification. Thirteen of the pages focus on the twentieth century. The overall historical tone is one of violence, death, and division. Even the city's "Golden Twenties" is introduced using Joseph Goebbels, the Nazi Minister of Propaganda (Rimmer 2000, 14).

In a case from 1990, the guidebook's chapter "Germany in Context" is primarily a discussion of the World War I and II, Nazism and the Holocaust, and life in East Germany (Holland 1990, 183–225). Like the other examples, this book parallels a critique of German history with a rejection of German fare. This rejection is demonstrated in the listing of "Restaurants," referring to international offerings, separate from "German Food." Furthermore, it is clear that the first outshines the second. For those looking to eat "local," the author responds less than enthusiastically, "It does help if you share the national penchant for solid, fatty food." Here, as with other examples, the description "solid, fatty foods" refers primarily to the meat-base of traditional fare.

Even those guides seeking to present a more positive picture of traditional dishes would not dispute that German cooking centers around animal-based protein. Indeed, this is a common focus repeated in most Western countries. It is simply a variation of the starch/legume(protein)/relish (flavor garnish) pattern identifiable as the foundation of most cuisines (Mintz 1994). What is striking, however, are the guidebooks' contrasting portrayals of meat, particularly swine.

Those books seeking to dismiss traditional German cuisine not only frame the culinary offerings in terms of their reliance on this animal, but also this protein source is usually referred to in its unprocessed form, "pig," rather than its preparation-ready form "pork." Similar to using the term "cow" rather than "beef," such terminology is designed to conjure up an image of the animal as a living entity rather than a processed food source. In contrast, other guides employ the term "pork," thereby making the source of the meat more abstract and the end product more appetizing. Consider the difference in the following examples: "For those who don't mind a touch of the *pig*, there is traditional Berlin food," versus "Lunch, the main meal of the day, could include a juicy *Schnitzel* (cutlet)—usually *pork*" (Rimmer 2000, 150; Ardah 2000, 13; emphasis mine). Even when the overall point is the same, word choice shapes perception. One guide critical of traditional German cuisine states: "The *pig* is the staple of the German menu. It's prepared in umpteen different ways, and just about every part of it is eaten" (Holland 1990, 102; emphasis mine). Whereas another guide's more favorable assessment reads: "Main courses in most restaurants are overwhelmingly *pork*-based. This is less restricting than it might appear as virtually every part of the pig is used and prepared and garnished in limitless numbers of ways, so that even a relentless diet of schnitzels, cutlets, steaks, and chops can appear quite varied (McLachlan 2000, 73; emphasis mine). Both entries convey that a significant portion of the animal is being utilized in German cooking, and the second example does concede that the German diet is overwhelmingly pork-based. However, phrases like "pork parts used and prepared" rather than "pig parts eaten" make the second example more palatable.

Even beyond the use of terms like "pork," guides looking to increase the appeal of German cooking choose illustrative examples that most closely resemble dishes familiar to the Anglo-American reader: sausages like *Bratwurst* compare to British bangers and American hotdogs; rib dishes such as *Kasseler Rippchen* (salted smoked pork ribs) also meet with approval. In contrast, those guides trying to create distance focus on less commonly used parts such as the knuckles, belly, and feet, and highlight uncommon preparation methods such as pickling. This is a variation of the earlier "blood sausage, brains, and eel" reference.

Another example of how certain guides manipulate portrayals of meat is worth mentioning. Those guides taking a negative view of traditional German fare describe the cuisine by pairing "fatty meats" with "unhealthy sauces," using additional adjectives such as "heavy," "basic," and "monotonous." They then propose that the solution to avoiding such meals is to choose to eat in "ethnic restaurants." The term "ethnic" refers not only to French (which remains the benchmark of superior cuisine), but Italian, Greek, Balkan, Japanese, Turkish, Thai, Scandinavian, Mexican, and a myriad of other cuisines from around the globe, including a number of eastern European dishes. However, none of these are necessarily any less meat-based than their German counterparts. Neither is the other alternative to traditional German cooking, *neue deutsche Küche,* "new German cuisine." This "contemporary cuisine," available in fusion restaurants, combines different elements such as German/Italian/Japanese and leaving the landscape dotted with dishes like *Steinbutt mit Kalbbries auf Rotweinschalotten* (turbot with veal sweetbreads on shallots in red wine) and fried perch with risotto, a dish in its own way as unfamiliar as some traditional German dishes (Knight 2003, 121–122). However, it largely escapes the criticism leveled at its more traditional counterpart. The conclusion to be drawn from this is that what makes the meat in these dishes more accept-

able is the fact that the dishes themselves transcend the political by cross-
ing out of exclusively German boundaries. One is not "eating German,"
and thereby internalizing part of the country's violent history. Instead, one
is partaking in a global community by eating transnationally.

Another connection between food, politics, and perception has to do
with issues of regional specificity. The division most commonly occurs
along a north-south axis. As one guide points out, "There *are* generalizations to keep in mind about Germany and the Germans. Northerners are
more likely to be Protestant, politically liberal, and socially reserved.
Southerners are more likely to be Catholic, conservative, warm, and out-
going" (Knight 2003, 2; emphasis in original). Even those guidebooks
seeking to present positive portrayals of German cuisine often make such
regional distinctions. Southern dishes are either universalized to represent a generic German fare, or they are ranked as superior northern dishes
in discussions of German cuisine. Portrayals of southern versus northern
food mirror larger portrayals of southern versus northern cities. Consider
the following representative descriptions of Bavaria, with its capital
Munich, and the Prussian city of Berlin. Both entries come from the same
guidebook:

> (Bavaria): Here you will find, in abundance, the "olde-worlde"
> German stereotypes of *lederhosen,* beer halls, oompah bands and
> romantic castles. But it also has a modern dimension . . . Bavaria
> is . . . Germany's most fertile breeding ground for new technolo-
> gies. These contrasts heighten the Bavarian's sense of otherness—
> many feel like citizens of another country, only tenuously linked
> to the rest of Germany. (Schulte-Peevers et al. 2002, 406)

> (Berlin): The world has always looked to this most dramatic
> city—sometimes in fascination, sometimes in horror and some-
> times even in deep sympathy. At once repellent and seductive,
> lighthearted and brooding, Berlin continues to be a city of fasci-
> nating extremes (Schulte-Peevers et al. 2002, 163)

In its own way, each is being described simultaneously as a microcosm
of the country and as a unique entity. While Munich has come to epitomize
all the positive elements of German traditions and largely been able to
escape the fallout from the more nefarious aspects of twentieth-century history, this same history has literally been written into Berlin's core. As a

result, Munich has become the "Capital of *Gemütlichkeit*" (comfort) while even after reunification its northern counterpart remains trapped by the lingering mental Wall. It has been torn up by the legacy of Nazi violence and before that Prussian militarism. What makes this division even more interesting is the fact that Munich's association with Nazism is largely dismissed, whereas Berlin cannot shake the cumulative legacy of the last hundred years. The only way for Berlin to move forward is to abandon the past.

These north-south distinctions carry over into the realm of food. Any attempts by Berlin to embrace traditional cuisine are soundly rebuffed as evidenced by the following comments: "First, the bad news. No one comes to Berlin to eat. It's simply not a world gastronomic capital like Rome, New York, or Bangkok. . . . There is . . . no restaurant which serves as gourmet shorthand for the city"; "With praiseworthy humility Berliners refrain from boasting about their knack for food. The taste of their dishes proves them right"; "Don't be too determined to eat 'Berlin style.' The city is known only for its mildly spicy sausage, *currywurst*"; "Berlin has not traditionally had a reputation for great food or sophisticated restaurants" (Rimmer 2000, 150; Reinfrank and Reinfrank 1987, 82; Steves 2001, 178; Schulte-Peevers 2000, 190). Commonly, the only praise Berlin gets for food is its abundance of international restaurants and percentage of German chefs trained abroad (Holland 1990, 102). Again, cuisine transcending national boundaries is praised over its distinctly German counterpart.

One of the few guides to praise regional Prussian offerings is *Touring Guide Berlin: Get to know it—get to like it*. The key here is that this book is a translation of the German *Berlin—Kennen und Lieben*. While the book also includes information on other types of cuisines (German and non-German), it is the local Berlin dishes that receive highest praise. The discussion of food opens: "Like any other major town Berlin too has a handful of special dishes which also one can export, but the recipes do not taste anywhere as good as on the green banks of the river Spree. If you get hold of such a dish somewhere in Berlin—don't hesitate, have it" (Weimert 1973, 153). The chapter then proceeds to wax poetic about various local delicacies like eel from the Havel river served boiled in dill sauce, the unique tenderness of "pig's trotters" served with pickled cabbage and pureed peas and the bliss of sour gherkins for dessert (Weimert 1973, 153–4). Unlike the ubiquitous sausages or ribs, the delicacies described here cater more to local tastes. This positive depiction is a function of the book's origins not only as a German-language guide, but one written with local emphasis. Reference to its regional specificity is demonstrated in an aside note to visitors from southern Germany, reminding them that potatoes do taste good in Berlin (Weimert 1973, 153).

In contrast to the generally negative reception granted Berlin and regional Prussian specialties, Munich receives high praise for its culinary offerings. The history of this recognition predates World War II. As one guide from 1932 states: "We are shameless about it—quite frankly we go to Munich to eat and drink!" (Josephy and McBride 1932, 119). Drinking is the key. While other local specialties help promote this positive reception there is no doubt that Bavarian dominance is due largely to its connection with beer. Beer fulfills an ambassadorial role. It is the item most commonly associated not only with Munich and Bavaria, but also Germany as a whole. At least one guide put it thus: "To import beer into Germany seems to me ten times more needless than taking coals to Newcastle" (Clark 1933, 35). Another devotes almost an entire page to German beer in a section on German food that runs a total of two pages (Olson 2003, 12–13). A third opens its chapter on food and drink with the following sentence, "The story of food in Germany begins, as one might expect, with beer" (Halliday 2002, 69). While most German towns have their own breweries it is Munich that bears the title, "the City of the Amber Flood" (Phillips 1929, 271–276). Munich beers also dominate outside Bavaria and get special mention even in guides from Prussia and other regions.

Munich's relationship with beer protects its local cuisine from the same kind of criticism leveled at Berlin. There is clearly no shortage of meat in the Bavarian diet: *Weisswürste* (white sausages), *Leberwurst* (liverwurst), *Leberkäse* (similar to baloney, served hot), *Leberknödel* (liver dumplings). However, whereas those eating in Berlin are directed to flee to the nearest international restaurant, diners in Munich are tempted by descriptions of sweet mustard and accompanying *Brez'n* (soft pretzels) (Muller 1999, 485–86). The parallels between meat consumption and violent history seem to bypass this city of beer gardens and beer halls. While one should not attribute too much to the guidebooks' rejection of Berlin and acceptance of Munich based solely on the categorization of a militaristic north and the affable beer-guzzling south, nevertheless one point does stand out. English-language guidebooks appear more willing to "eat the other," or in this case "drink the other," when it comes from the south of Germany rather than the north.

Munich is permitted to retain its provincial roots without penalty. Its history is read to extend beyond the aggressiveness of the twentieth century back into another time of pastoral romanticism. References to "purity laws" mean those set down in 1516 pertaining to the brewing of beer, *Reinheitsgebot,* rather than those of 1935 focusing on the purity of race, *Rassengesetze.* In contrast Berlin carries a different mandate. It bears the burden of the legacy of the recent past. Furthermore, with the fall of the Berlin wall and subsequent opening up of new land at its core, the city has been given a unique opportunity to reinvent itself, and therefore the country. As these guidebooks have demonstrated, the rest of the world waits to see what it will become.

As this chapter has endeavored to demonstrate, history, politics, culture, and food share an intricate relationship. Furthermore they are interwoven within larger frameworks of which guidebooks are both products and producers. How a particular guidebook perceives one of these strands influences depictions of the others. In terms of English-language guidebooks about Germany: the more critical the view of the country's history as violent and bloody, the less positive the depiction of its traditional cuisine. When this violent past is physically written on to the landscape, as in the case of the Berlin Wall, the only hope for the future is seen as a complete break from the past. In terms of food, this manifests itself as a rejection of traditional cuisine in favor of international imports. When something else can step in and replace history in that ambassadorial role, as beer does for Munich, then tradition need not necessarily be abandoned. To this end, while tourists to Munich can continue happily indulging in sausages and beer, English-language guidebooks push Berlin's visitors to abandon traditional *Currywurst* in favor of international offerings like the Turkish *Döner Kebap.*

Notes

1. I recognize the term "English-language" encompasses both native and nonnative speakers of English. However, I also argue that until the age of the Internet and the promotion of mainstream globalized mass communications took off in the mid- to late-1990s, travelogues exhibited a very visible national character. For this reason, I am using the term to refer to guides targeted at readers from America and the British Commonwealth. What links these two is their shared history as Allies against Germany in both World War I and II.

Works Cited

Appadurai, Arjun. "On Culinary Authenticity." *Anthropology Today* 2 (1986): 24–25.

Ardah, John et al. 2000. *Fodor's Exploring Germany.* 4th· ed. New York: Fodor's Travel Publications, Inc.

Bell, David and Gill Valentine. 1997. *Consuming Geographies: We Are Where We Eat.* London: Routledge and Kegan Paul.

Boehle, Bernde. 1954. *Handy Guide to Western Germany: A Reference Book for Travel in the German Federal Republic.* New York: William Sloane Associates Inc, Publishers.

Bransby, Leslie. 1962. *A Fortnight in Germany.* London: Percival Marshall.

Camp, Charles. "Foodways in Everyday Life." *American Quarterly* 34 (1982): 278–289.

Clark, Sydney A. 1933. *Germany on $50.* New York: Robert M. McBride.

Cooper, Gordon. 1954. *Your Holiday In Germany.* London: Alvin Redmen Limited.

Counihan, Carole M. 1999. *The Anthropology of Food: Gender, Meaning, and Power.* New York: Routledge and Kegan Paul.

Curtain, Deanne W. 1992. "Food/Body/Person." In *Cooking, Eating, Thinking: Transformative Philosophies of Food.* Ed. Deanne W. Curtain and Lisa M. Heldke. Bloomington, IN: Indiana University Press.

Douglas, Mary. 1966. *Purity and Danger.* London: Routledge and Kegan Paul.

Engel, Lyle Kenyon. 1973. *West Germany.* New York: Cornerstone Library Publications.

Finke, A., and O. Heymann. 1930. *Greenbook 1930.* Hamburg and New York: International Interchange Company.

Goody, Jack. 1997. "Industrial Food: Toward the Development of a World Cuisine." In *Food and Culture: A Reader.* Ed. Carole Counihan and Penny van Esterik. New York: Routledge and Kegan Paul.

Guide: German Democratic Republic. 1970. Dresden: Verlag Site im Bild Dresden.

Halliday, Tony, ed. 2002. *Insight Guide—Germany.* Singapore: Apa Publications GmbH & Co.

Holland, Jack. 1990. *The Real Guide: Berlin.* New York: Prentice Hall Press.

Josephy, Helen and Mary Margaret McBride. 1932. *Beer and Skittles: A Friendly Guide to Modern Germany.* New York: G. P. Putnam's Sons.

Knight, Christina, ed. 2002. *Fodor's Berlin.* New York: Fodor's Travel Publications.

———. 2003. *Fodor's 2003—Germany: The Guide for All Budgets, Where to Stay, Eat, and Explore On and Off the Beaten Path.* New York: Fodor's Travel Publications.

Koshar, Rudy. "What Ought to be Seen: Tourists' Guidebooks and National Identities in Modern Germany and Europe." *Journal of Contemporary History* 33 (1998): 323–340.

Lauglin, Clara E. 1930. *So You're Going to Germany and Austria.* London: Metheun & Co., Ltd.

Long, Lucy M. 2004. "Culinary Tourism: A Folklorist Perspective on Eating and Otherness." In *Culinary Tourism.* Ed. Lucy M. Long. Lexington, KY: The University of Kentucky Press.

MacCannell, Dean. "Staged Authenticity: Arrangements of Social Space in Tourist Settings." *The American Journal of Sociology* 79 (1973): 589–603.

McLachlan, Gordon. 2000. *Berlin.* 2d ed. New York: W. W. Norton & Company, Inc.

———. 2004. *The Rough Guide to Germany.* 6th ed. New York: Rough Guides.

Meigs, Anna. 1997. "Food as a Cultural Construction." In *Food and Culture: A Reader.* Eds. Carole Counihan and Penny van Esterik. New York: Routledge and Kegan Paul.

Mintz, Sydney. 2003. "Eating Communities: The Mixed Appeals of Sodality." In *Eating Culture: The Poetics and Politics of Food.* Eds. Tobias Döring, Markus Heide, Susanne Mühleisen. Heidelberg: Universitätsverlag Winter.

———. 1994. "Eating and Being: What Food Means." In *Food: Multidisciplinary Perspectives.* Eds. Barbara Harris-White and Raymond Hoffenberg. London: Blackwell.

Molz, Jennie Germann. 2004. "Tasting an Imagined Thailand: Authenticity and Cultural Tourism in Thai Restaurants." In *Culinary Tourism.* Ed. Lucy M. Long. Lexington, KY: The University of Kentucky Press.

Muller, Douglas, ed. 1999. *Let's Go Germany 1999.* New York: St. Martin's Press.

Northern Germany As Far As The Bavarian and Austrian Frontiers: Handbook for Travelers. 1910. Leipzig: Karl Baedeker Publishers.

Olson, Donald, ed. 2003. *Germany for Dummies.* New York: Wiley Publishing, Inc.

Phillips, Henry Albert. 1929. *Meet The Germans—In Which An American Sees The New Germany Through Its People.* Philadelphia: J. B. Lippencott Company.

Reinfrank, Arno and Karin Reinfrank. 1987. *Berlin: Two Cities Under Seven Flags, A Kaleidoscopic A–Z.* Lemmington Spa: Oswald Wolff Books.

Rimmer, David, ed. 2000. *Time Out Berlin.* 4th ed. London: Penguin Books.

Rojek, Chris and John Urry, eds. 1997. *Touring Cultures: Transformation of Travel and Theory.* New York: Routledge and Kegan Paul.

Schall, Sybil. 1958. *Berlin Today—A Complete Guide: Sightseeing, Shopping, Restaurants, Night Life, Useful Tips, History, Music, Theatre.* Berlin: W. Frick Publishers.

Schulte-Peevers, Andrea et al., eds. 2000. *Lonely Planet Berlin.* 2d ed. Hawthorne, Australia: Lonely Planet Publications Pty Ltd.

———. 2002. *Lonely Planet Germany.* 3d ed. Footscray, Australia: Lonely Planet Publications Pty Ltd.

Steves, Rick. 2001. *Rick Steves' Germany, Austria, and Switzerland 2001.* Emeryville: Avalon Travel Publishing.

The English and American Register's Guide of Berlin and Potsdam, with a Map of Berlin. 1899/1900. Berlin: Hugo Steinitz Publisher.

Travel Guide: German Democratic Republic. 1962. Leipzig: VEB Edition Leipzig.

Travel Guide: German Democratic Republic. 1983. Dresden: Zeit im Bild Publishing House.

Weimert, Franck. 1973. *Touring Guide Berlin: Get to Know It—Get to Like It.* Trans. Lisa Drew. New York: Drake Publishing.

CHAPTER 7

The Embodied Rhetoric of "Health" from Farm Fields to Salad Bowls

Jean P. Retzinger

For decades Americans have been admonished to "eat your vegetables." In skirmishes across dinner tables and in USDA pamphlets promoting federal dietary guidelines,[1] the battle has been waged in the name of "health"—and propriety. For vegetables (fresh, frozen, or canned) stand as evidence of a proper meal,[2] proper nutrition. The USDA's own findings, however, conclude that while Americans have indeed been eating more overall, raising concerns about obesity, few Americans meet the minimum recommendations for fruit and vegetable consumption. The vegetable of choice for most Americans remains the potato—usually in the form of French fries. Coming in at a distant second is head lettuce with tomatoes, onions, and carrots rounding out the top five.[3] These patterns in vegetable consumption have remained largely unchanged over the past seven decades. Thus, while its form may have changed, Americans' meat and potatoes diet largely persists, available at fast-food restaurants across America, with lettuce, tomatoes, and onions as a garnish.

Rising rates of obesity in the United States (and globally) have recently prompted the examination and critique of fast-food restaurants.[4] In seeming response, fast-food chains introduced fresh vegetables (and now fruits) onto their menus in the form of "designer" or "premium" salads. Wendy's led the way, launching its "Garden Sensations" salad line in February 2002. Burger King quickly followed suit in July 2002. Within a few months, McDonald's (March 2003), Jack in the Box (April 2003), and Subway

(March 2004) introduced competing salads—all of which have been widely advertised in print and television campaigns.[5] Ironically, then, with the introduction and promotion of their salads, fast-food restaurants have become leading proponents for fresh vegetable consumption.

The enormous sums of money devoted to advertising in America (currently nearing $250 billion annually) offer a compelling reason to take advertisements and their messages seriously—however trivial individual ads might appear. But advertising deserves attention for other reasons as well. Jean Baudrillard describes advertising as "pure connotation," further noting that advertising "contributes nothing to production or to the direct practical application of things, yet it plays an integral part in the system of objects not merely because it relates to consumption but also because it itself becomes an object to be consumed" (1996, 161). As a form of material culture and as a rhetorical force, advertising plays a crucial role in the dissemination of meaning: affirming, reinforcing, and transforming cultural beliefs and values. Judith Williamson notes in the introduction to *Decoding Advertisements* that "advertisements are selling us something else besides consumer goods: in providing us with a structure in which we, and those goods, are interchangeable, they are selling us ourselves" (1978, 13). The "social tableaux" depicted in print advertising and the mini cinematic narratives of television commercials offer highly distorted representations of race, class, and gender in contemporary America—but they still provide poignant glimpses into cultural dreams and anxieties.

Advertising for food may be especially worthy of investigation. Food has long since ceased to function in a merely nutritive role. As Felipe Fernandez-Armesto argues in *Near a Thousand Tables: A History of Food*, food gives pleasure; it forges society; it can encode meanings. "It has spiritual and metaphysical, moral and transmutative effects" (2002, 20). It is also, quite simply, "what matters most to most people for most of the time" (2002, xi). The material fact of food and its prominence in our daily lives is matched in equal measure by the messages it relays regarding social class, ethnicity, gender, regional or national identity, religious beliefs and practices, psychological propensities, and sexual fantasies. "Every mouthful, every meal," write Bell and Valentine, "can tell us something about ourselves, and about our place in the world" (1997, 3). As such, it is a commodity that seems especially malleable within advertising, for it possesses the capacity, as Arjun Appadurai states, "to mobilize strong emotions" (1981, 494).

These strong emotions frequently operate at cross-purposes. Susan Bordo's analysis of food advertising in *Unbearable Weight* examines the ways in which advertising messages directed primarily at women pose a discourse of (bodily) control against fantasies of indulgence, "intensity, love, and thrills" (1995, 108). Jean Kilbourne devotes a chapter of *Can't Buy My Love* to advertising's tendency to eroticize food, linking food to sexuality and love, and, by extension, to addiction and eating disorders (1999). These explicit examinations of food advertising extend the work of feminist scholarship spanning several decades that has investigated the relationships between women, media, self-esteem, and body image—focusing particularly on eating disorders primarily affecting girls and young women (Chernin 1981, 1985; Thompson 1994; Beardsworth and Keil 1997; Counihan 1998; Groesz et al. 2002; Neilson n.d.; Sodolo 2005).

The relationship between food and the body resonates in yet a different way among environmental historians. Food serves as one of our most intimate links to the environment. Every food contains within it the sun, soil, air, and water required to transform seeds into sustenance. Each bite connects us to the agricultural policies and practices inscribed on rural lands. Our bodies, literally shaped by food, ultimately stand as direct testimony to our consumption of the environment and serve to inform others about the nature of that relationship.

Those who labor within agricultural fields, though, bear the brunt of American political and economic policies related to food. The class and ethnic markers of their bodies are strongly implicated in both the material conditions under which they labor and the (limited) attention those labors receive. To a great extent, agricultural labor remains invisible in America. This may be attributable in part to the physical distance between the farm fields where our food originates and the kitchens where it comes to rest.[6] This invisibility may also be due in part to a psychic distance: the fact that the number of Americans actively engaged in and knowledgeable about food production has declined precipitously (Berry 2002), especially since the end of World War II. Currently less than 2 percent of the American population is engaged in agricultural labor. Those who perform farm labor are further marginalized by their immigration status (81 percent are born outside the United States) and by poverty (61 percent have family incomes below the poverty level) (Das et al. 2002). Whatever its cause, invisibility allows and even encourages exploitative and dangerous worker health and safety conditions to fester, particularly with regard to pesticide use in fruit and vegetable crops. The testimony written on the bodies of agricultural workers remains largely hidden from view—though it surfaces intermittently in investigative reporting and in statistics compiled by federal and private organizations.

"Politics," as Judith Williamson succinctly states, "is the intersection of public and private life" (1978, 10). In many respects advertising represents our most "public" and ubiquitous form of mass-mediated communication—reaching us not simply via radio and television broadcasts or inscribed in print media, but emblazoned as well in public spaces: on billboards, buses, taxicabs, buildings, and sewn/printed into the very fabric of our clothing. Advertising is public, but it speaks to us in intimate ways and "influences us privately: our own private relations to other people and to ourselves" (Williamson 1978, 10). The language of advertising is meant to seduce: dazzling us with a seemingly infinite range of choices, offering pleasures for eye and ear alike, making promises and suggestions, urging us to express our "individuality" by obtaining just the right constellation of mass-produced goods, flattering our savvy and good taste.

Advertising works hard to create a sealed and seamless reinterpretation of the world, excluding other evidence and perspectives. Analyzing advertisements helps reveal their strategies and expose their fissures. But juxtaposing ads with other discourses renders them more legible still. In an essay challenging the ease with which audiences can construct liberating readings of mass mediated texts by exploiting their polysemic qualities, Celeste Condit argues that audiences are "constrained by a variety of factors in any given rhetorical situation" and these include "access to oppositional codes," other information or perspectives that can be used to critique media messages (1989, 103). Though Condit is writing about television programming, her analysis applies as well to advertising, which through its sheer ubiquity and repetition also "disseminates and legitimates, in a pleasurable fashion, a political vocabulary that favors certain interests and groups over others, even if by no other means than consolidating the dominant audience by giving presence to their codes" (1989, 114). Advertising for fast-food salads focuses attention on the body, but in ways that render concerns about health a matter of narcissism, while simultaneously exploiting anxieties and stereotypes about sexuality, body image, ethnicity, and gender in representations that reinforce the regimes of bodily propriety and control. Yet it is the bodies excluded altogether from this advertising, those of agricultural fieldworkers, that best reveal the paucity of its discourse. This essay attempts to reintroduce the testimony of those bodies, shaped by the conditions and the environments in which they labor, alongside an analysis of the images and messages found in fast-food salad ads.[7] Such juxtapositioning helps expand the notion of "health" beyond the narrow confines patrolled by the language of advertising and reintroduces the realities of food production amidst the cultural representations of food consumption found in fast-food advertisements.

Advertisements speak to our dreams and aspirations more than to our rational minds. They may allude to (or even arouse) our current dissatisfactions—but always with the goal of securing a sale. Such narratives conspire to persuade us that we can be happy (in the future) if only we take the proper action (buy something). Thus, advertising feeds our narcissism, allowing us to view ourselves (and our bodies) as the measure of all things. Personal transformation—in pursuit of perfection—is always only a purchase away. Food fads and health crazes are frequently swept into this vortex, leaving behind a long line of dietary experiments in America since the late eighteenth century (Levenstein 1988; Fernandez-Armesto 2002; Pollan 2004). As Harvey Levenstein argues, "food processors have responded nimbly, churning out foods in low-calorie, low-sodium, low-cholesterol, low-fat, caffeine-free, high-fructose, high-protein, high-calcium, and high-fiber forms" (1988, 205). Low or no-carb foods can now be added to this list. Each swing of the health pendulum is accompanied by advertisements promoting new foods and new diets.

Marion Nestle's answer to what constitutes a "healthy" diet emphasizes balance. She notes that our diets must "provide enough energy (calories) and vitamins, minerals, and other essential nutrients to prevent deficiencies and support normal metabolism. At the same time, they must not include excessive amounts of these and other nutritional factors that might promote development of chronic diseases" (2002, 5). For food historian Fernandez-Armesto, the concept of health is somewhat more complex. Noting that when eighteenth-century sailors learned to ward off scurvy through a diet that included fresh fruits, food became elevated "above its commonplace role as a nourisher, to the ranks of a healer" (2002, 40). Fernandez-Armesto continues:

> Food health became a quest in which rising science met abiding religion. It was both a pseudo-science and a mystic vocation: pseudo-scientific because of the new prestige of science in the nineteenth-century West; mystical because it was developed beyond evidence by visionaries who, in many cases were

religiously inspired: if food was the key to physical health, why not moral health, too? (2002, 40–41)

The ability of scientists to break down the chemical composition of foods seems to have encouraged what Michael Pollan describes as a reductionist attitude towards food in which "we've learned to choose our foods by the numbers (calories, carbs, fats, R.D.A.'s, price, whatever), relying more heavily on our reading and computational skills than upon our senses" (2004, 74). Eating by the numbers attempts to create a mathematical formula out of the concepts of "health" and "balance."

While it might be expected that claims about health would be the primary way in which fast-food restaurants promote their designer salads, explicit references to health appear only infrequently in ads or in the accompanying articles (about restaurant salad bars) paired with them in "Special Advertising Sections." In advertising discourse about health, narcissism sets the tone, pairing physical appearance with a reductionist approach to food and encouraging a belief that personal transformation can be easy and enjoyable. Under the heading "Slim Down Your Salad," the article adjoining an advertisement for Kraft Carb Well Ranch Dressing offered "a guide to help you make a healthy—and tasty—salad" from a restaurant salad bar. Using data on calories, fat, vitamins A, C, and D, folate, potassium, calcium, protein, fiber, and sodium as its measure, the guide recommended, for example, adding cherry tomatoes and a hard-boiled egg, but skipping the red onions (as not worth their weight in either potassium or Vitamin C). Selecting kidney beans was encouraged as providing "a burst of color" as well as fiber and protein, yet the mathematical formula never quite added back up to "tasty." Instead health (and pleasure) are reduced to a set of numbers—and the numbers that matter most are those found on a bathroom scale: the slim salad promises the slim body. But if counting calories and carbs and grams of fat requires too much effort, consumers could simply "take a brisk walk to the salad bar" at Ruby Tuesday's and "eat your way to better health;" with "at least 689 salad bar combinations" "it's love at first bite." McDonald's promises that "getting active is easier than you think," especially with the purchase of an adult happy meal: salad, water, and a pedometer included. Over and over, ads assure us that "making smart menu choices is a snap," and leading "a healthy, active life" is "cool," "smart," "colorful," "easy," "fun," and "user-friendly."

The upbeat copy stresses ease and convenience, echoing the "therapeutic ethos" that T. J. Jackson Lears finds characteristic of advertising beginning in the early twentieth century, and further feeds our narcissism. These modern ads betray the same "almost obsessive concern with psychic and physical health" that Lears argues signaled a shift away from "a Protestant ethos of salvation through self-denial" (1983, 4). Advertising attempts to persuade that personal sacrifices are unnecessary; restraint is anathema. Instead, salvation (or success, status, youth, beauty, happiness, sexual attractiveness, and the friendship and love of others) is obtainable through effortless cash or credit transactions. Simply "swap one menu favorite for another tasty choice," in order to proclaim, "I'm feeling better about me, and 'i'm lovin' it.'"

Perhaps because salads, in the eyes of McDonald's spokeswoman Joanne Jacobs, are already thought to wear a "nutritional halo" (Aschoff 2003), fast-food restaurants have decided that claims about health in their advertising are unnecessary. Or perhaps in attempting to attract a consumer who may be already too well-versed in the numbers game, fast-food restaurants wish to avoid further scrutiny of designer salads with calorie, fat, and sodium levels that rival (and at times exceed) those of a McDonald's Quarter-Pounder or cheeseburger. One further concern, even with "healthy" fruits and vegetables, also remains unaddressed in these ads: food safety.

In 1991, the USDA began the Pesticide Data Program (PDP) to test for pesticide residues in agricultural commodities. The PDP has tested over fifty different commodities, including fresh, frozen, and canned fruit and vegetables, for more than 380 different pesticides. PDP reports are issued annually, available on the USDA website. In 2002, the latest year for which data is available, the PDP conducted tests on 10,056 samples of fruit and vegetable commodities, fresh and frozen, from both domestic and foreign sources. Approximately 47 percent had detectable pesticide residues (PDP 2002). "The foods most likely to contain residues of high-risk pesticides are apples, pears, peaches, grapes, green beans, tomatoes, peas, strawberries, spinach, peppers, melons, lettuce, and various juices" (Benbrook 2003).

While testing for pesticide residue is a relatively straightforward process, understanding the health risks associated with consumption of those residues is considerably more complicated. And while the risk assessment formula itself is fairly simple—exposure = residue concentration x amount of food consumed (Tomerlin 2000, 15)—it is difficult to measure either variable with much precision. Nor do scientists necessarily know how to calculate the effects caused by the interactions of various pesticides. Still, Jorgen Stenersen argues that "residues of pesticides are ranked very high as an important risk factor in society (see, for instance Faustman and Omenn, 2001), although toxicologists do not think such residues are very significant for human health. Even in the literature fundamentally critical to pesticides, the authors admit that pesticide residues in food are seldom a real toxicological problem (e.g. Emden, 1996)" (2004, 226). One cautionary note sounded by some individuals concerns the effects of pesticide residues on children. Because of significant differences between children and adults in terms of metabolic rates, body composition, development of reproductive and central nervous systems, as well as diet, the effects of pesticide exposure on children are more complicated and less well understood (Kegley and Wise 1998, 16–18).

Though direct appeals to "health" might seem a powerful motivating factor among a public "obsessed with the idea of eating healthily" (Pollan 2004, 74), such claims remain largely outside the discourse of advertising for fast-food salads. Advertisers turned to other strategies for selling salads to the American public instead. Rather than references to proper meals and proper nutrition, ads evoke other forms of propriety, laced with innuendo and double entendre.

If, as Fernandez-Armesto notes, food and religion have long been linked through a strong moral imperative, an equally entrenched association exists between food and sex. The sheer physicality of eating and the pleasures to be derived from the sensual properties of many foods link gustatory and sexual appetites. These delights often find entrance initially through the eye. We learn through advertising to "derive pleasure from the spectacle alone" (Buck-Morss 1989, 85). Alexander Cockburn argues that "there are curious parallels between manuals on sexual techniques and manuals on the preparation of food. . . . True gastro-porn heightens the excitement and also the sense of the unattainable by proffering colored photographs of various completed recipes" (1987, 125). Gastro-porn is characterized, then, by images of seduction, of foods displayed in stereotypical but wholly artificial perfection, destined to remain forever out of reach and unobtainable. It is not simply the culinary dishes destined for upper-class tables (or coffee-table books and magazines) which receive this treatment. Fast food, despite its ubiquity and low status, has been "aestheticized to . . . a point of frenzy and hysteria" (Kroker et al., quoted in Smart 1994, 171). Fast-food advertisements (like the restaurants themselves) are awash in garish colors and dazzling displays.

At times gastro-porn seems employed to stimulate salivary glands as well as sales. Carefully lighted and airbrushed images are paired with copy meant to emphasize the perfection pictured and its irresistible allure. Above an angled close-up of the Wendy's Chicken BLT Salad, a warning proclaims, "Prepare to start a new habit." While habits and addictions are not synonymous, the copy implies that this particular "habit" will prove inescapable. Simple surrender is the only possible response. While salads may not fall into the category of "rich, fattening, soothing food" that Susan Bordo finds especially troubling when eroticized and linked with sexuality, desire, and transgression, the ad depicts food as a sensual and overpowering delight (1995, 108). Yet images of unattainable perfection (in food as in sex) may pave a path to frustration and dissatisfaction. Some ads attempt to inoculate against such responses by deflecting dissatisfactions to other sources, further fetishizing the commodity for sale. A close-up of the Mandarin Chicken Salad glistens beneath the single line, "At least one thing today will exceed your expectations," implying, in one fell swoop, the inadequacy of all other events that might occur in an ordinary day, whether interactions with friends and family or sexual encounters with a spouse or lover.

Television ads employing gastro-porn techniques add motion to the mixture. Vegetables dance across the screen to the beat of up-tempo music. In a series of ads from 2004 (archived on the AdLand web site) for Wendy's, Subway, Arby's, and McDonald's, lettuces and spinach (often mixed with sprays of water) float and flutter in a green cascade, whole heads of lettuce splash into wooden bowls, fresh vegetables and other ingredients in a rainbow of bright colors tumble through the air and land in salad bowls, streams of salad dressing ooze onto mounds of ripe vegetables, and salad bowls, heaping with vegetables, cheeses, bacon and chicken, spin in slow circles as the camera holds a tight shot. The camera work and lighting, color and motion, do their best to lure us in, attract our gaze. "All you need is your appetite," coos the Arby's ad.

Gastro-porn depends on imagery and innuendo; too many words threaten to interrupt the pleasures. A McDonald's ad fills a borderless page with an extreme close-up of a bright green lettuce leaf, curled sensuously, glistening with droplets of water. Superimposed over the image, the ad copy appears in the form of a Q & A exchange ("a series of real answers to real questions asked by our customers"). The answer to the query, "What makes your lettuce so crisp?" is at once simple and yet inscrutable: "Our

Fig. 7.1. Wendy's Expectations Ad

lettuce is fresh and never frozen, so the crunch you hear is pure fresh lettuce from the same place you buy yours. Simply put, the only unnatural aspect of our lettuce is the speed at which it travels from the farm to the restaurant." The answer both presumes consumer ignorance about food preparation and handling (by implying that other fast-food restaurants freeze their

Fig. 7.2. McDonald's Fresh Lettuce Ad

lettuce) and flatters our shopping expertise (in suggesting we purchase our produce directly from the farm with no intermediary stops) with the goal of persuading us that McDonald's offers ingredients that are exactly the same, only better, as those we buy for ourselves. Such contradictory messages make it evident that gastro-porn isn't intended to trigger analysis, only Pavlovian responses to beautiful and sensuous images. Physical perfection and beauty have long served as the language of advertising.

There is a beauty to be found in the appearance of agricultural fields as well, even to some extent amidst the vast monocultural fields representing the imposition of human order upon the natural environment. The straight lines of row crops create dizzying patterns of green against brown for passing motorists. Salinas, California prides itself as the "salad bowl to the world." Situated in Monterey County, Salinas and its surrounding area have become "the home of the packaged salad and value added fresh vegetable industry with over 90% of the market share. Monterey County is the State's third largest agricultural producer" netting just under $3.3 billion in sales in 2003. "Forty-one individual commodities each gross over 1 million dollars," with leaf lettuce the number one commodity, earning $555.6 million in 2003 (Profile 2004).

This visual perfection is gained at a cost. In California alone, according to the California Department of Pesticide Regulation (DPR), "some 175 million pounds of pesticide applications were reported in 2003, a 4 percent increase from the previous year" (DPR 2005). Reported pesticide use in California climbed fairly steadily through the 1990s (when the California DPR began collecting complete records), peaking in 1998, with 214 million pounds applied to agricultural fields across the state. Reports of pesticide use began to fall in 1999 and continued to decline for the next two years, though reported use is now on the rise once again. The ten crops most heavily sprayed with pesticides are: grapes, cotton, broccoli, oranges, ornamentals, almonds, tomatoes, lettuce, strawberries, and alfalfa (Reeves et al. 1999, 7). Pesticides are meant to ensure that fruit and vegetable crops meet our expectations of physical beauty. Grocery stores create their own displays of gastro-porn with flawless produce piled high and glistening. The toxins themselves remain invisible.

The visual enticements of gastro-porn can be enhanced by sound—shifting attention from the food itself to consumer responses. In the most recent television ads for fast-food salads, close-up shots of the salads themselves have given way to the "mimed celebration of other people's decisions" (Williams 1980, 193), expressed in subverbal moans or one-word exclamations, sounds one might associate with sexual pleasure. The fact that these scenes take place in the workplace adds further intrigue. This trend may have originated with the McDonald's "Watcher" ad which aired in 2004. The narrative opens with a woman in an employee lunchroom asked to watch a coworker's salad. She is left alone with a salad that looms in the foreground of the screen. The camera swoops in for a close-up shot of the salad. The woman quickly succumbs to its temptations. She takes a bite. "Love grilled chicken," she moans. She takes another bite. "Love bleu cheese," she murmurs. Within seconds she has consumed the entire salad and departed the scene of the crime, leaving yet another coworker to take the blame. Transgression is also the theme of a Wendy's fruit salad ad in which a woman hides under her desk in order to eat her Wendy's fruit salad undetected and undisturbed. The implication of both ads is that women must hide their appetites, whether for food or for sex.

Gene Weingarten skewered the McDonald's "Watcher" ad in an August 2004 column in the *Washington Post*, railing: "So we have, in one ad, a celebration of shockingly unethical behavior, stupidity, larceny, gluttony, sloth, envy, greed, cowardice, bearing false witness against a neighbor and littering. Other than out-and-out murder, is there any commandment or deadly sin that this ad does not advocate, condone, or endorse?" (Weingarten, W11). Weingarten neglected to add "lust" to his list, though it is present—at least in the form of "cooked sex" that Judith Williamson discusses in *Decoding Advertisements*. "Cooked sex" manages to appeal to our prurient interests while masking our obsession at the same time. "Sex becomes a referent system, always hinted at, referred to, in innuendo, double entendre, or symbolism, but never 'raw'" (1978, 120). Ads titillate while hoping to avoid offense.

Women left alone with food in advertising replay the story of the Garden of Eden, succumbing over and over again to temptation. When men and women eat together, at least in Wendy's ads, they voice their pleasures and dissatisfactions as a chorus. Seated around a lunchroom table, four office workers take turns assessing their level of satisfaction with their fast-food salads. The first three utter a simple "eh." When the camera reaches the woman with a salad and soft drink from Wendy's, she murmurs an approving "ummm!" "So we got 'eh' and you got 'ummm'?" a coworker asks in frustration. The vagaries of their communication suggest their disappointments and pleasures extend far beyond fast-food salads. A second ad suggests that such disappointments need not matter—as long as our salads satisfy. Interspersed with an employer's announcements that "Last year was not our best. We fell short of our projections in nine out of ten areas. In fact, I'm sad to report a record loss in terms of money," are the employees' interjections of "great!" "impressive!" "outstanding!" "incredible!" "awesome!" and "fantastic!"—as they happily bite into their Wendy's salads. The final shots of both ads revert to visual gastro-porn as salad ingredients fly across the screen in an orgy of excitement. Whatever else their message, these ads paint an unflattering portrait of American white-collar employees: largely complacent, easily distracted, but engaged in petty crimes and competitions directed at each other in their dreary, but otherwise comfortable, worksites.

As unappealing as these portrayals of office workers may be, farm workers, by contrast, rarely occupy even 30–seconds' worth of prime time attention in a television commercial or appear in the glossy pages of magazines. Their labor remains strategically hidden from view in the sanitized world of advertising. On occasion, though, agricultural workers can be seen amidst the fields in which they labor, planting or staking tomato plants by hand, bundling onions and garlic, stooping to pick strawberries, cutting and tossing head lettuce onto conveyor belts pulled by slow moving trucks across endless fields. They are mostly Hispanic (90 percent), mostly men (80 percent), mostly illegal immigrants (52 percent) (Das et al. 2002), wearing jeans and long-sleeved flannel shirts or hooded sweatshirts and gloves (sometimes plastic) regardless of the weather (even in central valley heatwaves with temperatures topping 100 degrees for days on end) as protection from the sun and pesticides. Grapes, cotton, broccoli, oranges, ornamentals, almonds, tomatoes, lettuce, strawberries, and alfalfa together "account for half of all reported agriculture-related pesticide illnesses" (Reeves et al. 1999, 7). These are crops which still require considerable hand labor. Every strawberry, every bunch of grapes, every head of lettuce or broccoli, every tomato and orange, and a multitude of other fruits and vegetables is still picked by hand. Those hands (mostly brown) labor in fields and orchards saturated with pesticides.

If the bodies of those responsible for planting, tending, and harvesting our foods are rarely glimpsed or acknowledged, Americans, for the most part, are acutely aware of their own bodies. The relationship between the foods we eat and the condition or shape of our bodies is understood by most individuals on at least some level. This relationship is not strictly a matter of food calories or composition. "Our bodies are 'molded by a great many distinct regimes' (Foucault 1977, 153) of which food, eating and associated codes of conduct represent one complex example" (Smart 1994, 169). Our physical bodies must negotiate the social body, revealing in each encounter, with constant and irreducible testimony, individual adherence to or departure from societal norms of propriety and decorum.

For women in particular, failure to conform to bodily expectations carries severe penalties.

Eating disorders represent one response to societal expectations and cultural regimes. It is difficult to arrive at accurate figures for the number of individuals with eating disorders, but most estimates claim that between 5 to 10 million Americans, the majority of them young women, suffer from anorexia, bulimia, and other disordered eating behaviors. Race and class as well as gender have figured into studies of eating disorders. Women of color were considered less likely to engage in disordered eating, though more recent studies have suggested otherwise. Women across all ethnic groups are more likely to adopt eating disorders, especially as their income level rises (Sodolo 2005; Neilsen n.d.). Although the tendency is to view eating disorders (and the individuals who engage in them) as pathological, Susan Bordo notes that "preoccupation with fat, diet, and slenderness are not abnormal. Indeed, such preoccupation may function as one of the most powerful normalizing mechanisms of our century, ensuring the production of self-monitoring and self-disciplining 'docile bodies' sensitive to any departure from social norms and habituated to self-improvement and self-transformation in the service of those norms" (1995, 186). Many point to media images—and particularly the images found in advertising—as promoting a preoccupation with body image and the quest to attain the thin ideal. Current research seems to substantiate this view (Groesz et al. 2002).

Advertising operates on a system of exchange, shifting focus from the specific properties of the object itself to its meaning in human terms, its symbolic content (Williamson 1978). Because salads are often viewed as a "diet" food, likely to aid in the effort to lose weight, body image and body ideals (explicit or implied) may be expected to play a significant role in fast-food salad advertisements. Salads, thus, can serve as a stand-in for the body ideal—and vice versa. "Your body is a temple," states a Subway ad for its fresh salads. "But that doesn't mean it can't have a little fun." The body depicted in this instance is a cartoon drawing of a young girl sporting a red onion ring as a hoola-hoop. Such "playfulness" about the body seems reserved for caricatures and children. For adult women, the message is more serious. Even absent bodies bear witness to the thin ideal. "Little black dress, here I come," reads the headline positioned above a close-up of Applebee's Mesquite Chicken Salad. Thus, salad represents a means to an end: bodily perfection and desirability.

Fig. 7.3. Applebee's Little Black Dress Ad

The system of exchange between salads and body ideals can operate in the reverse direction as well, in which slim, attractive bodies are used to represent—and sell—fast-food salads. When the body is present, it often upstages the salad being sold. A series of Burger King ads exem-

Fig. 7.4a. Burger King Pouch Ad

plify this practice. Enlisting the services of the Crispin Porter + Bogusky advertising agency, Burger King created the character of a fashion designer named Ugoff to help sell their salads. While the television commercials feature Ugoff himself in parodies of fashion expertise, the print

Fig. 7.4b. Burger King Pouch Ad

advertisements celebrate "The Pouch: The Ultimate Lunch Accessory." The phrase accompanies the image of various models, each young, sleek, and dressed in a fashionable black and white ensemble, delicately holding a small white bag, patterned discreetly with what appears at first glance to be a single flower. Upon closer inspection the image is revealed as a fork filled with salad. A thin column of text, topped by a small image of the salad itself, reveals the product. These postmodern ads make no attempt to mask the fact they are selling the packaging more than the product. That packaging includes the slim young bodies of multiethnic models: white, black, Asian. The emphasis on surface over substance is further parodied and celebrated in versions in which the left-hand page of a two-page spread is made to resemble a separate fashion magazine article. One poses the question, "What's in your bag?" and answers it with glimpses into the purses of four fashion designers—one of whom is none other than Ugoff. A second features seven different purses, complete with their designer label, price, and contact information, one of which turns out to be the Burger King Pouch. The ads both mock and reinforce young women's anxieties about appearance and style—including body image.

While these Burger King ads for the most part appear to gloss over racial differences, some ads exaggerate "the other," giving prominent attention to markers of race and ethnicity. Black models are paired with copy meant to convey that they are bold and sassy. "I want to put 'me' at the top of my to-do list. I want to have my cake and eat it, too. And I want a salad that's not like, you know, rabbit food," exclaims one black model in a McDonald's ad, dressed all in red, her mouth open wide. "And, I want it now or else I'm gonna pout!" she concludes. A close-up of another black woman's face beams down upon a McDonald's Fiesta Salad. Her mouth, too, is open wide in a large grin and the accompanying caption reads, "my taste is out there," with the words "out there" given a 3–D effect in bright red and yellow. She sports animal print sunglasses and boasts, "I don't do dull. Mild is not my style. I can't stand bland." Similar to a television commercial for McDonald's salads featuring another young black woman, the words echo the rhythms of hip hop and the rhyme of poetry slams. Meanwhile, a white model, dressed in layered white T-shirts and blue jeans, in an ad for the same product states, "sometimes i need to bring out my wild side. so i'll grab a new Premium Fiesta Salad. . . . wow." She is positioned at the bottom of the page, both below and smaller than the image of the Fiesta Salad, and tilting her body inward in an extreme body cant. The headline above her reads, "it's my party. it's my salad." For white women, whose ego occupies only a lowercase "i" and who party solo, wild is attainable through a purchase; for women of color, wild is their "natural" state of being. In concluding his historical survey on the images of

Fig. 7.5. McDonald's Out There Ad

blacks in advertising, Jan Nederveen Pieterse argues that currently, though there are many ads in which "ethnicity plays no significant part, . . . [m]ore often, however, existing stereotypes are fine-tuned and made to look new as they are recycled" (1992, 210). Some stereotypes persist

Fig. 7.6. McDonald's Party Ad

intact, others are modified, while new stereotypes seem to be emerging, including "the aggressiveness of black women" (203). Black women's bodies add hipness and cool to counter the stereotype of salads as the bland food of diets and self-denial.

On those few occasions when a salad is gendered as an appropriately masculine food, advertisements play upon a different set of stereotypes. Gender difference is amplified rather than downplayed in advertising for a food traditionally perceived as feminine. A Wendy's ad celebrates choice with the options of fries, chili, baked potato, side, or Caesar side salad combo meals. The condensed history lesson depicted here is meant to demonstrate culinary progress: fries are now an option, not a requirement. Though the ad boasts that "Wendy's has changed everything," the feature that remains obviously unchanged in each scene—whether "65 million years ago" when the meal of the day was a "brontosaurus combo with fries," or the present day chicken sandwich with a side salad—is the fact that "men eat and women prepare" (Bordo 1995, 117). In each scene, a female servant or waitress happily hands over a meal to a waiting and hungry man. Meanwhile, parody is employed in a Jack in the Box commercial to exaggerate men's tendencies to eschew salad. The ad depicts an "intervention" staged to assist the male protagonist, "Gary," who is in denial about being a salad dodger. "Maybe I've dodged a few salads," he finally admits, "But who wouldn't? Fast food salads are so—" Though unable to complete his commentary, with the help of family and friends, and, of course, Jack and his new Chicken Caesar Salad, Gary can overcome his salad-dodging ways. In a brief 30 seconds, with masculinity constructed through food preferences, implied lack of commitment, and the shirking of familial responsibilities, Jack in the Box delivers a high-calorie serving of stereotypes. Thus, male and female, black, white, and Asian bodies figure into ads in ways that reveal the regimes of culture and the strictures of stereotypes.

Other bodies display these regimes in still more concrete and dangerous ways. Thirty percent of the pesticides used in California agricultural fields are on a list of chemicals known to cause cancer or reproductive harm (Das et al. 2002). The symptoms of pesticide poisoning include: headache, nausea, skin irritation, muscular incoordination, vomiting, diarrhea, loss of reflexes, irritation of nose and throat, abdominal cramps, uncontrollable muscular twitching, difficulty in breathing, mental confusion, excessive sweating, intense thirst, profound weakness, rapid pulse, rapid heartbeat, convulsions, fever, blurring of vision, unconsciousness (Pesticide Certification Training 2002, 161). Researchers have linked an "increased incidence of asthma, allergic reactions, and other respiratory problems" to pesticides (Kegley 2001). Chronic effects of pesticide exposure may not appear until fifteen to thirty years after exposure, and few studies have been conducted on farmworkers. The evidence that does exist indicates an increased risk for several cancers, birth defects, infertility, and miscarriages among farmers and farmworkers compared with the general population (Reeves et al. 1999, 19–20).

Despite whatever bucolic notions of rural America and farming we might possess, agriculture is one of the most hazardous occupations in the United States. "Between 800 and 1,000 farm workers die in the United States each year as a direct consequence of pesticide exposure, according to a 1997 report by the U.S. Department of Health and Human Services" (Sanchez 2003). The most recent report from the Bureau of Labor Statistics cited 707 fatalities in 2003 among agricultural workers (a category that also includes forestry, fishing, and hunting)—resulting in the highest fatality rate among private sector businesses at 31.2 fatalities per one hundred thousand employees. Three hundred thirty-three of these deaths were associated specifically with crop production.[8] Nonfatal injuries are more difficult to calculate. Over twenty-two thousand nonfatal injuries associated with crop production were reported in 2003 (Bureau of Labor Statistics). "More than 313,000 farm-workers in the United States may suffer pesticide-related illnesses annually, according to the World Resources Institute, a Washington-based, nonprofit environmental group" (Sanchez 2003). "The few analyses available indicate that nationwide, the majority of pesticide poisoning cases are never diagnosed or reported (Blondell 1996, U.S. GAO 1993)" (Reeves et al. 1999, 21). Lack of health insurance or access to medical care contribute to this situation, but "the primary reason farmworkers are unlikely to report pesticide-related injuries and illnesses is fear of employer retaliation" (Reeves et al. 1999, 21–22). Such retaliation usually means firing workers who seek compensation or even medical attention for their injuries. Both jobs and bodies are endangered in agricultural fields across America every day.

While any given advertisement may be insignificant in itself, together they construct webs of meaning that help shape our views of ourselves, others, and our place in the world. In fast-food salad advertising, "health," when found at all, refers to the physical appearance of the individual body. In the absence of even this flimsy concept, advertising representations emphasizing sexuality, stereotypes, and body ideals reinforce dominant codes of propriety—and our narcissism. Creating an oppositional code, a means of reading against the grain of advertisements and the cultural values they affirm and reinforce, requires familiarity with a larger discourse, one that resides outside the narrow confines constructed by the language of advertising (and further cemented by mainstream media neglect).

The concept of "health" has the potential to serve as a powerful motivating force for human action. But it may be more likely to accomplish this if we were to understand that "health" encompasses more than our own individual bodies. We might, as Wendell Berry writes, "begin with Sir Albert Howard's illuminating principle that we should understand 'the whole problem of health in soil, plant, and animal, and man as one great subject.' Eaters, that is, must understand that eating takes place inescapably in the world, that it is inescapably an agricultural act, and that how we eat determines, to a considerable extent, the way the world is used" (2002, 324). Our bodies are already linked to the soil, water, air that makes agriculture possible and thus provides the food we eat—in our own kitchens and in restaurants (fast food or otherwise)—each and every day. We must begin to understand that our bodies are linked as well to the bodies of those farmworkers who make our eating possible. The health of the one is inextricably tied to the health of all. We can and should eat our vegetables. But doing so will constitute a "healthy" choice only if we purchase fruits and vegetables grown and harvested by farmworkers laboring in safe, healthy, and sustainable environments.

Notes

1. According to the USDA, "increasing Americans' consumption of fruits and vegetables has been a mainstay of the Federal Dietary Guidelines for more than a decade" (Guthrie 2004, 1), most notably through its joint sponsorship of the 5-A-Day program with the National Cancer Institute (NCI) and the Produce for Better Health Foundation. In March 2005, McDonald's joined the 5-A-Day partnership.

2. Bell and Valentine in *Consuming Geographies* argue that the concept of a "proper" meal implies a meal eaten together as a family and that "part of the intention behind producing such a meal is to produce 'home' and 'family'" simultaneously (1997, 59).

3 *Agricultural Statistics 2004* estimates that Americans ate just over forty-five pounds of potatoes per person in 2003 (the latest year for which figures are available). Of these, 51 percent are consumed away from home. Per capita consumption of the other most popular vegetables are: head lettuce—22.3 pounds; tomatoes—18.6 pounds; onions—17.4 pounds; carrots—12.7 pounds.

4. Eric Schlosser's 2001 book *Fast Food Nation*, which remained on the *New York Times'* best seller list for nearly two years and was translated into more than twenty languages (http://ckp.kp.org/newsroom/nw/archive/nw_050412_fastfood.html), and Morgan Spurlock's 2004 documentary *Super Size Me*, which by September 2004 had made about $10.5 million at the box office and was ranked the fourth highest grossing documentary of all time (DVD Talk http://www.dvdtalk.com/interviews/003252.html), offer the most prominent of these critiques.

5. If even a fraction of the fast-food industry's combined advertising expenditures (reaching $3.1 billion in 1998) were devoted to promoting these salads, the amount would exceed government expenditures on its "5-A-Day" program (5-A-Day; Dukcevich 2002). Marion Nestle claims the "total funding available for public communication" of the "5-A-Day" program was under $3 million in 1999, or, as she notes, "miniscule in comparison to the advertising budget of any single candy bar, soft drink, or potato chip" (2002, 131).

6. Barbara Kingsolver discusses the environmental impact of the physical distances our food travels in "Lily's Chickens," an essay in *Small Wonder*. Kingsolver notes that the second largest source of fuel consumption in the United States (and thus the world) involves the production and transportation of food. "Americans have a taste for food that's been seeded, fertilized, harvested, processed, and packaged in grossly energy-expensive ways and then shipped, often refrigerated, for so many miles it might as well be green cheese from the moon. . . . Transporting five calories' worth of strawberry from California to New York costs 435 calories of fossil fuel" (Kingsolver 2002, 114).

7. Many of the thirty-four ads used in this study were gathered from two simple content analysis projects, one examining women's magazines and a second on prime time television. Of the 1,379 print ads, 256 advertised food, with 13 of these for fast-food salads. (Another nine ads were for salad dressings, which also receive some attention in the following analysis.) Of the 467 total prime time television ads, sixty-eight advertised food, three of them for fast-food salads. Additional print (9) and television ads (9) for fast-food salads were derived from a variety of other sources. No ads for fresh fruits or vegetables were found in either study. The magazine study examined advertising in two issues each of nine magazines (for the randomly selected months of July and August 2004). The magazines included in this study were: *Better Homes and Gardens*, *Bon Appetit*, *Elle*, *Essence*, *Glamour*, *Good Housekeeping*, *Ladies' Home Journal*, *O*, and *Self*. The television study consisted of the top twelve ranked prime time programs

(as measured by Nielsen Ratings) during the week of May 2–8. The programs in this sample include (in order): *CSI: Crime Scene Investigation* (CBS); *Desperate Housewives* (ABC); *American Idol* (Wednesday), (Fox); *American Idol* (Tuesday), (Fox); *CSI: Miami* (CBS); *Survivor: Palau* (CBS); *Everybody Loves Raymond* (CBS); *Grey's Anatomy* (ABC); *Two and a Half Men* (CBS); *Without a Trace* (CBS); *Lost* (ABC); and *House* (Fox).

8. An additional 158 fatalities were reported in 2003 for animal production and forty-four more for agriculture and forestry support activities (Bureau of Labor Statistics 2004, 8).

Works Cited

Appadurai, Arjun. 1981. "Gastro-politics in Hindu South Asia." *American Ethnologist* 8: 494–511.

Achoff, Susan. 1999. "Salad Shooter." *St. Petersburg Times*, 23 September. http://www.sptimes.com/News/92399/news_pf/Taste/Salad_shooter_

Agricultural Statistics / United States Department of Agriculture. 1972. Table 289. Washington DC: U.S. Government Printing Office.

———. 1981. Table 281. Washington DC: U.S. Government Printing Office.

———. 1984. Table 244. Washington DC: U.S. Government Printing Office.

———. 1994. Table 238. Washington DC: U.S. Government Printing Office.

———. 2003. Table 4–64. Washington DC: U.S. Government Printing Office.

Baudrillard, Jean. 1996. *The System of Objects.* Trans. James Benedict. London: Verso.

Beardsworth, Alan, and Teresa Keil. 1997. "Dieting, Fat and Body Image." In *Sociology on the Menu: An Invitation to the Study of Food and Society*, 173–190. London: Routledge.

Bell, David, and Gill Valentine. 1997. *Consuming Geographies: We Are Where We Eat.* London: Routledge.

Benbrook, Charles M. 2003. "A Closer Look at the Pesticide Residue Question." http:// www.newfarm.org/depts/gleanings/0504/pesticide.shtml

Berger, John. 1972. *Ways of Seeing.* London: Penguin Books.

Berry, Wendell. 2002. *The Pleasures of Eating. The Art of the Commonplace.* Ed. Norman Wirzba, 321–327. Washington DC: Counterpoint, 2002.

Blondell, J. M. 1996. "Memorandum: Review of Registrant Response to Acute Worker Risk Ranking Meeting July 20, 1995." May 30, 1996. U.S. EPA, Washington, DC.

Bordo, Susan. 1995. *Unbearable Weight: Feminism, Western Culture, and the Body.* Berkeley, CA: University of California Press.

Buck-Morss, Susan. 1989. *The Dialectics of Seeing: Walter Benjamin and the Arcades Project.* Cambridge, MA: The MIT Press.

Bureau of Labor Statistics. Table SNR05. Washington, DC: Department of Labor. USDL 04–1830 http://www.bls.gov/iif/oshcfoi1.htm

Chernin, Kim. 1985. *The Hungry Self: Women, Eating and Identity.* New York: Times Books.

Chernin, Kim. 1981. *The Obsession: Reflections on the Tyranny of Slenderness.* 1st ed. New York: Harper & Row.

Cockburn, Alexander. 1987. "Gastro-porn." *Corruptions of Empire: Life Studies & the Reagan Era*, 119–127. London: Verso.

Condit, Celeste. 1989. "The Rhetorical Limits of Polysemy." *Critical Studies in Mass Communication* 6:103–122.

Counihan, Carole M. 1998. "What Does It Mean to be Fat, Thin, and Female in the United States: A Review Essay." *Food and Gender: Identity and Power.* Eds. Carole M. Counihan and Steven L. Kaplan, 145–162. Amsterdam: Harwood Academic.

Das, Rupali, Andrea Steege, Sherry Baron, John Beckman, Ximena Vergara, Patrice Sutton, and Robert Harrison. 2002. "Pesticide Illness Among Farmworkers in the United States and California." www.dhs.ca.gov/ohb/AgInjury/soeh0702.pdf

"DPR releases 2003 pesticide use data; Director emphasizes reduced-risk strategy." 2005. California Department of Pesticide Regulation. http://www.cdpr.ca.gov/docs/pressrls/2005/050126.htm

Dukcevich, Davide. 2002. "Wendy's Salad Days." *Forbes*, April 9. http://www.forbes.com/2002/04/09/0409wendys.html

Emden, H., and D. B. Peaball. 1996. *Beyond Silent Spring: Integrated Pest Management and Chemical Safety.* London: Chapman & Hall.

Faustmann, E. M., and G. S. Omenn. 2001. "Risk Assessment." In *Cassarett and Doull's Toxicology: The Basic Science of Poisons.* Ed. C. D. Klaassen, 83–104. New York: McGraw-Hill.

Fernandez-Armesto, Felipe. 2002. *Near a Thousand Tables: A History of Food.* New York: Free Press.

"5-A-Day for Better Health Program Evaluation Report: Message Environment." n.d. Washington D. C.: National Cancer Institute. http://www.cancercontrol.cancer.gov/5ad_5_mess.html

Foucault, Michel. 1977. *Language, Counter-memory, Practice: Selected Essays and Interviews.* Oxford: Blackwell.

Gallo, Anthony E. 1999. "Food Advertising in the United States." In *America's Eating Habits: Changes and Consequences.* Ed. Elizabeth Frazao. Washington, DC: U.S. Department of Agriculture, www.ers.usda.gov/publications/aib750/aib750i.pdf

Groesz, Lisa M., Michael P. Levine, and Sarah K. Murnen. 2002. "The Effect of Experimental Presentation of Thin Media Images on Body Satisfaction: A Meta-analytic Review." *International Journal of Eating Disorders* 31:1–16.

Guthrie, Joanne F. 2004. "Understanding Fruit and Vegetable Choices: Economic and Behavorial Influences." Bulletin Number 792–1. Washington, DC: USDA. www.ers.usda.gov/publications/aib792/aib792-1/aib792-1.pdf

Kegley, Susan E. 2001. "Pesticide drift: Views from beyond the fenceline." www.cdpr.ca.gov/docs/drftinit/confs/2001/kegley.pdf

Kegley, Susan E., and Laura J. Wise. 1998. *Pesticides in Fruits and Vegetables.* Sausalito, CA: University Science Books.

Kilbourne, Jean. 1999. "Please, Please, You're Driving Me Wild: Falling in Love with Food." *Can't Buy My Love: How Advertising Changes the Way We Think and Feel.* 108–127. New York: Simon & Schuster.

Kingsolver, Barbara. 2002. "Lily's Chickens." *Small Wonder: Essays.* 109–130. New York: Harper Collins.

Lears, T. J. Jackson. 1983. "From Salvation to Self-realization: Advertising and the Therapeutic Roots of the Consumer Culture, 1880–1930. In *The Culture of Consumption: Critical Essays in American History, 1880–1980.* Eds. Richard Wightman Fox and T. J. Jackson Lears, 1–38. New York: Pantheon.

Levenstein, Harvey. 1988. *Revolution at the Table: The Transformation of the American Diet.* New York: Oxford University Press.

Neilsen, Linda. n.d. "Black Undergraduate and White Undergraduate Eating Disorders and Related Attitudes." www.healthyplace.com/Communities/Eating_Disorders/minorities_blacks.asp

Nestle, Marion. 2002. *Food Politics: How the Food Industry Influences Nutrition and Health*. Berkeley, CA: University of California Press.

"Pesticide Certification Training: Pesticide User's Reference." 2002. Washington DC: USDA.

"Pesticide Data Program / Annual Summary Calendar Year 2002." 2002. Washington, DC: USDA.

Pieterse, Jan Nederveen. 1992. *White on Black: Images of Africa and Blacks in Western Popular Culture*. New Haven, CT: Yale University Press.

Pollan, Michael. 2004. "Our National Eating Disorder." *New York Times*, October, late ed., sec. 6: 74.

"Profile: Cooperative Extension Monterey County." 2004. University of California, Davis. Division of Agriculture and Natural Resources. http://cemonterey.ucdavis.edu/aboutcounty.htm

Reeves, Margaret, Kristin Schafer, Kate Hallward, and Anne Katten. 1999. *Fields of Poison: California Farmworkers and Pesticides*. San Francisco: Pesticide Action Network.

Sanchez, Mary. 2003. "Project Addresses Pesticide Risks among Kansas Migrant Workers." *The Kansas City Star*, January 23. http://www.kansascity.com/mld/kansascity/news/local/5008439.htm

Smart, Barry. 1994. "Digesting the Modern Diet: Gastro-Porn, Fast Food and Panic Eating." In *The Flaneur*. Ed. Keith Tester, 158–180. London: Routledge and Kegan Paul.

Sodolo, Edith. 2005. "Eating Disorders Cross Color Lines." *The Hilltop*, 13 April. http://www.thehilltoponline.com/media/paper590/news/2005/04/13

Stenersen, Jorgen. 2004. *Chemical Pesticides: Mode of Action and Toxicology*. Boca Raton, FL: CRC Press.

Stewart, Hayden, J. Michael Harris, and Joanne Guthrie. 2004. "What Determines the Variety of a Household's Vegetable Purchases?" Bulletin Number 792–3. Washington, DC: USDA. www.ers.usda.gov/publications/aib792/aib792-3/aib792-3.pdf

Thompson, Becky W. 1994. "Childhood Lessons: Culture, Race, Class, and Sexuality." *A Hunger So Wide and So Deep: American Women Speak Out on Eating Problems*, 27–45. Minneapolis: University of Minnesota Press.

Tomerlin, J. R. 2000. "New Methodologies for Assessment of Risk from Pesticide Residues." In *Human Exposure to Pesticide Residues, Natural Toxins and GMOs: Real and Perceived Risks*. Eds. N. Atreya and R. Billington, Farnham, Surrey, UK: British Crop Protection Council.

Weingarten, Gene. 2004. "Crime and Nourishment." *Washington Post*, August 15.

Williams, Raymond. 1980. "Advertising: The Magic System." *Problems in Materialism and Culture, Selected Essays*, 170–195. London: Verso.

Williamson, Judith. 1978. *Decoding Advertisements: Ideology and Meaning in Advertising*. London: Marion Boyars.

———. 1986. "Woman Is an Island: Femininity and Colonization." In *Studies in Entertainment: Critical Approaches to Mass Culture*. Ed. Tania Modleski, 99–118. Bloomington, IN: Indiana University Press.

CHAPTER 8

Consuming the Other

Packaged Representations of Foreignness in *President's Choice*

Charlene Elliott

"Food is better than power"
—*Upanishads*, 8th century BC

". . . texts can create not only knowledge but also the very reality they appear to describe."
—Edward Said 1979, *Orientalism*

In *Orientalism,* Edward Said explores the representation of the "Other" in various "texts" from the nineteenth century to the postmodern era. The Orient, he argues, is a European "invention" imagined as "a place of romance, exotic beings, haunting memories and landscapes, remarkable experiences" (1979, 1). His oft-cited definition presents Orientalism as the "corporate institution for dealing with the Orient—dealing with it by making statements about it, authorizing views of it, describing it . . . ruling over it: in short, Orientalism [is] a Western *style* for dominating, restructuring, and having authority over the Orient" (1979, 1; emphasis added).

As a style, Orientalism presents an "internal consistency" (1979, 5)—its myths consistently and persistently circulate in myriad forms (literature, poetry, art, political maneuvers) that function in a self-reinforcing manner. This style, like fashion or a form of dress, is based on surface and representation, which makes Orientalism a text of exteriority—dealing not with what lies hidden but with the wrappings, the symbolic "package."

This "package" is continually being made and remade (1979, 333) or, for the purposes of this study, labeled and relabeled. Orientalism's exteriority is tightly bound up with notions of identity of Self and of Other, allowing the West to define who it *is* by the identification of who *it is not*.[1]

Obviously, much has changed since Said's publication in 1979—globalization, developments in communications technology, reconfigured terrains of power—and in this regard it seems ridiculously outdated to discuss Said's "brand" of Orientalism at all. However, Orientalist discourse still percolates throughout society (see Karim 1997, 2000; Semati 1997; Ahmed 1992; Morley and Robins 1995), and the point here is to draw attention to its presence in more subtle texts of unexpected form.[2] For instance, the ubiquitous gourmet coffee retailer Starbucks creates an upscale and cosmopolitan image by liberally grinding Orientalism into its beans, coffee and marketing literature (Elliott 2001, 2006). Stereotypical representations of the Other can also be found in tourist promotion (Little 1991), mail-order catalogues (Hendrickson 1996), and food discourse (Bell and Valentine 1997; Beardsworth and Keil 1997; James 1996). Yet the most packaged and consumed text of all—*food packaging*—has been consistently overlooked; and it is startling to observe that the simplified representations of culture, which today would be absurd (and subject to much protest) in any other context, are strangely present and seemingly acceptable in the world of food package design. This analysis will explore how a Canadian food brand best known (and loved) for its "Decadent" Chocolate Chip cookies also sells a particular taste of the foreign.

Food packaging provides a rich text for analysis, for its surface and its contents are consumed: food "messages" are digested both figuratively and literally.[3] Anthropologists have long established food's role in creating identity and status, establishing taste and defining cultural otherness. And while the history of colonization is peppered with the (re)presentation and conquest of food, spices, and sugar (Sokolov 1991; Mintz 1985), this discourse still permeates contemporary food culture. Today, food (re)presentation has moved to the supermarket shelves, which proudly display the "world's cuisine" to be purchased, owned, and devoured by the consumer and culinary tourist. Packaged edibles comprise the ultimate expression of the *contained* Other—they are exotic, but temperately spiced and "cooked" to suit a Western palate. In this light, the dictum "food is better than power" in the age-old *Upanishads* is mistaken: food *is* power, and control over food representations has powerful implications for perceptions of one's own and other cultures.

In a world of controlled food representations, it proves revealing to scrutinize what, precisely, is being displayed for consumption on supermarket shelves. This paper attempts such a scrutiny. It explores representations of the "exotic" in contemporary food packaging to unveil its messages about cultural hierarchies and perceptions of taste, as well as its images of race, culture, and class.[4] In this study, the "Other" comprises all "foreign" cultures (not just Arabs/Islam), and food products are selected according to both their content (i.e., couscous, Indian curry, basmati rice), and the images on their labels.

Within Canada, the world's cuisine can be readily sampled by "touring" the *President's Choice (PC)* products within Loblaw-owned supermarkets. *President's Choice,* Loblaw's upscale house brand or premium private label, currently offers more than 3,500 products, ranging from gourmet "staple" foods and prepared meals to organics. Healthier options and low-fat fare can be found under the *PC Blue Menu* banner launched in 2005, only months after the brand introduced its *PC Mini Chefs* line, which sells "fun and nutritious" foodstuffs specifically targeted to five- to ten-year-olds. *President's Choice* also offers a vast array of "exotic" products within its line of frozen prepared foods, sauces, marinades, cereals, and beverages. All of these products are worth studying for their representations alone, but *PC's* remarkable ubiquity and popularity give its packaged messages added significance. As the flagship brand of Canada's largest food distributor—Loblaw operates over one thousand corporate and franchised stores from coast to coast—*President's Choice* receives proud display in every province. Consumers can also find select *President's Choice* fare around the world: in the United States, Bermuda, Hong Kong, Israel, Cayman Islands, Jamaica, Barbados, Colombia, Belize, St. Kitts, St. Lucia, St. Vincent, St. Maarten, Antigua, and Grenada. The popularity of these products cannot be overstated: in 2004, sales of Loblaw's "control label" products amounted to $5.6 billion (Loblaw 2004).[5] *President's Choice,* therefore, is not only widely distributed, but widely consumed—making it an excellent case for analysis.

Packaging Power and Shelved Representations

While advertising and branding give goods a powerful voice, packaging is the discourse most firmly wrapped around consumer products. Packages are standing advertisements on the store shelves: these "two-second

commercials" (Cato 1985, 29) or dwarfed posters (Pilditch 1973, 18) act
as miniature, portable billboards, which support larger advertising messages and may even serve as the consumer's primary source of information
about the product. Packages prove significant, for they continue to advertise and represent long after the sale—a cereal box communicates equally
well on the kitchen table as on the supermarket shelf. "Shelved" representations therefore continually negotiate within consumers' quotidian lives.
And as mass media messages proliferate—more television channels, more
magazines, more newspapers, more advertising—packaging, ironically,
becomes more important. Mass media crowding only weakens advertisers'
messages, since people switch channels or "tune out" (Aster 1998, 14).
Instead, consumers increasingly decide upon their supermarket purchases
at point-of-sale: current estimates point to the fact that shoppers make up
to 90 percent of buying decisions in the store (*Point of purchase* 2005; *In-
store consumer* 2005)—up from 60 percent in the 1980s and 33 percent in
the 1940s (Kingston 1994, 135). Considering that Loblaw's average corporate store size is 53,600 square feet and houses 100,000 items, these in-
store buying selections give added meaning to, for instance, the *choice to
buy President's Choice*. Shoppers' purchases can provide one indication of
whether a foodstuff and its accompanying symbolic representation has
"spoken" meaningfully and persuasively.[6]

Even though packages comprise a largely overlooked advertising
medium, they have been recognized as important "indicators" of a society—equally indicative as painting, sculpture, architecture or clothing
(Heller and Chwast 1988, 9). "A poet two millennia years hence would
certainly learn more about our world by looking at cans from a supermarket than canvases from a museum," affirms one cultural historian (Hine
1995, 248). Supermarket "canvases" such as food labels or boxes, then, are
important cultural symbols (Sacharow 1982; Hine 1995) that reflect prevailing attitudes. Issues of taste and race (as will be illustrated) figure
prominently in this symbolic structure.

The Rise of the Packaged Other

Said's characterization of Orientalism as a "system of representations"
(1979, 202–203) with internal consistency and durable "canons of taste
and value" (1979, 12) also informs the history of ethnic foods and ethnicity in food marketing. Stereotyped images of the Other, originating with

Aunt Jemima and Uncle Ben, have long been used by national brands. Remarkably, the foodstuffs themselves were "white": (white) pancake mix, (white) rice. Aunt Jemima and Uncle Ben, the pioneers of pancake mix and packaged rice, respectively, did not present frighteningly foreign or heavily spiced fare. Instead, common foodstuffs were promoted by black brand personalities—hinting at the residual racism of black servants preparing meals.

Regarding ethnic foods and taste, however, the supermarket proved "conspicuously late in responding to the impact of ethnic diversity on North American taste" (Kingston 1994, 146). While mainstream restaurants and cookbooks offered a watered down version of "foreign" food (i.e., Chinese) even in the 1920s (Barbas 2003), historian Harvey Levenstein (1993) observes that a real interest in culinary variety only emerged in the decades after the second World War. This was not due to the foreign travel by our armed forces (as is generally assumed),[7] but rather, due to a host of other postwar factors: the growing influence of the mass media, especially television, which introduced and advertised new products; the popularity of Julia Child, who (with her massively successful cookbook and television show in the 1960s) brought French cuisine into the American kitchen; and reduced airfares, which allowed a form of gastronomic tourism to develop as middle-upper-class North Americans traveled throughout Europe and tasted new cuisines (Levenstein 1993, 2004). Remarkably, however, the supermarket did not reflect the rising intrigue in exotic "tastes" for decades (Kingston 1994, 146). Not until the 1980s did "foreign" food in the supermarket emigrate from its ghettoized "ethnic" shelf filled with chow mein noodles and soy sauce to figuratively color the store with the signifiers of world cuisine. And *President's Choice*, launched in 1984,[8] was the first Canadian brand to market this wide array of unfamiliar foods to aspiring cosmopolites *de goût*. Basmati rice, naan bread, balsamic vinegar, extra virgin olive oil, spicy Thai marinades, salsa—all of these foods were refashioned, homogenized and repackaged to appeal to the Canadian palate.

Packaging the World's Cuisines: *Places and Names*

President's Choice packages the global palate with a distinct taste "image." The brand's exotic and geographical names work to convey a sense of the world's cuisine. In the brand's 23-year history, "exotic" products have included *PC* Chevalier triple crème, Splendido bundnerfleisch, Biryani rice, and Tikka Masala, to name but a few. Other "foreign" sounding food-stuffs have been introduced in the past decade, including *PC* Tyrokaverti, *PC* Pad Thai, *PC* Pad gai goong, *PC* Baba Ghanouj, *PC* Gee chow ching chai and *PC* Nasi goreng. Geographically, *PC* maps the world with its *Memories of . . .* labeled goods, which read more like a bottled tour than a line of food sauces. Currently, there are *President's Choice Memories of . . .* : Kobe tamari garlic sauce; Kashmir spicy tandoori sauce; Hong Kong spicy black bean and garlic sauce; and Shanghai honey hoisin sauce. There are *Memories of . . .* : Agra tikka sauce for chicken; Canton hot plum sauce; Bangkok soya and sesame sauce; and Lyon 4-peppercorn sauce. This saucy cartography also includes *Memories of . . .* Thailand, Greece, Santa Fe, Montego Bay, Gilroy, Loire, and Patagonia. Despite these (mostly) exotic locales and names, *PC*'s labels reveal that the *Memories* are a "PRODUCT OF CANADA." In fact, many of the "memories" are made, not in Bangkok, Kashmir, or Santa Fe, but in Canada by the trusted E.D. Smith Company—the same label that brings consumers strawberry jam, cherry pie filling and pancake syrup. What's more, it is the *President's Choice Memories of . . .* line of sauces. The words *President's Choice,* identifying a known Canadian brand, "stand" before every exotic place being sold: it is the *President's Choice* (i.e., Canadian) memory of Agra, the *President's Choice* memory of Thailand and the *President's Choice* memory of Shanghai.

Fascinating threads weave through this food text. First, *PC* mirrors Said's observation of nineteenth-century Orientalists—who were "white races indulging their taste for voyaging" (1979, 219). Here, however, the *taste* of voyaging assumes a literal and layered complexion. As in *Orientalism*, geography proves crucial: Said notes that "geography was essentially the material underpinning for knowledge about the Orient . . . the geographical Orient solicited the West's attention" (1979, 216). Knowledge of geography, simply, was a sign of cosmopolitanism (1979, 216), or what Pierre Bourdieu would classify as a mark of distinction (Bourdieu 1984). For *President's Choice*, this geographical referencing is equally central—and superficial. Just as Said's Europeans embraced an "imaginative geography" (1979, 50) based on (oft shallow) perceptions of the Orient made by Orientalists, so, too, are *PC*'s *Memories* situated in geography and "created" according to what the brand claims the taste *should* be. *PC*'s labels have consistently catered to the unsophisticated shopper, with maps, definitions, pronunciation guides and explanations—in short, with all the information budding cosmopolites require to exchange potentially vulgar tastes for ones with higher cultural capital. When *PC's Memories of Fuji* shiitake mushroom sauce first debuted on the shelves, for instance, the bottles not only depicted Mt. Fuji on a caricatured map, but also further explained the history and dimensions of Japan's sleeping volcano—"a perfectly cone-shaped crater [that] has awakened 18 times in the past."9 *Memories of Kobe*, too, located the sauce name on a map, informing shoppers that Kobe is pronounced *Ko-bay* or *Ko-bee* and is "renowned for [its] Famous Japanese black beef." Similar edifying kernels pop throughout the *PC* line. When Tiramisu was first introduced into the *PC* lineup, the package explained the products as a "traditional Italian dessert" pronounced *tier-a-MEE-sue;* similarly, when *PC's* Ancient Grains cereal debuted, the box explained that that Quinoa, a staple of the Inca Empire, is pronounced *Keen-wa* and that Kamut is a "rich, buttery tasting" grain originating in the near East and commonly known as "King Tut's Wheat."

Problematic about this gustatory guidance is the very exteriority of it all, wherein *PC* carves up and serves the world (as if on a platter) to the West. With regards to *Memories of . . .* in particular, geography and ethnic culture has been reduced down to a sauce—a topping for Western tastes. And while Arjun Appadurai has defined food as a "highly condensed social fact" (1981, 494), the bottling of a place for mass consumption is likely not what he had in mind. Appadurai's sense of food, its social "fact-ness," has to do with food's capacity to reinforce self and community identity, to symbolically indicate one's place in the world. The identity reinforced by *Memories of . . .* however, is not Indian or Japanese or Chinese or Indonesian. As evidenced by the basic, descriptive and explanatory labels, Memories of Fuji, for example, is hardly intended as communal fare to solidify Japanese social bonds. Rather, the sauce "sells" the consumption of the Other: it offers a subtle display of power in which shoppers select and consume food to reveal their *mastery* over it, in the spirit of the cosmopolitan, instead of their self-identification with it.10

Examining *Memories of . . .* as a literal and figurative "sauce" proves both fascinating and revealing. *PC* labels instruct consumers to use the products as simple addendums to their regular "western" meals: use Memories of Thailand as an "authentic sweet and spicy" dipping sauce for chicken fingers, nuggets or wings or add the "enticing, hot and sweet" Memories of Canton to spice up regular meatloaf, plain chicken, or rice. Here, the Other is not embraced as a cuisine, only tasted.11 One dips into it or adds a teaspoon to enliven commonplace fare. Here, the gustative qualities highlighted—"sweet," "spicy," "hot," "enticing"—have racial and sexual connotations, connected to the sauce's "geography." bell hooks observes that "within commodity culture, ethnicity becomes spice, seasoning that can liven up the dull dish that is mainstream white culture" (hooks 1992, 21). She forgot to mention sauce, but her critique highlights the irony of a metaphor made concrete. hook's reference to cultural blandness also configures in culinary blandness—and then reflects back "the dull dish that is mainstream white culture."

Packaging the World's Cuisines: *Representing the Sauce*

"Packaging" the Other extends far beyond the geographical naming and explanatory descriptors found on *Memories of . . .* bottles. Indeed, the racial connotations noted above have emerged most clearly in the labels' images, the miniature billboards that are visually consumed long before any physical ingestion takes place. These images are powerful, for shoppers need not buy *PC* to consume the "digested" and glamorized representations of ethnicity decorating each frozen dinner or bottled sauce. Collectively, *PC's* "exotic" labels offer a romanticized, stereotyped rendition of culture being sold. There is: the ceremonially painted white, red, and black face of a Japanese Kabuki actor on the *Memories of Kobe* marinade; the camel and rider silhouetted in the desert on the *Memories of Kashmir*; the stately Taj Mahal adorning Memories of Agra; the watchful boatman on *Memories of Shanghai. Memories of Jaipur,* although no longer distributed, displayed turban-clad Indians and British polo players on the label. Graphically, *PC* presents a modern, commodified expression of nineteenth-century Orientalism, which Said characterizes as "a field with considerable geographical ambition" (1979, 50) and, conversely, "a limited vocabulary and imagery" (1979, 60). In short, Orientalism seeks to expand the world while simultaneously reducing its cultures down to a series of stock props. And this limited imagery is present in *PC's Memories of . . .* sauces. Agra *is* the Taj Mahal; Kashmir *is* camels and desert; Santa Fe *is* southwestern desert and skulls, and Kobe is both striking and masked. These props or cultural signifiers present stereotypical perceptions of the Other to the Western gaze. *PC's* worldly sauces are a garnish to what "we" already believe the Other to be.[12]

One particular example illustrates how limited imagery and stock props can be bandied about by something (seemingly) as innocuous as a food brand. Consider *Memories of Marrakech* Couscous, *PC's* "instant

5-minute precooked durum wheat semolina." A Muslim woman gazes out from the label, her dark, almond-shaped eyes framed by the azure veil covering her face. Here, the stereotypical other, Said's "mysterious Orient" thrives, veiled and secretive, on the stage that is the supermarket shelf. She is culturally distant but sensuous, silent, and waiting to be consumed. Moreover, the image literally displays the particularizing and fragmenting qualities that typify representations of the Other (Said 1979, 72). The Other is "divided up" into manageable parts for easy understanding (1979, 72); or, in the language of food, it is cut into bite-sized pieces. *Memories of Marrakech* does this visually: the part (the veiled woman) represents the idea of a distant, exotic culture—and, incidentally, its cuisine. And the ease of relocating this North African dish is reinforced by the *PC's* label, which identifies it as "popular in Morocco, Algeria and Tunisia—and now Canada!" On one level, this move supports what Ian Cook and Philip Crang refer to as the "local globalization of culinary culture." They explain that "the touristic quality of these constructions [is] particularly apparent when [it] allows consumers to bring the experience of travel to their own domestic culinary regimes" (1996, 136)—and the fact Loblaw's encourages consumers to serve *PC's* couscous "as you would rice or pasta" or "as an alternative to stuffing" only underscores these touristic qualities. *PC* couscous is just a little taste of "difference" that merely displaces spaghetti on the standard dinner plate. But something more noteworthy pertains to this ease of relocation within *PC*, which is the fact that the identical image has been used simultaneously to promote an entirely different (now discontinued) product—*Memories of Ancient Damascus* tangy pomegranate sauce. Southern Morocco, it seems, can be represented exactly as one would Syria; the idea of Northwest Africa is cloned with West Asia. Here we have the same veiled woman representing two different products and geographical locations, and four named countries. This is image colonialism at its finest, a Xeroxed rendition of the "authentic." These cloned images, (apparently) connotative of various ethnic foodstuffs, make farcical Arjun Appadurai's understanding of food as a "marvelously plastic kind of collective representation" (1981, 494). Appadurai's sense of the plastic comes from food's flexibility, its use in various arenas and its ability to evoke various emotions. But in the hands of *PC*, food is "plastic" in an entirely different sense. "Plastic" means applicable to any product referencing the Other.

A final comment must be made about the *Memories of . . .* namebrand encompassing the series of geographical tastes and ethnic flavors. Shoppers

familiar with the brand's history will recall that *Memories of . . .* is the
brainchild of David Nichol, the former "President" of *President's Choice*,[13]
and that the *Memories* are purportedly his personal memories "bottled" and
sold. A self-proclaimed arbiter of taste, Nichol claimed to search the world
for exceptional epicurean delights. When he happened upon a taste
"epiphany," explains *PC's* early marketing literature, Nichol would challenge a food manufacturer to recreate his "memory." *Memories of . . .* then,
was initially presented as the memory of the product developer, the
memory of the president—hence the "choice" in *President's Choice.* Briefly
digressing from "reading" *PC's* packages illustrates this point. Take *PC
Memories of San Francisco*, for instance, which re-creates the tastes of San
Francisco's Imperial Palace Chinese Restaurant. Nichol explains in his
June 1992 *Insider's Report*:

> To commemorate all the famous Oriental dishes I've feasted on
> there, I gave E.D. Smith the challenge of re-creating a special
> lemon ginger sauce that still haunts my memory. Naturally, I call
> it President's Choice Memories of San Francisco Golden Gate
> Lemon Ginger Sauce because it brings to mind all those wonder-
> ful meals.[14]

Within this *Memory,* many factors converge. Nichol begins by establishing
the sauce as a purely representational "versioning" of Chinese cuisine. *President's Choice Memories of San Francisco Golden Gate Lemon Ginger Sauce by E.
D. Smith:* it is a Canadian company manufacturing an Oriental flavor principle based on Nichol's "memory" of a U.S. restaurant rendition of an
"original" Chinese sauce. The single sauce presents one flavor principle
(Chinese), interacts with three countries (Canada, United States, China),
and has been reinterpreted three times (by Imperial Palace, by Nichol and
by E. D. Smith). By the time it reaches the table as a topping for aspara-
gus, the sauce is pure simulacrum. It is four steps removed from the real
thing, a succession of devourments bottled for further devouring. Significant issues are at stake in this bottled simulated sauce, for while the rhetoric of Nichol/President's Choice has created a circuit between the
Imperial Palace sauce (which represents 'authentic' Chinese fare) and the
imaginary (Nichol's memory of his meal), the simulation (found in the
mass-produced bottled sauce) actually produces a widespread sense of
what authentic Chinese sauce should taste like. This substantiates Gilles
Deleuze and Félix Guattari's argument that simulation "carries the real

beyond its principle to the point where it is effectively produced" (1977, 87). *PC's Memories of* . . . sauce does not merely substitute signs of the real for the real; it produces or replaces the real for consumers.

Yet even if shoppers are unfamiliar with the precise "history" of the *Memory,* the very fact that *Memories of* . . . blazons from each label is supportive of the brand's discursive construction of the Other. Obviously the sauces have been packaged by whites for whites—so the *Memories of...* title signifies a particular Caucasian "remembrance" of something foreign. This closely parallels the Orientalist's tendency to understand the Orient *as* a memory, and in terms of the past, instead of as a modern entity (Said 1979, 73–110). *PC's Memories,* too, are bolstered by stock images and clichéd iconography drawn from the past. The labels speak nothing of the industrialized metropolis that is modern Kobe or cosmopolitan city of contemporary Shanghai.

Versioning Cuisine: Collapsing the Irreducible Distance

Representations of the Other through food and its packaging have great symbolic potency, and this "labeling" of foreignness proves significant precisely because it seems so innocuous. But the seemingly harmless marketing of foodstuffs is really a form of power—power operating over both representation and taste. *Memories of* . . . Thailand or Shanghai or Singapore exemplify this control, right down to the fact that the flavor associated with a particular ethnic cuisine is ultimately determined by a company located in Ontario, Canada.

And as the products become more "Other," moving up the cultural scale of foreignness, Loblaw's control becomes more evident. Consider the brand's indisputably foreign sounding products, which have included Pad gai goong, Gee chow ching chai, Nasi goreng, and Pad Thai, and in which *PC's* "cookery" is particularly noticeable. These *names* might intimidate the average Canadian shopper, but their packages reassure: they purge the threat while preserving the exotic. Credit this to Loblaw's expert control over package descriptors and image, over its discourse. Boxes of these "foreign" foods boldly display the *PC* wordmark to assure shoppers that a trusted name stands behind the product. Beneath *PC's* wordmark sits the food title (i.e., Nasi goreng or Pad Thai) and directly beneath that, in prominent capital letters, is PRODUCT OF THE USA or PRODUCT OF CANADA. Shoppers need not fret that their chicken Nasi goreng emerged from the bowels of some dubious Indonesian factory, for it was made in the (respectable) USA! Similarly, *PC Peking Duck* is a PRODUCT OF USA, while *PC Cantonese Vegetable Rice Bowl* or *Chinese Black Bean Beef* are a PRODUCT OF CANADA. The exotic, in fact, becomes a taste and a name, but is processed at home.

Another remarkable aspect of this packaging pertains to Said's claim that the West transforms the Other into a "style" (for categorization, manipulation and control). In the world of *President's Choice*, Said's "style" assumes caloric significance, as signifying dishes of a particular culture's cuisine transform into renditions or culinary fashionings of the Other. Each box plainly describes its product—but *PC* Pad Thai is not a Thai dish; rather, it is defined as a Thai *style* dish, just as *PC* Gee chow ching chai, when introduced, offered a Chinese-*style* chicken and vegetable meal. *PC's* flatbread is not Greek, but Greek-*style*. Moreover, many packages specify their contents as interpreted by Loblaw: it is *PC's* version of a dish, and therefore ingredients can be invented or substituted in and out at will. Packages of *PC* Pad Thai, bearing the MADE IN CANADA stamp, are defined as "our version of the traditional Thai dish . . . prepared with rice noodles, tofu, scrambled eggs, [and] a variety of vegetables in a mildly spicy sauce." This is, perhaps, a step up from the original packaging which explained the dish as "our version of the traditional Thai noodle and veg-etable dish, made with our *PC Memories of* Szechwan Peanut Sauce and our Memories of Bangkok Spicy Thai Sauce." But in both cases the *name* is Indonesian, while the dish is pointedly interpreted by *PC*, from the claim that its "our version" right down to the initial inclusion of *PC* created sauces. In another example, *PC* Moussaka boldly declares beneath the name: "Our own version of the popular Greek dish is prepared with sliced potatoes, seasoned ground beef, and a creamy topping of whipped potatoes with béchamel sauce." Ownership of the brand means that this signifier of Greece can be whimsically recreated: with French sauce, sliced potatoes instead of eggplant, beef in lieu of lamb. But is it really Moussaka? And is this even significant? One might equally query whether the Orientalist's *Orient* is really the Orient. And control over the Orient, as Said has exten-sively detailed, is highly significant.

Fusing East and West in these "exotic" products raises certain concep-tual issues. While Said argues that traditional Orientalist discourse con-veys a sense of "the irreducible distance separating white from colored" (1979, 222), this is problematized in the modern marketing of food. David Harvey remarks that globalism can be a powerful unifying discourse, sensitizing people to "what the world's spaces contain"—thus Kenyan haricot beans, Californian celery, Chilean grapes, and North African potatoes happily sit side by side in the supermarket (Harvey 1992, 294). And fusion cuisine, the playful, parodic mixing of cuisines and styles (in the spirit of Wolfgang Puck) explodes this "irreducible distance." But Puck's popular restaurant fare is not found in Loblaw's packaged goods; and although *PC's* "exotic" products may advertise the presence of more than one culture on a package (i.e., Canada/PC and Other) a distance still separates white from colored. The MADE IN CANADA or MADE IN USA disclaimer serves, primarily, to distance *PC* from Indonesian Pad Thai or Peking Duck, as does *PC's* emphasized "versioning." While these exotic packages all depict the "stock props" of the culture being "versioned," the conceptual significance is clear: we can consume the Other for nourishment, but the creation of that Other for consumption is Western. Much like Napoleon consumed the image of the Orient as if truly experiencing it (Said 1979, 73–92), modern shoppers partake of Orientalist nourishment. And just as Napoleon imperialistically sought to ingest Egypt for the sustenance of his own race, so Canadians metaphorically consume Indonesia (etc.) for their own physical sustenance. This culinary control is one way of demarcating the boundaries between the Self and Other, and of administrating (and cooking) that Other.

PC's Blue Menu: The Commonplace of Health

It is important to note that the "exotic" comprises only a part of *PC's* extensive menu of foods; the brand is more famous for *The Decadent Chocolate Chip Cookie* than its *Memories of Kashmir.* Equally crucial is the recognition, as per Lis Harris in "The seductions of food" (2003), that "foods that would have been considered exotic a couple of decades ago… look as familiar in our shopping carts as boxes of Jell-O" (2003, 54). So while *PC's* balsamic vinegar, asiago cheese, and naan bread—or even its Ancient Grains Cereal—may have been exotic when first introduced in the 1980s (or even into the 1990s), they certainly are not now, and *PC* packaging reflects this. Over the years, pronunciation guides and suggestions for "how to use" have been removed from labels, as certain products become more familiar. Particularly intriguing, however, is the place of the exotic when it comes to PC's 'health' foods, specifically the recently launched *PC Blue Menu* line. Here, the foreign is deliberately muted. Acting on concerns over health and obesity (a recent Ipsos-Reid survey found that 87 percent of Canadians are trying to make healthier food choices), *PC* has introduced over eighty nutritious products in distinctive blue packaging that are lower in fat or calories, or high in fibre. The blue packaging allows customers to identify "healthy products" at a glance—and responds to some of the key barriers that Canadians have identified with respect to healthy eating. Fifty-one percent of Canadians feel that it's difficult to make healthy food choices, while over 75 percent note that taste is important, as is having confidence in the food choices that they are making. Trust, too, is key: 78 percent of those polled agreed that many "food and beverage manufacturers claim their products are healthier but I don't believe they really are" (Iposos-Reid 2005).

Canadians, in short, want healthy food to be tasty and easily identifiable; they want simplicity in their food selections and want to be able to trust the product. Given this, it is not surprising that *PC Blue Menu* items have simple labels—they contain the name of the *PC* product, a vivid picture of the food, and a blue menu. No "exotic" images adorn the *Blue Menu* products: there are no images of a harem/belly dancers as with *PC's Baba Ghanouj,* no camel riders, no Kabuki masks, no Taj Mahals. In short, there is nothing that might unsettle even the most timid of food consumers; and in this way, the *Blue Menu* packaging ensures that "foreign" fare does not undermine the confidence and trust in food choices that Canadians have identified as so important. The *Blue Menu* line is about health, and health (as *PC* demonstrates) is straightforward, targeted to all, not exotic—and certainly not foreign. This is not to suggest that the *Blue Menu* is solely comprised of more nutritious variants of "boring" meals, since *PC* aims to tingle the tastebuds of Canadians looking for nutrition *and* taste. Even ethnically inspired dishes, however, such as the *PC Blue Menu* Chicken Bangkok or Chicken Tikka Masala are visually depicted just like *PC Blue Menu* chicken strips or bran cereal—chicken on a plate with rice, cereal in a bowl. The *Blue Menu* underscores that the commonplace of health has little room for representations that might seem, to some, to be adventurous.

Conclusion: "Thinking" food

President's Choice's commodified food text offers consumable identities for sale. In this text, each identity is subject to interpretation and reinterpretation, and the seemingly innocuous label creates a discernable portrait of the world and its cultures. "Each age and society re-creates its 'Others,'" Said affirms, ". . . human reality is constantly being made and remade (1979, 332–333). Probing expressions of this reinterpretation on the supermarket shelves proves fascinating, for here the "made and remade" reality is also cooked and consumed. The predominant "taste" flavoring *PC's* product line is white, but it is peppered with the ethnic "spice" that bell hooks identified. Loblaw's brand reaffirms the conceptualization of food as a marker of "our neighborhoods and those outside them" (Bell and Valentine 1997, 15): in some cases (as with the marketing of "health food" in the *PC Blue Menu*) there is no room for outsiders; in others, representations of those "outside" predominate. Tinkering with the *Upaniṣads'* dictum, it seems appropriate to affirm that *PC food is power* because the cultural identity it presents is controlled and dictated by Loblaw. *PC* can determine what Canadians perceive as "authentically" foreign; it can reduce the Other down to a sauce, a style, and a series of stock props. The brand's exceptional popularity reveals that even our tastes are sweetened with power, and that Claude Levi-Strauss' assertion that "food is good to think" (1964) is still worth thinking about.[15]

Notes

1. As Edward Said notes, Orientalism is "a considerable dimension of modern political intellectual culture, and as such has less to do with the Orient than it does with 'our' world" (1979, 12).

2. This wording is intentional, for it is the text itself that proves subtle, not the message. Simply put, when approaching a cup of coffee or a plate of couscous, one would not *expect* a taste of Orientalist discourse, although it may exist. It is my contention that Orientalism becomes infused within the commodity itself: the discourse *about* the coffee bean or the food can work *through* the bean, spice and so forth.

3. It is interesting to note that the *exteriority* of Orientalism is literally embodied by packages and labels—they wrap, veil, and cover the surface, they present an (purportedly authentic) image, and above all, they contain.

4. Please note that this paper focuses on what is being presented or offered up for consumption. While it would be fascinating to explore the consumer response to packaged "exotic" products (i.e., analyzing audience reception studies), it proves beyond the scope of this study.

5. Loblaw Companies Limited's control label program (i.e., products sold under the Company's owned or licensed trademarks) include the following: *President's Choice, PC, President's Choice Organics, PC Mini Chefs, PC Blue Menu, no name, Club Pack, GREEN, EXACT, Teddy's Choice,* and *Life@Home.*

6. One cannot discount packaging's importance on food product sales. Certainly, one might argue that shoppers buy products because they *like* them. Fair enough. However, something must impel shoppers to purchase the product in the *first* place, and if traditional advertising is weakening in pull, then the burden falls on point-of-purchase sales. The package, increasingly, must "convince" shoppers to buy. Without appealing packaging, even very low prices do not guarantee high product sales: witness the oft-shunned house brands, which have historically suffered from a poor image due to their unappealing packages. Consumers may also believe the lower prices indicate an inferior product. (For commentary on house-brand image and "saleability" see Hine 1995.)

7. Harvey Levenstein (1993) makes the interesting point that the military eating experience during the war actually worked to level tastes, as it was characterized by "diner" fare, and did not reflect regional cooking styles. Immediately after 1945, Levenstein observes that American food tastes were remarkably "classless" (2004, 168), insomuch as exclusive restaurants would generally offer the same burger platter available elsewhere: status did not come from the type of cuisine, but from the exclusivity of the restaurant.

8. The PC brand was launched in 1984 with twelve high quality, low priced "staple" products, including: chocolate chip cookies, cola, raisin bran, strawberry jam, cherry pie filling, Dijon mustard and roasted peanuts.

9. *Memories of Fuji* is no longer part of PC's *Memories of . . .* lineup. It, along with *Memories of Hawaii, Memories of Jaipur, Memories of Singapore, Memories of San Francisco, Memories of Winnipeg,* and *Vague Memories of Montego Bay,* are now but memories of PC sauces.

10. As the editors of this volume have observed, in this capacity *PC* rightfully stands for both President's Choice and "politically correct" in the way it presents a "superficial, image-based sampler-platter approach to diversity."

11. An anonymous reviewer of this piece reasonably asked "what would be a real embrace of another cuisine?" I would argue that a cuisine is not comprised merely of a singular sauce that adds to the rest of a meal. Embracing another cuisine means dealing with the whole of it—understanding its

dominant flavor principles, ingredients, cooking methods (etc.) as per the early work of Claude Levi-Strauss (1963, 1964). This is not to say that cuisines don't evolve—they are, obviously, diachronic, not static.

12. This argument contests David Morley and Kevin Robins' claim that with the rise of industrialized powers like Japan, "the traditional equation of . . . the Orient with the exotic (but underdeveloped) past is thrown into crisis" (1995, 6). Morley and Robins are concerned with the reshaping of cultural identities in light of global media; and given this, overlook how these traditional representations hold fast in other communicative forms (such as food packaging).

13. Although David Nichol was not President of Loblaw Companies: Nichol was president of Loblaw International Merchants, the now defunct arm of the company that was responsible for developing new products and raising the supermarket's profile (and profit).

14. The *Insider's Report* is Loblaw's offbeat supermarket flyer, which first introduced *President's Choice* to the public in 1984 and is full of food trivia, cartoons, irreverent humor, and, naturally, *PC* products.

15. A few points need to be made regarding the shortcomings of this paper. I am well aware that the analysis fails to address one critical aspect of contemporary Canadian reality: the presence of the Canadian "Other." Why *can* Loblaw's get away with packaging foods only for whites when many people in Canada have very different memories of the places being evoked? Answering this question (beyond mere speculation) would require detailed market research into who *exactly* is buying President's Choice. Ethnographic research to see how these products are being negotiated within the consumers' lives/lifestyles would also be helpful—and remain the topics for another project. Second, one might legitimately question the extent to which Canada shares the colonial/postcolonial worldviews of Europe. Here, I am operating on the premise that PC's success, given its extensive use of the foreign as a marketing tool, opens the door for using Edward Said's work to probe the contemporary packaging of the Other.

Works Cited

Ahmed, Akbar. 1992. *Postmodernism and Islam: Predicament and Promise.* London: Routledge and Kegan Paul.

Appadurai, Arjun. 1981. "Gastro-politics in Hindu South Asia." *American Ethnologist* 20, No. 3:494–511.

Aster, Andrea. 1998. "A Non Formula for Success." *Marketing Magazine* 103, No. 11:13–14.

Barbas, Samantha. 2003. "I'll take Chop Suey: Restaurants as Agents of Culinary and Cultural Change." *Journal of Popular Culture* 36, No. 4:669–87.

Beardsworth, Alan and Teresa Keil, eds. 1997. *Sociology on the Menu.* London: Routledge and Kegan Paul.

Bell, David and Gill Valentine. 1997. *Consuming Geographies.* London: Routledge and Kegan Paul.

Bourdieu, Pierre. 1984. *Distinction: A Social Critique of the Judgment of Taste.* Cambridge: Harvard University Press.

Cato, J. Mac. 1985. "Give that product . . . personality." *Canadian Packaging* 35, No. 4:28–30.

Cook, Ian and Philip Crang. 1996. "The World on a Plate: Culinary Culture, Displacement and Geographical Knowledge." *Journal of Material Culture* 1, No. 2:131–53.

Deleuze, Gilles and Félix Guattari. 1977. *Anti-Oedipus. Trans.* Robert Hurley, Mark Seem and Helen R. Lane. New York: Viking.

Deveny, Kathleen. 1993. "More Shoppers Bypass Big Names and Steer Carts to Private Label." *Wall Street Journal.* September 29, B7.

Elliott, Charlene. 2001. "Consuming Caffeine: The Discourse of Starbucks and Coffee." *Consumption, Markets and Culture* 4, No. 4:369–82.

———. 2006. "Sipping Starbucks: (Re)considering Communicative Media." In *Mediascapes: New Patterns in Canadian Communication, 2nd ed.* Eds. P. Attallah and L. Shade, 62–76. Ontario: Nelson.

Harris, Lis. 2003. "The Pleasures and Politics of Food." *Wilson Quarterly,* 52:52–60.

Harvey, David. 1992. *The Condition of Postmodernity.* Cambridge: Blackwell.

Heller, Stephen and Seymour Chwast. 1988. *Graphic Style.* New York: Abrams.

Hendrickson, Carol. 1996. "Selling Guatemala: Maya Export Products in US Mail-order Catalogues." In *Cross Cultural Consumption: Global Markets, Local Realities.* Ed. David Howes, 106–121. New York: Routledge and Kegan Paul.

Hine, Thomas. 1995. *The Total Package.* Boston: Little, Brown and Company.

hooks, bell. 1992. *Black Looks: Race and Representation.* Toronto: Between the Lines.

"In-store Consumer Survey: What shoppers want." 2005. *In-Store Marketing,* April 5, 25.

Ipsos-Reid Survey Reveals Canadians "Want to Eat Better, but are Struggling to do so." 2005. *Canada NewsWire,* February 17.

James, Allison. 1996. "Cooking the Books: Global or Local Identities in Contemporary British Food Cultures?" In *Cross Cultural Consumption: Global Markets, Local Realities.* Ed. David Howes, 77–93. New York: Routledge and Kegan Paul.

Karim, Karim. 2000. *Islamic Peril: Media and Global Violence.* New York: Black Rose Books.

———. 1997. "The Historical Resilience of Primary Stereotypes: Core Images of the Muslim Other." In *The Language and Politics of Exclusion.* Ed. Stephen Riggins, 153–82. CA: Sage.

Kingston, Anne. 1994. *The Edible Man.* Toronto: Macfarlane Walter & Ross.

Levenstein, Harvey. 1993. *Paradox of Plenty: A Social History of Eating in Modern America.* New York: Oxford University Press.

———. 2004. *We'll Always Have Paris: American Tourists in France Since 1930.* Chicago: University of Chicago Press.

Levi-Strauss, Claude. 1963. *Structural Anthropology.* New York: Basic Books.

———. 1964. *The Raw and the Cooked.* London: Jonathan Cape.

Little, Kenneth. 1991. "On Safari: The Visual Politics of a Tourist Representation." In *The Varieties of Sensory Experience.* Ed. David Howes, 148–163. Toronto: University of Toronto Press.

Loblaw Companies Limited. 2004. *Annual Report.*

Mintz, Sidney. 1985. *Sweetness and Power.* New York: Viking.

Morley, David and Kevin Robins. 1995. *Spaces of Identity.* London: Routledge and Kegan Paul.

Pilditch, James. 1973. *The Silent Salesman.* London: Business Books.

"Point of purchase: Find out What's in Store." 2005. *Marketing Week,* 24 (February): 41.

Sacharow, Stanley. 1982. *The Package as Marketing Tool.* Pennsylvania: Chilton.

Said, Edward. 1979. *Orientalism.* New York: Vintage.

Semati, Mehdi. 1997. "Terrorists, Moslems, Fundamentalists and Other Bad Objects in the Midst of Us. *The Journal of International Communication* 4, No. 1:31–48.

Sokolov, Raymond. 1991. *Why We Eat What We Eat.* New York: Summit Books.

CHAPTER 9

From Romance to PMS

Images of Women and Chocolate in Twentieth-Century America

Kathleen Banks Nutter

> Women lust after chocolate. Their desire for it is overpowering; no matter how hard a woman tries to restrain herself with visions of tight black dresses or tiny bikinis, she knows in her heart she will ultimately succumb to chocolate's seductive call.
>
> Barber, Whitin and Loew, *Chocolate Sex*

So begins *Chocolate Sex: A Naughty Little Book*. But even before women's lust for chocolate was recognized, the connection between chocolate and lust itself was made. Indeed, the conceptualization of chocolate as an aphrodisiac dates to the sixteenth century. While remaining somewhat skeptical, chocolate historians Sophie and Michael D. Coe concede that, "Its *reputation* as an aphrodisiac goes back as far as the European conquest of Mexico."[1] Thus, by the start of the twentieth century as the business historian Gail Cooper has argued, chocolate candy "as a marker of the special occasion was clearly seen in its importance to courtship. Men routinely bought chocolate for the women they courted" (Cooper 1998, 73). In this way, that box of chocolate bonbons was very much a part of what the sociologist Eva Illouz sees as the intertwined processes of the "romanticization of commodities and the commodification of romance" (Illouz 1997, 26).

Today, women are free to indulge themselves in the chocolate candy of their choice. It has even been argued that women actually need chocolate "to look and feel great" (Waterhouse 1995). And not surprisingly, they long for what they need. But one should not have to worry about that form-fitting black dress or tiny bikini being a bit too tight while satiating one's longings or needs. In 2003 *Family Circle* magazine told its readers that "Chocolate tops many women's 'most-craved' food list. When you give in to your desire, you don't have to feel guilty" (Jibrin 2003, 68). In her 2004 cookbook, actress and health-and-fitness maven Suzanne Somers claims to have "found a way around the guilt. . . . The answer? Somersize Chocolate," a low-carbohydrate form of chocolate made without refined sugar, easily available through Somers' Web site (Somers, 10).

During the last century American women have achieved near-equality—legally, economically, even socially. Such can be seen in a myriad of ways in the lives of many women as well as within the products of American culture. By focusing on advertisements for chocolate candy that feature white women in them, we can see both the evolving history of white women in America over the twentieth century and the cultural representation of such change as documented within these advertisements.[2] From the demure young woman who shyly offers her beau a Romance brand chocolate bonbon in 1920 to the wild-eyed, screeching woman who adorns the PMS milk chocolate with caramel bar today—"for ANY TIME of the MONTH!," these representations of women reflect their perceived social roles and lived experiences at a particular historical moment. In a sense, then, these advertisements are marketing chocolate as they "market" women's roles and thus, in this rather intriguing and quite visual way, we can further examine those roles over the course of the last century.

What is particularly striking within these advertisements is the sense of longing expressed by the women featured in these ads. For much of the twentieth century, women's needs were ultimately to be fulfilled by others, thus maintaining a gender-based imbalance of power. Today, women can achieve self-fulfillment—sometimes simply by purchasing chocolate. An imbalance of power based on gender, as well as on class and race, remains a fact of modern life, but an examination of changes in the representation of women in chocolate ads highlights advances that have been made and at the same time indicates the inequalities that still exist.

As the historian John C. Super has claimed, "food is the ideal cultural symbol that allows the historian to uncover hidden levels of meaning in social relationships and arrive at new understandings of the human experience" (Super 2002, 165). This is especially the case when food is looked at through the lens of gender and no food product is more "woman-identified" than chocolate. Especially within the last decade, the popular press has acknowledged women's special relationship with chocolate. However, while some British feminists have examined more analytically this relationship within our own time, the representation of women and chocolate bonbons in American advertising beyond the 1910s has not yet generated much interest.

Nor within the large and ever-expanding history of American women at work has much attention been paid to women candy makers since 1928 when the National Consumers' League published *Behind the Scenes in Candy Factories,* exposing the generally horrific conditions of labor for women in the confectionery industry. As the chocolate candy industry entered mass production at the end of the nineteenth century, its workforce became increasingly feminized and until the end of the 1930s was for the most part without union representation. Although the historians Gail Cooper and Jane Dusselier have looked at the relationship of women and chocolate in terms of production as well as consumption, both their studies end around World War I. Mass-produced chocolates were and continue to be made by and for women. An examination of that symbiotic relationship throughout the twentieth century and into the twenty-first can only enrich our historical understanding of American women, both as workers and as consumers in general.

In focusing on women as consumers, food advertisements can serve as source material for such an examination, a fact recognized not least by those who create today's advertisements. According to Denise Fedewa, senior vice president and planning director for Leo Burnett Worldwide, one of the nation's top advertising agencies, advertising in general is "both a mirror of the culture and it moves the culture forward." Co-founder of her agency's subunit called "Leo-She," Fedewa claims that "the best advertising, the most successful advertising, is advertising that taps into a direction that we are moving in, but we are not there yet, and it helps take us there" (Fischer 2003, 9). Whether advertising reflects our cultural reality and/or helps create it, the historian Katherine Parkin has recently noted the conscious effort of food advertisers to present their products "as gendered and sexual" (Parkin 2004). From the 1,500-pound chocolate Venus de Milo that was a feature of the 1889 Paris Exposition to DIFFA's annual Chocolate Fashion Show fundraiser, what food is more easily gendered and eroticized than chocolate? Women, both those who appear to be longing for something more and those who seem to have achieved a sense of fulfillment, share a special and quite public affinity with chocolate throughout the twentieth century.

At the start of the twentieth century, the so-called New Woman reigned supreme in America. Whether striding confidently down a city street or riding a bicycle up a country lane, she was the Gibson Girl—single, college educated, white, and middle class. The historian Sara Evans and others situate the New Woman at the heart of a more urban and "Modern America." As she moved slowly towards a still narrowly proscribed level of self-fulfillment, the New Woman was surrounded by the tensions around changing roles for women. Such was especially the case for those who were white and middle class, evident in the fears of "race suicide" as birth rates for these women began to noticeably decline just as millions of immigrants, especially from Eastern and Southern Europe, arrived to live and work in America's growing cities. Native-born Americans' increasing nostalgia and simultaneous xenophobia is reflected in the popularity of Whitman's Chocolates trademark yellow box with its Colonial-revival cross-stitch facsimile top.

Ads for Whitman's Chocolates generally featured that box, first introduced in 1912, and up through 1920 invariably included young children, thus projecting as well a certain innocence and timelessness. In one Whitman's ad from 1917, headed "Her favorite box of candy," a young girl sits on a bench, her feet not touching the floor, as she works on a large embroidery frame, cross-stitching (of course) the "Whitman's Sampler." Dressed in ruffles and pantalets in the style of perhaps the mid-nineteenth century, "This diligent little maid," according to the ad text, "has made a most excellent copy of the cover of her favorite candy-box, Whitman's Sampler."

When women are pictured in chocolate candy ads in this same period, they are generally holding the box of candies out to the viewer/consumer, offering a piece but in a shy, appropriately demure way, thus seemingly fulfilling the needs of others rather than even acknowledging their own longings. For example, a Whitman's ad that appeared in *Cosmopolitan* circa 1900 shows a young woman in a chemise, her shoulders bare, candy box in one hand, a bonbon held up in the other. The strategically placed placard that covers her chest, almost up to her neck, reads: "A Taste of Whitman's Chocolates and Confections is the best advertisement of their goodness."

So too does the model in a 1913 ad for NYLO Chocolates hold out an open but apparently untouched box of bonbons, again at chest level.

Fig. 9.1. NYLO Chocolates, 1913

NYLO Chocolates were the in-house brand of the New York and London Drug Company and the ad text reflects health concerns of the day. In language that would have reassured even the most skeptical of National Consumers' League investigators, who early on worried about the conditions under which chocolate candies were mass produced, for the good of the worker as well as the consumer, the NYLO ad claims that this is "the very finest in 'pure food' candies: no artificial coloring materials . . . ever fresh, ever wholesome." Here, unlike the more reticent Whitman's model, the NYLO model is rather more direct in her outward gaze, smiling quite broadly at her viewer/consumer, perhaps because she is fully clothed or maybe because by 1913 the social and political changes in women's perceived status that would burst forth in the 1920s had begun to percolate up through the commercial culture of the time.

During this period known as the Progressive era, scores of white middle-class women worked in increasingly public ways for much needed social reforms, including women's suffrage. Growing numbers of working-class women became active in the trade union movement as well as in radical politics as the sheer number of women in the workforce grew dramatically, not just in industry but in the office as well, as a significant minority of usually native-born white women entered clerical jobs. But rather like the women in both the Whitman's and the NYLO ads, they are still serving the needs of others even as their public roles expanded.

What the New Woman was to the late-nineteenth/early-twentieth century, certainly the flapper was to America of the 1920s. While American losses paled in comparison to those of the European nations, a collective sigh of relief was heard at the end of World War I as many Americans sought to put the horror of what historians have come to see as the world's first modern war behind them. Advances in technology had introduced heretofore unknown instruments of death such as airplanes and chemical warfare which led to staggering casualty levels as well as brought new terms into the language such as the phrase "shell-shocked." In many ways, even for Americans who suffered far fewer war casualties, there was a heavy psychic cost paid during the Great War as it was then called. As the national economy returned to prewar production levels, America experienced a severe but brief economic recession followed by almost a decade of apparent widespread prosperity. By the 1920s, the immigrant working class had come of age and they and their American-born children were engaging in the mass consumption of goods and services, much of it bought on credit and marketed through radio ads while fan magazines informed them what that week's movie stars were wearing, smoking, and drinking. Prohibition appeared to be having little effect on the availability of alcohol, though the National Confectioners' Association later noted that candy consumption did increase during the 1920s in likely response to the passage of the Eighteenth Amendment that banned the production and distribution of alcohol (Gott 1958, 26). Nonetheless, the image of the flapper pervaded it all—she was young, carefree, independent, scantily clad, and possibly promiscuous, not to mention white and middle class, no matter that many of those attributes derived from notions of working-class femininity. By the 1920s, makeup, cigarette smoking, dancing, and an active heterosocial lifestyle were all appropriate behavior for young middle-class women in the 1920s. Like other products of the culture, ads for chocolate candy featuring women reflected the seismic shifts in what came to be called the "Roaring Twenties."

While young women can still be seen offering up that box of chocolates, in some ads she is clearly a working woman, behind the counter, assisting a young man in purchasing just the right, even "socially correct" chocolate—or so claims an ad for Johnson's Chocolates from 1924. Here, the attractive young woman dressed not so much like a store clerk but as a housemaid, complete with apron, holds up a box of bonbons for the consideration of an earnest young man, dressed in a three-piece suit. As the ad text points out, a gift of Johnson's Chocolates demonstrates "that more than perfunctory thought has been given. . . . It shows consideration—that priceless virtue!" Thus, again, fulfillment for women comes in serving the needs of men to appear socially correct through their thoughtfulness.

Reflecting the increasingly heterosocial world, chocolate candy ads in the 1920s often show a young couple, some more intimately engaged than others, but all obviously enjoying each other's company. Here a woman can be seen not so much as longing, but rather in a state of fulfillment having had those longings satisfied in her relationship with a man. In the early 1920s, a young Norman Rockwell illustrated a most charming advertisement for the aptly named Romance Chocolates then available from Cox Confectionery Company of Boston. A demure young woman, dressed in a flowing yellow evening gown, her hair bobbed, offers a young man one of the Romance Chocolates she presumably just received from the same man, dressed in a tuxedo, who sits not too closely on the sofa next to her. The illustration ably conveys the sense that this young woman's longings are about to be fulfilled by the thoughtful man who brought her these bonbons.

Fig. 9.2. Romance Chocolates, 1923. *Source.* Norman Rockwell Family Agency, Inc.

Out of the parlor and onto "Pleasure Island," a stylish young couple adorns a 1924 Whitman's ad for one of its "Quality Group" boxed candy selections. Walking on the beach, hand in hand, the couple are caught in the act of discovery; they are seen approaching a cluster of cacao trees, underneath a treasure chest and an open box of Whitman's "Pleasure Island" assortment, "a package of chocolates that speaks of the far off isles where cacao trees bend in the breeze of the Spanish Main." And how better to savor this island paradise than with a member of the opposite sex for, "A visit to PLEASURE ISLAND is best when made by a man and a maid, and together they enjoy the plunder from this wonderful chest of chocolates," further visual evidence of the primary importance of the heterosexual relationship.

Closer to home, the "Salmagundi" candy collection was also advertised by Whitman's in 1924 for "that out-of-door craving for sweets." According to the text for this ad, "The craving for chocolates after active sports is best satisfied with Whitman's, the universal chocolates, supplied at nearly all points where people gather in summertime." The accompanying illustration is, however, of a gathering of only two, one being a flapper perched on the end of a lakeside dock, managing to show a good bit of leg while satiating "that out-of-door craving for sweets," her box of chocolates open, a piece of candy in her hand, poised just below her mouth as she looks directly, and rather seriously, at the smiling young man sitting next to her. While she appears rather casually dressed, the young man is still in his suit—perhaps he just arrived for a weekend visit as a valise sits on the dock behind the couple and he had the good taste to bring his hostess a box of Whitman's Chocolates. His hostess appears to have just gone for a swim, the leg of her bathing suit evident beneath her flowing cover-up, her hair encased in a scarf, evidence of the growing social acceptance in the 1920s of women's increased participation in sports such as swimming, tennis, and biking.

The sophisticated couple on the town who adorn a 1925 advertisement illustrated by E. Henry are the embodiment of "unobtrusive good taste" that can be found inside a box of the ever "socially correct" Johnston's chocolates, the perfect gift "from the thoughtful man to the fastidious woman." Their sense of mutual fulfillment is evident in their confident stance. But what about the calories, a growing concern in America especially among young women in the 1920s, as the historian Margaret Lowe has recently pointed out, due to the fashion industry's emphasis on the slim silhouette. Even at the time, the connection between chocolate consumption and possible weight gain was craftily used by the American Tobacco Company in a series of Lucky Strike cigarette ads aimed specifically at women in the late 1920s. Fetching stars of the day, such as Billie Burke (who a decade later would become forever known as Glinda the Good

Witch in the 1939 film, *The Wizard of Oz*) told consumers to "reach for a Lucky instead of a Sweet." According to the National Confectioners' Association (NCA), "this was war," and they promptly launched a counteroffensive ad campaign in which "medical experts" confidently told chocolate candy consumers not to worry. As one full page ad sponsored by the NCA in the *Saturday Evening Post* in January 1929 assured: "You can get thin on candy!" While earlier in the century candy manufacturers sought to assure an anxious consuming public that their product was produced under sanitary conditions, by the diet-conscious 1920s the candy industry would begin its long battle against fears that eating candy would cause weight gain. A massive ad campaign and a favorable ruling from the Federal Trade Commission though soon had the NCA feeling confident as they and the rest of the nation entered the 1930s.

But the nation's confidence was soon shattered by the growing impact of the Great Depression that began with the stock market crash of 1929. By 1932 one-quarter of the American workforce was unemployed and the other three-quarters saw their wages slashed and hours cut back. As heavy industry came to a near standstill, Hunger Marches in major American cities turned violent and homeless individuals and even families became a common sight, camped out in Hooverville shanties across the country. The ravages of the Great Depression were felt worldwide and turmoil spread as Fascism rose in Europe and Asia. Yet another world war increasingly became likely. While in the United States, the federal response known as the New Deal offered some relief, many Americans continued to live on the edge. Those who still had a place to call home, a family intact, sought comfort within that family, and a revived notion of women's maternalism came to the fore as a social comfort and constraint. As unemployment rose to dizzying heights—officially 25 percent by 1933—women's participation in the workforce, especially for married women with children—was discouraged, socially and legally. Yet, women continued to work, oftentimes as the sole support of their families, especially those clustered in low-paid service sector jobs traditionally held by women workers which saw less of an impact than the better-paid industrial jobs generally held by men and that had by 1933 all but evaporated.

Despite the economic turmoil, no one could deny women their role as mothers; quite the contrary—and for *Her Day, May 10th* [1931], a box of Whitman's Chocolates, "ultra modern," yet with its now familiar cross-stitch design on top had "a touch of auld lang syne" that would "please any mother." The visual center of this ad is an illustration of an Oklahoma statue, *The Pioneer Woman*, a book (most likely a Bible) in one hand, a young son clutched in the other, striding across the Great Plains. Shortly, the ecological disaster known as the Dust Bowl would combine with the manmade economic havoc caused by the Great Depression, displacing thousands of poor farm families, both white and black. While Ma Joad may not have looked like the woman in this statue, one can imagine that she too would have loved a box of Whitman's on Mother's Day—had her family been able to afford such a treat at $1.00 a box. And like that fictional character, many women were encouraged to find self-fulfillment in their homes, as wives and mothers, not in the working world where a woman in a job translated to a man left unemployed. In response, cities, states, and even the federal government passed laws banning the employment of married women under certain conditions.

Not surprisingly, however, marriage and birth rates declined as unemployment rose during the Great Depression. Strong, seemingly independent, and, increasingly out of economic necessity, unmarried women could be seen on the silver screen and in chocolate candy ads. Paradoxically then, single women could seek personal fulfillment but only if their economic situation allowed. While the Great Depression touched the lives of middle- and even upper-class white Americans, the impact was less and, in a constrained way perhaps, there would still be anniversaries, trips, graduations, and fun-filled weekends that, as a 1934 ad reminds consumers, are "Days remembered best with Whitman's Chocolates." Each of this ad's four illustrations depicts a solitary woman within each of the four occasions best remembered by a gift of chocolate. They include a woman waving bon voyage from a ship's railing while clutching that ubiquitous yellow box. Another features a young woman in graduation cap and gown, holding her diploma in one hand and, needless to say, a box of Whitman's in the other. Even summer holidays, typically not a season for chocolates, were appropriate occasions for a box of Whitman's as the perfect hostess gift. In the background of yet another Whitman's ad, this time from 1938, we see a strong-looking woman on the diving board—evidence of the continuing importance of professional and amateur women athletes in the 1930s. In the foreground, we see the appreciative hostess, taking a bite of one of her chocolate bonbons, smiling broadly, pronouncing it "delightful!"

Within a few short years of this 1938 ad, such innocent and carefree summer weekends would be an increasing rarity, even for the middle class. When America went to war at the end of 1941, the nation and the world would never be the same. Hundreds of thousands of men and women would serve in the armed forces, women were encouraged to become Riveting Rosies (if only for the duration), and several basic commodities including sugar were rationed—a potential problem for the chocolate candy industry. But "Chocolate is a *Fighting* Food" and thus became part of U.S. Army rations through an official contract between the government and manufacturers such as Hershey's and Nestle.[3] The American GI handing out chocolate bars and cigarettes as Allied forces liberated Europe became an iconic image.[4] Back on the home front, however, the similarly iconic yellow box of Whitman's could be had on special occasions, such as Easter 1943, especially if one's officer husband was home on leave to fulfill his wife's needs as he was in an ad that touted both an "Easter Bonnet from Lilly Dache" and an "Easter Sampler from Whitman's."

Having survived the Great Depression and the Second World War, many Americans entered a sustained period of relative prosperity during the Cold War period. The American economy was booming and the national birthrate boomed as well. More Americans married and did so at an earlier age than the previous generation. According to the historian Beth L. Bailey, teenage dating as an art form reached its zenith during the 1950s and into the early 1960s—leading young women to their ultimate fulfillment, a happy marriage. One such union was enjoyed by Pat and Shirley Boone who are featured in a 1961 ad for King's Chocolates. King's Chocolates were "for American Queens," and were the "Greatest [for a man] to Give," but were "even Greater [for a woman] to Get!" However, not everyone eating chocolate bonbons in the 1950s was in the "nuclear family in the nuclear age" as Elaine Tyler May has put it. Hardly a typical suburban housewife, a fur-covered and rather sultry-looking Lana Turner urged her fans in 1953 to "Enjoy Brach's Fine Candies," especially their chocolate-covered cherries. But then again, if a woman like Lana Turner does not know how to have her longings fulfilled, who would?

While some women in the 1950s may have fantasized about looking like Lana Turner and living her life as sex goddess, most American women in that decade of containment knew that society expected them to find their ultimate fulfillment as wives and mothers. They could much more readily identify with the young woman featured in an ad from 1958 who has just received a box of Whitman's from "the nicest man in the world." With her wedding ring prominently displayed on one hand as she holds a bonbon in the other, we can assume that "nicest man in the world" is her husband who has fulfilled her longings. Regardless, it should be noted she holds that half-bitten piece of candy between her first two fingers as one might hold a cigarette—perhaps the candy industry was still competing with the tobacco industry for customer loyalty thirty years after the Lucky Strike campaign of the 1920s. But within a few years, confectioners would face an even greater challenge as a social revolution took off with the growing recognition among some women that there was more to life than a nice man, a home in the suburbs, and a growing family. When she published *Feminine Mystique* in 1963, Betty Friedan called it "the problem with no name." Widely read by white, educated middle-class housewives, such as the one who just a few years earlier was eating the chocolate given to her by the nicest man in the world, Friedan argued that the socially proscribed dictum that women's sense of fulfillment was best achieved by meeting the needs of others while ignoring her own longings explained women's oppression in general. Furthermore, advertisers were complicit in perpetuating this oppression through the words and images they used to sell a plethora of products. But in the 1960s profound social changes would usher in a new era—for women and men and their relationships with each other—and in their chocolate consumption.

Beth L. Bailey has argued that "By the late 1960s, a new incarnation of youth culture and the beginnings of a new feminism challenged some of the values embedded in the dating system and undercut some of the public controls effected by convention" (Bailey 1988, 7). So too was the consumption of chocolate candy, at least as purchased by a man for a woman, affected. Anticipating perhaps 1967's "Summer of Love," Brach's advertised a heart-shaped box of chocolates for Valentine's Day that same year, promising the presumably male purchaser, "Free kisses with every box of Brach's Valentine Chocolates you give to her." The growing rejection of sexual mores of the past, made possible in the age before AIDS, in part with the introduction of the birth control pill in 1960, was increasingly evident in 1960s America. Increasingly, one's parents' courtship practices were seen as being as old-fashioned as the Whitman cross-stitched adorned candy box itself. The social impact of the women's liberation movement at the end of the 1960s further emphasized for many the sexist tokenism represented by the man's gift of a box of chocolates bonbons to a woman he sought and the advertising industry responded to these changes in the rules of heterosexual relationships in its own quirky way. As Juliann Sivulka has noted: "During the 1960s, the social forces of feminism hit Madison Avenue" (Sivulka 2003, 59). In a sense then, chocolate bonbon advertisers were faced with a double burden. Not only would they have to redesign their ad approach to reach the "feminist," they would have to do so for a product that for many represented a prefeminist world.

By the late 1960s the chocolate candy industry was also challenged by the growing health consciousness of many Americans. As part of the mainstream adoption of some aspects of the counterculture, carob beans were touted as an alternative, healthier source of chocolate taste than cocoa beans. Increasingly, chocolate in any form was seen as something bad for you, but that was nonetheless so good it had to remain available if only as a very special treat. But now, instead of being a token of courtship given by a man to a woman, chocolate could be shared as a decadent delight or even consumed by a woman as a solitary "sensuous bedtime snack," thus fulfilling her own needs ("Private Time" 1983, 39). In the process, chocolate itself became more publicly eroticized, not surprising given the centuries-held notion of chocolate as an aphrodisiac, as noted by a cover story from a 1975 issue of *High Times*. The cover image sets the tone for the article inside and reflects the increasingly openly erotic relationship between women and chocolate. Behind the cover blurb, "Deep Dark Secrets of Chocolate," is a woman's naked breast, the erect nipple pointing upward as chocolate is poured from an unseen source above the *High Times* logo. Yet another cover blurb, above the title, reads: "Does Grass *Really* Make Your Breasts Grow?", an article that discusses the effect of marijuana on male breast growth. While this 1975 issue of *High Times* may have focused on both male and female breasts, its content matter regarding chocolate as a kind of drug was part of a growing literature on the chemical properties of this "delicious temptress."[5]

During the decadent and self-indulgent Reagan era of the 1980s, it was still possible to find that yellow box of Whitman's at the local drug store. But, high-end chocolate candy—preferably handmade and European in origin—became a commodity whose very purchase symbolized one's status. Thus, it remained appropriate for a man to give a woman chocolates, as long as they were European and expensive, and meant to be shared in an intimate moment, such as "Baci, Italy's most romantic—and delicious chocolate." A Baci ad from 1988 features a young, attractive woman, apparently naked and buried up to her chest in a pile of Baci bonbons, who "knows, in Italian, Baci means kisses. And she also knows that with kisses, it's best to be generous." Here is evidence of the ultimate in self-indulgent, even decadent consumption as she shares this erotic treat with her partner as she gives her kisses, fulfilling her own longings as she continues to fulfill those of another.

Fig. 9.3. High Times. *Source. High Times*, vol. 1, No. 6 (October/November 1975).

By the mid-1990s, American women had achieved relative power within society, especially in legal terms, reflecting the impact of the modern women's movement. No longer should women expect to find their fulfillment outside themselves. Rather, women could and should feel free to fulfill their own longings, including those for chocolate. In 1995,

Debra Waterhouse published *Why Women Need Chocolate*, arguing that if women sensibly recognized their biologically determined craving for chocolate, they'd "feel better, function more effectively, eat less, enjoy the food more—and you'll never have to diet again!" At the same time, women have repeatedly been told over the last several years, in countless articles and books, that the craving, much less the need, for chocolate appears to only intensify when in the throes of premenstrual syndrome because of shifting hormones. Thus, scientific rationale has legitimized what for so long had been dismissed as an irrational longing of overly emotional women whose very beings are shaped by their hormones. Confectioners and their advertisers quickly and quite cleverly adapted this theme of rationalized need for their own profit-driven uses.

As *Z Magazine* co-founder and current editor Lydia Sargent has recently stated, "Feminist liberation is anything that sells a product" (Sargent 2005). And what could be more liberating than consumption of a PMS chocolate candy bar? According to a PMS candy bar wrapper from 2003, on which in bright primary colors is depicted an angry–looking woman who appears to be in mid-howl, chocolate is really "for ANY TIME of the MONTH!" Part of the "True Confections" candy line, the PMS candy bar is just one of the many chocolates aimed specifically at women for self-purchase. Renee M. Corvino's "Special Report: The Feminine Side of Chocolate," for the industry's trade magazine, *Confectioner* in 2005, points out that chocolate candy manufacturers "have finally decided to cease their coolness of heart and return the affection—with special packages, shapes, and marketing messages that speak the modern female's language of love" (Corvino 2005).

Chick Chocolates and Godiva Chocolatier are excellent examples of the recognition of feminist liberation as a lifestyle that sells products, even those products formerly associated with a prefeminist way of life, or at least prefeminist liberation practices of courtship. Chick Chocolates are, according to their byline, "like you, fabulous." Like True Confections which is based in western Massachusetts, the Seattle-based Chick Chocolates is a woman-operated company and makes sure its consumers are aware of that fact. According to "Chief Chick and CEO" Jean Thompson, "For women, chocolate is more than a food choice, it's a relationship" ("About Chick"). And in this case, it is a relationship over which the woman has a fair amount of control as the consumer of a product made with her needs in mind. Certainly, the proliferation of these smaller, high-end candy makers is part of the growing trend in handmade, quality

Fig. 9.4. PMS Candy Bar Wrapper, 2003

chocolates in America at the end of the twentieth century and into the current one. But only some, such as Chick Chocolates sold in lipstick box-like packaging, unabashedly shape their product to "appeal" to women longing for self-fulfillment.

There are also, as the twenty-first century reaches into its first decade, those larger chocolate concerns that craft their ads with a more subtle, seemingly gender-neutral appeal. Russell Stover's and Whitman's both offer low-fat, low-carb versions of the perennial favorite box of chocolates in response to the diet concerns of many Americans, both male and female. But, there are also those among the giants of the confectionery industry who consciously craft the marketing of their products to appeal to the feminist within every woman. Godiva Chocolatier, long recognized as one of the premier makers of mass-produced but still high-end chocolate bon-bons, launched an ad campaign in 2004 that plays on its famous name at the same time that it capitalizes on the recent trend to recognize certain women performers as "divas" as feminist inspirations for a new generation of women.

One Godiva advertisement in the "GO DIVA" series shows a sensuous young woman, her sweater pulled off one shoulder to reveal a ruffled sheer slip underneath; she sits sidewise but gazes directly at the viewer/consumer, delectable Godiva truffle in hand midair, presumably on its way to her mouth and not someone else's. Divas know that true pleasure lies in self-fulfillment. With nary a man in sight, the ad text states that "Every woman is one part DIVA much to the dismay of every man."[6] In selling products, especially perhaps chocolate, it seems that advertisers have chosen to take the notion of self-empowerment around which women's liberation revolved and turn that concept into a marketing strategy.

In one century then, women in chocolate ads have moved from demure maid to diva status. Even as divas, women may still be longing for more, including chocolate, but now women can fulfill their needs themselves, if need be. And it is that very longing for fulfillment that is depicted in chocolate candy ads over the last century in a variety of ways, reflecting at the same time changing gender roles for white American women. From the young Romance candy girl of 1920 to the screeching woman on the PMS bar in 2003, and in between, there was many a piece of chocolate consumed by a variety of women in search of some kind of fulfillment.

Notes

NB: My examination of women and chocolate has been greatly enriched through conversations with my colleague and friend, Jane Elkind Bowers. I am also grateful for the comments of Katie LeBesco and Peter Naccarato.

1. Sophie D. Coe and Michael D. Coe, *The True History of Chocolate* (New York: Thanes & Hudson, 1996), p. 31; emphasis added.

2. It should be noted that all the advertisements and ephemera I have looked at that feature women use only white women—why such was the case certainly reflects the racially limited view of American womanhood up through the 1970s. More recent advertising perhaps reflects instead a concern that to use a woman of color (i.e., with a skin tone of a "chocolate"

hue) in a chocolate candy ad might be seen as racist today. It could also reflect buying patterns as broken down by race but I have been unable to access any supporting data regarding race and chocolate candy consumption patterns.

3. Although chocolate in soldiers' rations was initially introduced during the First World War, the relationship solidified during World War II. According to Joel Glenn Brenner, "Backed by the National Confectioners Association [NCA], Hershey successfully fought off attempts to ration much needed supplies, like sugar, corn syrup and cocoa beans, pitching chocolate as a vital source of nutrition for the nation's troops. . . . The chief supplier, of course, was Hershey," which by the end of the war, "had produced more than one billion candy bars for U.S. soldiers." See Joel Glenn Brenner, *The Emperors of Chocolate: Inside the Secret World of Hershey and Mars* (New York: Random House, 1999), p. 153. For the industry's successful effort to have candy declared an "essential food," see Gott and Van Houten, *All About Candy and Chocolate*, p. 185.

4. This, too, could be an erotically charged image. As Marcia and Frederic Morton have claimed, "Still more nakedly sexual was the World War II barter equation, the GI holding out a chocolate bar, the Fraulein nodding *ja*. . . . Mouthwatering bar in hand, the American soldier could go shopping for anything from antique silver for Mom back home to a beddable girl for himself that night." See Morton and Morton, *Chocolate: An Illustrated History*, p. 125.

5. Thanks to Tom Brinkmann for showing me this article.

6. Thanks to Sandra Krein for sending me this ad.

Advertisements Cited

Brach's Confectioners, Inc. "Enjoy Brach's Fine Candies." 1953.

Cox Confectionery Company. "Romance Chocolates: From the most critical group in America to people the country over." Illustrated by Norman Rockwell, 1923.

Godiva Chocolatier, Inc., "Every Woman is One Part DIVA." 2004.

King's Chocolates, Inc. "Greatest to Give!" 1961.

National Confectioners' Association. "You can get thin comfortably 'on candy'." 1929.

New York and London Drug Co., Inc. "NYLO Chocolates." 1913.

Perugina Chocolates. "Baci to You." 1988.

Robert A. Johnson Company.
   "A gift may tell much." Illustrated by McClelland Barclay, 1924;
   "From the Thoughtful Man to the Fastidious Woman." 1925.
Stephen F. Whitman & Son, Inc.
   "A Taste of Whitman's." c.1900.
   "Days remembered best with Whitman's Chocolates." 1934.
   "Delightful." 1938.
   "Easter Bonnet from Lilly Dachet." 1943.
   "Her favorite box of candy" 1917.
   "Mother: Her Day, May 10th." 1931.
   "That out-of-door craving for sweets." 1924.
   "The Nicest Man in the World." 1958
   "Whitman's Pleasure Island." 1924.

Works Cited

"About Chick." http://www.chickchocolates.com/aboutchick.htm [accessed 1 May 2005].

Albright, Barbara. 1997. "Trends in Chocolate." In *Chocolate: Food of the Gods.* Ed. Alex Szogyi, 137–144. Westport, CT: Greenwood Press.

Bailey, Beth L. 1988. *From Front Porch to Back Seat: Courtship in Twentieth-Century America.* Baltimore: John Hopkins University Press.

Barber, A. Richard, Nancy R. M. Whitin, and Anthony Loew. 1994. *Chocolate Sex: A Naughty Little Book.* New York: Warner Books.

Barthel, Diane. "Modernism and Marketing: The Chocolate Box Revisited." *Theory, Culture & Society* 6 (1989): 429–438.

Behind the Scenes in Candy Factories. 1928. New York: The Consumers' League of New York.

Belasco, Warren J. 1989. *Appetite for Change: How the Counterculture Took on the Food Industry, 1966–1988.* New York: Pantheon Books.

Boime, Albert. 1989. "The Chocolate Venus, 'Tainted' Pork, the Wine Blight, and the Tariff: Franco-American Stew at the Fair." In *Paris 1889: American Artists at the Universal Exposition.* Ed. Annette Blaugard. New York: Harry N. Abrams, Inc.

Brenner, Joel Glenn. 1999. *The Emperors of Chocolate: Inside the Secret World of Hershey and Mars.* New York: Random House.

"Chocolate to Sin By." *Cosmopolitan* (February 1970).

Coe, Sophie D., and Michael D. Coe. 1996. *The True History of Chocolate.* New York: Thanes & Hudson.

Cooper, Gail. 1998. "Love, War, and Chocolate: Gender and the American Candy Industry, 1880–1930." In *His and Hers: Gender, Consumption, and Technology.* Eds. Roger Horowitz and Arwen Mohun. Charlottesville: University of Virginia Press.

Cooper, Glenda. 2004. "Women and Chocolate: Simply Made for Each Other." *The Times,* March 13, 2004.

Corvino, Renee M. 2005. "Special Report: The Feminine Side of Chocolate." *Confectioner,* http://www.confectioner.com/content.php?s=CO/2004/10&p=5.

Cox, Cat. 1993. *Chocolate Unwrapped: The Politics of Pleasure.* London: The Women's Environmental Network.

Dusselier, Jane. 2001. "Bon Bons, Lemon Drops, and Oh Henry! Bars: Candy, Consumer Culture, and the Construction of Gender, 1895–1920." In *Kitchen Culture in America: Popular Representations of Food, Gender, and Race.* Ed. Sherrie A. Inness, 13–49. Philadelphia: University of Pennsylvania Press.

Evans, Sara. 1997. *Born for Liberty: A History of Women in America.* New York: Free Press.

Fischer, Eileen. 2003. "Working for Women within the Organization: Eileen Fischer Interviews Denise Fedewa of LeoShe." *Advertising and Society Review* 4, No. 4. [available online through John Hopkins University Project Muse, accessed April 4, 2005].

Frank, Thomas. 1997. *The Conquest of Cool: Business Culture, Counterculture, and the Rise of Hip Consumerism.* Chicago: University of Chicago Press.

Friedan, Betty. 1963. *The Feminine Mystique.* Reprint, 1984. New York: Dell Books.

Gott, Philip P., and L. F. Van Houten. 1958. *All About Candy and Chocolate: A Comprehensive Study of the Candy and Chocolate Industries.* Chicago: National Confectioners' Association.

Harte, Tom. 2004. "Whitman's Sampler Celebrates 150 Years of Chocolate Goodness." *Southeastern Missourian.* http://semissourian.com/story.html$+130298 .

Illouz, Eva. 1997. *Consuming the Romantic Utopia: Love and the Cultural Contradictions of Capitalism.* Berkeley: University of California Press.

Jacobsen, Rowan. 2003. *Chocolate Unwrapped: The Surprising Health Benefits of America's Favorite Passion.* Montpelier, VT: Invisible Cities Press.

Jibrin, Janis. 2003. "Eat Your Chocolate and Get Slim Too." *Family Circle,* October 1.

Kaufman, Stuart B. 1986. *A Vision of Unity: The History of the Bakery and Confectionery Workers International Union.* Urbana: University of Illinois Press.

Lemme, Robert. 1975. "The Deep Dark Secrets of Chocolate." *High Times,* October/November.

Lines, Lisa. 2001. "Sexism Everywhere You Look." *Green Left Weekly.* http://www.greenleft.org.au/back/2001/463/463p12b.htm.

Lowe, Margaret A. 2003. *Looking Good: College Women and Body Image, 1875–1930.* Baltimore: John Hopkins University Press.

May, Elaine Tyler. 1988. *Homeward Bound: American Families in the Cold War Era.* New York: Basic Books.

Morton, Marcia and Frederic Morton. 1986. *Chocolate: An Illustrated History.* New York: Crown Publishers.

Parkin, Katherine. 2004. "The Sex of Food and Ernest Dichter: The Illusion of Inevitability." *Advertising and Society Review* 5, No. 2: n.p.

"Private Time." 1983. *Glamour,* February.

Redfern, Catherine. 2002. "Not for Girls? The Yorkie and Echo Adverts." *the f word: contemporary UK feminism* 2002, http://www.thefword. org.uk/reviews/2002/05/not_for_girls_the_yorkie_and_echo_adverts [accessed April 27, 2005].

Sargent, Lydia. 2005. "Feminism in the U.S. It's the Best if Times; It's the Worst of Times." *Z Magazine* http://www.zmag.org/lydiatalk.htm [accessed Sept 4, 2005]

Silverman, Debora. 1986. *Selling Culture: Bloomingdale's, Diana Vreeland, and the New Aristocracy of Taste in Reagan's America.* New York: Pantheon Books.

Sivulka, Juliann. 2003. "Historical and Psychological Perspectives of the Erotic Appeal in Advertising." In *Sex in Advertising: Perspectives on the Erotic Appeal.* Eds. Tom Reichert and Jacqueline Lambiase. Mahwah, NJ: Lawrence Erlbaum Associates.

Somers, Suzanne. 2004. *Somersize Chocolate: 50 Delicious Guilt-Free Recipes for the Carb-Conscious Chocolate Lover.* New York: Crown Publishers.

Super, John C. "Food and History." *Journal of Social History* 36, No. 1 (2002)

Sykes, Diane. "Food as Pleasure: Other Directedness in Food Ads." *Journal for the Study of Food and Society* 6, No. 2 (Winter 2003): 49–56.

The Chocolate Show and DIFFA (Design Industries Foundation Fighting AIDS). "Gala Opening and Fashion Show." [http://www.chocolateshow.com/, accessed April 27, 2005].

"Valentine's Day Delights." *Harper's Bazaar,* February 1978.

Waterhouse, Debra. 1995. *Why Women Need Chocolate: Eat What You Crave To Look and Feel Great.* New York: Hyperion.

Weil, Andrew and Winifred Rosen. 1983. *Chocolate to Morphine: Understanding Mind-Active Drugs.* Boston: Houghton Mifflin Co.

Zind, Tom. "Premium Chocolate Hitting a Sweet Spot in North American Market." *Confectioner Magazine* (June 2002).

CHAPTER 10

Julia Child, Martha Stewart, and the Rise of Culinary Capital

Kathleen LeBesco and Peter Naccarato

> The culture industry perpetually cheats its consumers of what it per-
> petually promises . . . the promise, which is actually all the spectacle
> consists of, is illusory: all it actually confirms is that the real point will
> never be reached, that the diner must be satisfied with the menu.
> —Theodor Adorno & Max Horkheimer, "The Culture Industry"

In their stinging critique of the "culture industry," Adorno and Horkheimer (1993) expose the illusory nature of its promises and, in doing so,
offer a fitting metaphor with which to begin this essay. However, rather
than seeing the dissatisfied diner merely as a metaphor for the citizen who
buys into the promises of the culture industry, only to realize that those
promises will never be fulfilled, we take a literal interest in the diner, the
menu, and the illusory meal. In doing so, we argue not only that food and
food practices provide appropriate metaphors for the relationship between
culture and the individuals who comprise it, but also that they play a significant role in mediating that relationship, whether by promoting dominant ideologies to which the individual is expected to conform or by
providing the individual with a venue for resisting or transgressing such
expectations. In this essay, we are concerned specifically with the cultural
value and ideological function of food and food practices insofar as they
help to sustain class hierarchies by promoting the illusion of class mobility.
To illustrate this point, we consider two icons of food culture, Julia Child
and Martha Stewart. Our goal is to understand how the representations of

food and food practices that they put forth in their cookbooks, their personal biographies, and their television programs function to promote a specific class ideology.[1]

A key ingredient for making this case is Louis Althusser's explanation of how ideology works: "Ideology represents the imaginary relationship of individuals to their real conditions of existence" (1971, 162). In making a case for the ideological function of food culture, we are suggesting that representations of food and food practices that circulate via television programs, books, magazines, internet sites, and other media invite viewers and consumers to imagine a class status and identity for themselves and to escape, if only temporarily, their real economic conditions. While such consumers may not be in a position to travel to France, thanks to Julia Child they can certainly master the art of French cooking. While they may never receive an invitation to the social functions of high society, they can reproduce such an event for their own family and friends by following Martha Stewart's recipes and instructions. Viewed from this perspective, food and food practices may be read as disrupting class hierarchies as they provide their consumers with access to a world normally out of reach from their economic position; however, because such access is limited and temporary, it ultimately does not challenge dominant ideologies of class. To the contrary, it protects them by providing consumers with an illusion of access that contradicts the reality of their economic and social position.

In their study of Martha Stewart and her fans, communication scholars Ann Mason and Marian Meyers draw on the work of Anthony Giddens to suggest that "mediated experience . . . is centrally involved in the presentation of affluence as a lifestyle worthy of emulation and aspiration" (Mason & Meyers 2001, 805). Giddens himself says that "the consumption of ever-novel goods becomes in some part a substitute for the genuine development of self; appearance replaces essence as the visible signs of successful consumption come actually to outweigh the use-value of the goods and services in question themselves" (Giddens 1991, 198 in Mason & Meyers, 805). It may be, then, that consumers of food culture are seduced less by recipes, and more by the imagined status that food culture claims to confer. Rather than making it possible for consumers to achieve the level of affluence that this culture overtly or covertly celebrates, however, food culture offers those consumers illusory access to "culinary capital" as they use food and food practices as vehicles for performing an imagined class identity. These conclusions are borne out in the reflections of Mason and Meyers' interviewees, with an important twist: the interviewees emphasize the pleasurable aspects of such performances, rather than imagining themselves as class victims. It would be foolhardy to dismiss their claims with a scholar-knows-best condemnation of "false consciousness," for their pleasure marks an important site for the discursive production of power and resistance. At the same time, it hints at the performative natures of both Child and Stewart's own identities, which are carefully constructed and sustained through a myriad of cultural representations.

In defining this concept of "culinary capital," we expand the work of Pierre Bourdieu by adapting recent scholarship on the contemporary phenomenon of reality television that seeks to understand the popularity of this new genre and to identify the cultural need that it claims to meet. In discussing the popularity of "lifestyle programming," for example, Gareth Palmer argues that it may "be perfectly placed to service the insecurities felt by those who are uncertain of their place in a rapidly evolving social system. Those who lack self-assurance may put themselves in the hands of lifestyle experts (whose success is measured and reaffirmed daily) and the old established bourgeois middle class" (Palmer 2004, 178). If, on the one hand, lifestyle programming offers a means of stabilizing one's place in a rapidly changing society, then, on the other hand, it also allows for the imagined fluidity of certain modes of social identification, namely, class status. Palmer continues: "In all its manifestations, lifestyle is the home of the view that eradicates, by illustration, the 'end' of class. Class, upbringing, location, education are constructs to be overcome from the vantage point of the self. If class can be defined as a boundary, as knowing one's place, then lifestyle 'proves' that one can adopt a look that fools anyone" (2004, 187–88). While lifestyle experts maintain their privileged class status through their knowledge of and appreciation for food, they simultaneously offer their viewers the myth of access to this privileged position through the food products they buy, consume, and serve. However, while such programming claims to offer its consumers upward class mobility through the acquisition of "culinary capital," its underlying purpose is to maintain the very class hierarchy that it seems to erase. By chastising their viewers for succumbing to growing obsessions with fast-food and frozen food (and, by implication, imploring them to resist all such working-class conveniences) and, instead, by encouraging them to embrace the beauty and pleasure of food, the hosts of these programs invite their viewers to swallow the ideological messages that these programs advance while feeding the marketing machines that they have produced.

To illustrate further the ways in which food culture promotes the myth of class fluidity while, in actuality, solidifying a class hierarchy, we turn to two iconic figures: Julia Child and Martha Stewart. While at first glance we may be struck by the similarities between these two towering figures, we argue that while both Child and Stewart demonstrate the competing narratives of class fluidity and class stability that we have just outlined, they do so in dramatically different ways. In short, Stewart marshals her rags-to-riches personal history to demonstrate the possibility of class transformation based upon the manipulation of appearances, while Child uses her forays into French cuisine—culinary bastion of the elite—both to establish her upper-class credentials and to mask the economic realities of class difference behind the egalitarian assumptions that her cookbooks and television programs promote.

Despite these differences, both Child and Stewart employ similar strategies for promoting food and food practices as vehicles for attaining (or appearing to attain) a desired class status. Interestingly, one commonality between them is the ambiguity of the class identifications they establish with their audiences in their cookbooks and television programs. While both Child and Stewart assume a privileged class position, they simultaneously situate themselves outside of such boundaries as they differentiate their approach to cooking from the more class-based elitism that one might expect from them. This strategy is evidenced in the book that first brought Martha Stewart—former model, stockbroker, and caterer—to national attention as a lifestyle doyenne, *Entertaining,* published in 1982. The glossy, full-color tome was aimed at a general audience rather than the culinary elite, as evidenced by Stewart's celebration of the decline of stuffy etiquette prescriptions regarding entertaining: "There are no longer rigorous prescriptions . . . upon which one's social status hangs, for the growing body of experience in America—social as well as culinary—has fostered a new openness and respect for diversity" (Stewart 1982, 12). Writing about hosting an at-home wedding, for instance, Stewart contends that "what counts is not fussy etiquette, or the number of bridesmaids, or the social prominence of the reception site, but something as simple and incalculable as a special feeling" (1982, 264).

Similarly, Julia Child works to interrupt the bourgeois sensibility in which "the important thing is to know without ever having learnt" (Bordieu 1989, 330 cited in Palmer 2004, 188). She shows how unnatural to most Americans the culinary techniques of the French in fact are, rather than addressing a confident reader/viewer who could breezily claim longtime acquaintance with such knowledge. In a televised biography, Child describes herself as "not a formal person," a tone she maintains so that others can find the cooking that she does approachable. She also adopts this tone in some installments of *The French Chef* as she works overtime to establish a kind of everyperson's "street cred." In "Bouillabaisse à la Marseillaise," she describes the dish as a plain fisherman's stew made of unsalable leftovers of the day's catch—a tasty but none-too-glamorous menu option. "Unfortunately, when you get a recipe like this, the *gourmets*" (she sneers disparagingly at this word) "get ahold of it and they fancy it up so much and say 'do this, do that,' or 'that's not the real thing,' that us ordinary people feel it's impossible to do and terribly expensive" (*The French Chef* 2005). Not to be confused with a food snob, Child reassures viewers that she's like them, a connection that will make *their* transformations to being more like her (fully culinarily capitalized) far easier. An anecdote from Child's A&E Biography reinforces this sense of Child's democratizing impulses: during the writing of *Mastering the Art of French Cooking,* Child apparently became frustrated with collaborator Simca Beck, who cooked "by instinct." Child, in contrast, insisted that the recipes be foolproof and completely accessible even to those without a whiff of instinct.

In fact, early episodes of *The French Chef* underscore the value of persistence over instinct. Viewing these episodes, no one would claim that Child demonstrates anything like an instinctual ease and comfort in the kitchen that might discourage a less polished would-be chef. In one of the earliest episodes of WGBH Boston's *The French Chef*, "The Potato Show," Child's persona contrasts with Stewart's in significant ways, though their end result (the acquisition of culinary capital) is nearly the same. Child narrates her cooking in a halting, breathless style, using none of the flowery language characteristic of Stewart; however, her speech is liberally peppered with French words and phrases. In contrast to Stewart's calm, confident manner, Child appears more like the home viewer when cooking. Sweating profusely, Child mops her face and neck with paper towels repeatedly, reminding the viewer that the acquisition of culinary capital is a heady endeavor. She is not a particularly polished television figure (at least in these early episodes), frequently appearing to forget her lines, and walking out of the frame of the camera rather unexpectedly. Child's haphazard manner in the kitchen and on the screen helps to drive home the accessibility of what she has accomplished. When she attempts to flip a potato dish and it slops on the counter, she assuages viewers with "that didn't go very well!" but reminds them that it doesn't matter, because nobody can see what goes on in the kitchen. The implication is that if one's dishes turn out well, one bears the mark of culinary capital, whatever messy manipulations it might have taken to get there. One need not be a sophisticate to get the job done. In some ways, this is similar to the message that media scholar Laurie Ouellette has attributed to Helen Gurley Brown's work in *Cosmopolitan* magazine in roughly the same time period (see Ouellette 1999). Gurley Brown encouraged readers to present themselves publicly as intelligent, sophisticated, and moneyed in order to catch the right kind of man, even if the reality of their lives was far more pink-collar working class. Child is rarely as explicit as Gurley Brown in promoting performed identities over economic realities as the key to social mobility, but the implicit possibilities are hard to miss.

Before celebrating the egalitarian impulse promoted by both Stewart and Child, we must consider the other side of the coin. In Stewart's case, while that "special feeling" that replaces "fussy etiquette" as the most important feature of that at-home wedding seems unmoored from class markers, many of Stewart's references throughout her book betray this possibility. Despite her contention that one's style of entertaining needn't mark one's class status, Stewart takes great pains to ensure that her readers imagine themselves as "classy." Although she spends much time describing her own roots as humble and ethnic Polish, the imaginary reader of her book emerges as a sophisticated host and chef capable of navigating both the offerings of a wide range of culinary cultural traditions and the demands of the good life. Only such a culinary sophisticate could gush "I've long been fascinated with ribbon candy" (as Stewart does in her *Martha's Homemade Holidays* video) and be taken seriously. Similarly, while Child consistently highlighted the point that the pleasures of French cuisine were readily available to anyone who would take the time to learn the techniques that it required, her own practices often hinted at the very culinary instinct that she so often denied. In early episodes of *The French Chef*, Child infrequently instructs her viewers about exact amounts of ingredients, focusing instead on techniques. Her directions to add "some" butter and "some cream" seem to fly in the face of her edict that excellent cooking need not result from instinct—the source of her ongoing disagreement with *Mastering the Art of French Cooking* co-author Simca Beck. Today, cooking show viewers can log on to the show website for detailed recipes, but this was not the case in the 1960s. Perhaps this reluctance to measure and provide specific directions reveals a fissure in Child's everywoman façade.

Another crack in the façade of class solidarity emerges when Stewart and Child reveal presumptions concerning their readers' own imagined identities when they present actual recipes and menus. In *Entertaining*, for example, we find "Cocktails for Eight to Twelve: Oriental," which begins "A small gathering of friends for cocktails is a gracious prologue to the theater, a concert, a large charity dinner, or just a late dinner in a restaurant" (Stewart 1982, 39). Theater, concerts, and charity dinners are not likely venues for a working-class reader; these leisure activities resonate more with upper-middle-class life. Even when describing a larger cocktail party (for 200!) as featuring mere "Country Fare," the examples Stewart provides of appropriate occasions reveal her presumptions about how her readers like to imagine themselves in terms of social class status. "The necessity of entertaining a very large group of people is a common dread, and every so often it becomes real," writes Stewart. "Few people in fact can escape for a lifetime a call to host a business or club affair, fête a friend or dignitary, or simply repay an ungainly accumulation of social debts" (Stewart 1982, 53). Poor, working class, and lower middle-class people typically can imagine hosting a party for two hundred guests only in the case of a wedding—a once-in-a-lifetime occasion. But the suggestion that one might be obligated to "fête a dignitary" or "host a club affair" allows the reader to transcend his or her associations with low socioeconomic status. Stewart positions as the problem with this scenario not *the cost* of the party, but the burdensome social obligation. Thus, readers are addressed as if they inhabit a world where money doesn't matter—a position adoptable only by those with lots of it. This tone persists in her video collections, as well: *Martha's Homemade Holidays* features Stewart purring about elegant holiday table settings in what appears to be a cozy, New England-style old-money dining room with a roaring fireplace. After showing off the vintage tableware, she insists "if you've done an elegant table, you *have* to do an elegant mantelpiece too." Although fireplaces are not the clear signifiers of wealth that luxury cars might be, Stewart's mode of address presumes that *of course* the viewer has a fireplace and dramatic mantelpiece. Such presumptions serve a dual role. On the one hand, they allow for identification between Stewart and her viewers by ignoring the likely differences between them; on the other hand, they remind viewers of Martha's elevated class status and reinforce their desire to share it by replicating her world in their own homes.

Similarly, Child and her co-authors in the 1966 masterpiece *Mastering the Art of French Cooking* hardly can be said to have had the concerns of the proletariat in mind. Case in point: The book opens with an admonition: "This is a book for the servantless American cook who can be unconcerned on occasion with budgets, waistlines, time schedules, children's meals, the parent-chauffeur-den-mother syndrome, or anything else which might interfere with the enjoyment of producing something wonderful to eat" (Child, Bertholle and Beck 1966, vii). Readers may not be so moneyed that they have servants, but they are clearly addressed as having a class status that precludes worrying (about money, time, reality). Julia Child, Louisette Bertholle and Simone Beck admit that the recipes are "a bit longer than usual" but reassure the reader that "No out-of-the-ordinary ingredients are called for" (1966, vii). Readers feel empowered to learn that French cuisine has little to do with the food itself, and much more to do with the techniques—so they too can gain the know-how behind appearing sophisticated and classy. In Stewart-esque fashion, the allure is populist:

> We have purposely omitted cobwebbed bottles, the *patron* in his white cap bustling among his sauces, anecdotes about charming little restaurants with gleaming napery, and so forth. Such romantic interludes, it seems to us, put French cooking into a never-never land instead of the Here, where happily it is available to everybody. Anyone can cook in the French manner anywhere, with the right instruction. Our hope is that this book will be helpful in giving that instruction. (Child, Bertholle and Beck 1966, vii)

How welcoming! There will be no forays into the exotic, nothing obscure, nothing too far out of reach for the social striver, at least for the moment. But just when the reader feels s/he has attained citizenship in Child's democracy française, the noble expert begins class-based scolding.

On cooking with wine: "If you have not a good wine to use, it is far better to omit it, for a poor one can spoil a simple dish and utterly debase a noble one" (Child, Bertholle and Beck 1966, 31). No longer does "anything go" ingredient-wise—now one needs a "good" wine (and to even know the difference requires culinary capital). On chicken: "If you are interested in price alone, you will often end up with something that tastes like the stuffing inside a teddy bear. . . . So when you buy chicken, make every attempt to find a market which takes special pride in the quality and flavor of its poultry" (Child, Bertholle and Beck 1966, 234). Child's instructions seem reasonable enough: pay attention to the quality of the poultry. However, the sudden rebuke of the reader for being concerned with price (a very *un*classy concern) reads like a bait and switch maneuver after the gentle, democratic welcome that precedes it. Stewart makes a parallel maneuver in *Martha's Homemade Holidays* when she coos about the ease with which her chocolate truffles can be made, but then insists that the viewer use "*very* good chocolate" and advises that European chocolate "tastes richer." Hershey's apparently will not do!

Another way in which both Stewart and Child expose the classist presumptions that lurk beneath their façade of broad class appeal and identification is their class-based rebukes of modern trends in food and food practices. "Convenience food has long been associated with the poor diet and general indolence of the lower classes," writes Joe Moran. "Today, convenience food is the focus of disparate anxieties about farm mechanization, unhealthy additives, the dangers of obesity and the dominance of the big retailers" (Moran 2005, 34). Both women—Child in the 1960s, Stewart in the 1980s—positioned themselves and their work as antidotes to the conveniences of the working and middle classes, but Child was particularly extraordinary in the way she eschewed popular (or populist) attitudes towards food, from admonishing her fans for relying on the fast, cheap, and "tasteless" to dismissing more recent cultural obsessions with diet and health over the pleasure of well-prepared food (after all, significant amounts of butter found their way into almost every one of her recipes as she railed against the "food police").[2]

Child emerged in the food world during the fast-food and TV dinner mentality of the late 1950s, and offered herself as a more civilized alternative; in fact, she was heralded on a 1966 cover of *Time* magazine for leading America into an era of better cooking and eating (*Julia Child: An Appetite for Life* video). However, some *French Chef* episodes reveal a sense of ambivalence between quality and convenience that speak to Child's ultimate emphasis on performance over material reality. In "Your Own French Soup," Child urges making one's own stock, suggesting that taking the time to do things oneself allows them to be distinguished from store-bought products. Nonetheless, she does provide instructions for how to make the soup with prepared stock, too. She teaches her audience how to add French touches like "wine and herbs" (though strangely, she chooses a California wine) and winks to the busy viewer: "Who's going to know?" she asks, when they've added all her little touches to either store-bought or homemade soup base? California stands in for France, store-bought stock replaces homemade, and no one is the wiser;

the resourceful home cook marshals whatever resources she has to assume the mantle of culinary capital. In "Bouillabaisse à la Marseillaise," Child advises viewers to create their broth by simmering an ample assortment of fish heads, but also provides convenient alternatives like clam juice from a can. "You don't need to use any fancy fish," she claims—lean cod or hake are okay—but she says that a large *variety* is key to an "interesting" bouillabaisse. In a later episode, "The Spinach Twins," Child endorses the use of ready-made pie dough and frozen spinach (as opposed to homemade and fresh) in a spinach turnover, much to the chagrin of Simca Beck, who dismissively responds, "I'm French—I *hate* ready-mix" and gesticulates as if to push Child away. The implication is that *real* quality would be desirable, but that one can achieve similar results without having to be fancy, or rich. Child's conclusion in "The Spinach Twins"—that the French are ingenious because they can take something as ordinary as spinach, "serving it with elegance and also giving it a beautiful name *(fontaine aux epinards forestière)*"—speaks volumes. Just as the plain spinach turnover undergoes a transformation into *fontaine aux epinards forestière*, so do her viewers transform from average Janes into culinarily capitalized sophisticates—and they can accomplish this with ready-made ease. Child proves herself more ideologically flexible than the upper-class food scold some might imagine her to be as she emphasizes an any-means-justify-the-end approach to cooking dinner and fabricating the self. One needn't be equipped with the priciest ingredients in order to perform the feat of upward mobility, as long as the *illusion* of quality is kept intact.

Such exotic transformations point to another tactic that both Stewart and Child employ to seduce their readers and viewers into identifying with them and aspiring to be like them, namely, addressing them as savvy about other cultures. In *Entertaining,* Stewart dons her clubby voice to describe a "Tempura Party for Sixteen" that utilizes the nuggets of culinary wisdom she picked up on her "last trip to Japan" (1982, 108). Most of her readers presumably have not made even their *first* trip to Japan, but they are initiated into the jet set by Stewart's intimate mode of address. Likewise, "A Country Buffet Breakfast for Forty," "Clam Bake for Thirty," "Italian Buffet for Fifty," and "Russian Buffet for Twenty-four" all presume some degree of cultural mobility, and the prerequisite for the informality Stewart imagines is class-bred confidence. Furthermore, these feasts also all involve the appropriation of peasant food. Martha brings us the exotic when she tells us that "Russian food is probably one of the least familiar cuisines in America . . . Russian food such as I know it (there are very few Russian chefs around to transmit their knowledge) is not intrinsically heavy, but interesting, colorful, and adaptable to many situations" (1982, 146). It is the elite, fully culturally capitalized home cook who can pull off a Russian buffet despite the obscurity of the cuisine. In *Martha's Homemade Holidays*, a video compilation of some of her cooking and decorating segments, every item in Stewart's domain has a name; she is not surrounded by generic "food," but, for instance, by "clementines from Morocco, persimmons from California, and kumquats from Florida." Her language habits encourage viewers to brandish their own status-making "traveling papers"; soon, they may realize that referring to "the quince on the iron stone pedestal" (as Stewart does in the video) rather than "fruit on a plate" gets them somewhere, class-wise.

Like Stewart, Child conflates culinary and cultural capital as the kitchen is transformed from a confining space of domestic duty into a gateway to the world.[3] Stirring a pot in *The French Chef*'s "Bouillabaisse à la Marseillaise," Child enthuses "It's already beginning to smell wonderfully like Marseilles!" Here, we see cooking as a mode of transport, as a ticket to the exotic (particularly in the 1960s context, when international travel was far more difficult and expensive than today). A later color episode, "The Spinach Twins," cuts between Child in her Boston studio and filmed footage of Child with Simca Beck in Provence, where loving shots of the French countryside entice viewers with gorgeous flowers and spectacular landscape. The "Salad Niçoise" episode presents film footage of Child exploring an open air market in Nice, on the Mediterranean coast. Child explains how to shop for salad ingredients there (implying that viewers will have similar opportunities): "You have to go early in the morning when the potatoes are the freshest." The footage shows Child and a merchant speaking in French as he helps her to select ingredients for her salad: she is fluent in the language and entirely comfortable in the situation, providing a role model for the places that the passport of culinary capital can take a person.

Both Stewart and Child thus encourage their readers and viewers to demonstrate privilege by displaying a global culinary passport (doing what bell hooks has called "eating the other"). Home cooks can disclaim their own peasant status by accessing the peasant cuisine of other cultures. Problematically, this "access" amounts to a promised cultural demystification that never really delivers. Anne L. Bower argues that such culinary tourism may serve a disingenuous function: "Since the reader has an illusion that she has sampled another culture, she may be disinclined to search for a deeper understanding of that other culture's workings. [. . . S]ince one is taking those culinary habits out of context (of socioeconomic factors, lived experience, and historical patterns of food acquisition, preparation, and consumption) the likelihood is that all one comes away with is a comforting but illusory 'taste' of the other culture" (2004, 37; see also Strange 1998).

Another fascinating point of comparison between Stewart and Child is the extent to which their personal biographies mesh (or fail to mesh) with the images of class mobility they have created in their enterprises. Biographer Christopher Byron quotes Stewart as writing, in a 1996 column, "When I was growing up, I wasn't one of the lucky ones whose every meal was accompanied by a fine damask napkin in a silver napkin ring. Nor was I fortunate enough to receive a trousseau of heirloom table and bed linens when I married" (Byron 2002, 19). Stewart is modest about her unassuming roots in a working-class New Jersey family of Polish immigrants, but she paints a rosy picture of what the family accomplished on such meager resources. Despite claims in *Entertaining* that her childhood Sunday dinners consisted of ten veggies and five fruit desserts, among other offerings, Stewart's biographer Jerry Oppenheimer writes that "Martha's close friends from that time had a different memory. 'From reading the first issue of *Martha Stewart Living*' I thought, 'This doesn't sound like the 86 Elm Place that I remember.' When we were in grammar school, we ate *mustard* sandwiches every day,' Stothoff revealed, 'which is kind of a far cry from Martha's gourmet meals. It was Gulden's mustard on white bread—never anything but white bread—which we'd wash down with a soda or milk" (1997, 36–37). It seems interesting that Martha hasn't invented a childhood of poverty for herself—and thus does not tell a pure Horatio Alger story—but instead that her revisionist history makes her childhood perfect, lush, and full of homey touches despite the austerity of the times. This spin exemplifies Stewart's emphasis on *illusion*—that being well-off is almost less important than *appearing* to be well-off is. The language she uses in her video collections is so liberally peppered with positive adjectives that it's not hard to imagine a "saying it makes it so" strategy at work; everything is "good," "beautiful," "wonderful," "fantastic," and "luxurious,"—nothing is ever unpleasant or distasteful or harsh. Stewart's oeuvre is nothing if not a handbook for strivers and a case study in how signifiers of wealth have become unmoored from actual personal fortune. Her work assuages readers and tempers their impulses to pursue economic advancement or equality; instead, the present class structure stays perfectly well in place while Stewart's readers distract themselves with the sleight of hand of lifestyle transformation. For the moneyed classes, "it's a good thing" indeed.

Child's personal history, while quite different from Stewart's, reflects similar ambivalences regarding the subject of class. That Child's grandfather amassed the family fortune by heading west for the gold rush (though ultimately earning his money in real estate) works as a significant metaphor for the grab for culinary capital that Child's oeuvre suggests. Biographer Noel Riley Fitch explains Child as "indeed a party girl, a child of well-to-do parents, who had never had to work" (Fitch 1997, 5). Julia Child described herself as "a kind of Southern California butterfly, a golf player and tennis person who acted in Junior League plays" (cited in Fitch 1997, 4). However, Child's elite class status did not guarantee her "classiness." Apparently, upon meeting her future husband, Paul Child, Julia felt rather unworldly. "'I was a hungry hayseed from California,' she would declare half a century later" (Fitch 1997, 4). She described him as "very sophisticated. He had lived in France and I'd only been to Tijuana!" (Fitch 1997, 4). Julia Child was immediately taken with the "cultured" world that Paul represented, "an intellectual and European world" (Fitch 1997, 5). Even though her Pasadena childhood had been marked by the abundance of home gardens and year-round vegetable wagons (thus freeing the McWilliams household from dependence on processed, store-bought convenience products), Julia remembered the kitchen as a dismal place that she avoided (Fitch 1997, 20). It was only after meeting Paul and wanting in to his world that she became interested in cooking.

What their biographies, cookbooks, and television programs underscore is that while Julia Child began from the position of class privilege to which Martha Stewart aspired, they share the recognition that regardless of actual economic conditions, one may use food and food practices as vehicles for *performing* a desired class identity. Thus, while class position is an economic reality, class identity is a cultural phenomenon that one may or may not perform appropriately, regardless of actual class position. While Stewart sought to change her class position by performing the class identity to which she aspired, Child was pressured to perform the identity that matched her class position. Similarly, for fans of Stewart and Child, food culture provides a means of both aspiring beyond one's class position (like Stewart, one can use food as a means of attaining a higher class status) or, perhaps more commonly, performing a class identity to which one aspires but that one may never actually attain. Audience analyses of Stewart's fans echo this conclusion. Ann Mason and Marian Meyers conducted in-depth interviews with ten fans, and found that the fans "indicated that Stewart's media products promote the fantasy of an upper-class lifestyle attainable through hard work and attention to detail rather than wealth" (2001, 810). Not just cultural dupes, the fans frequently recognized the lifestyle presented by Stewart—one of prosperity, extravagance, and ease—as contrived, but Mason and Meyers found that "this knowledge does not seem to interfere with their enjoyment of the illusion or their desire to create and live the lifestyle Stewart promotes" (2001, 814). Corporate America has not only recognized this phenomenon, it has worked to capitalize on it. Speaking of K-Mart's newly forged relationship with Martha Stewart, Barbara Loren-Snyder, a 1980s K-Mart executive, explains that the company approached Stewart because "she had style, grace, good looks. . . . She was everything your average K-Mart shopper was not . . . everything such a person secretly wanted to be" (Byron, 111). For K-Mart, this secret desire has translated into corporate profit as they have used Martha Stewart's name and status to market her products to their shoppers. The ironic subtext of the Martha Stewart product line, however, is that while one buys her products at K-Mart, one uses them to create and sustain the identity of a person who would never shop there. Thus, the consumer's class status (and the broader class hierarchy) is maintained while said consumer is able to fantasize about an imagined class mobility as she uses her Martha Stewart products to perform an identity that she has not achieved.

These examples underscore the point that in the end, what may matter most is not the food, itself, but rather, the use of food and food practices as vehicles for performing an illusory identity. As such, food culture serves as an important apparatus for circulating dominant cultural ideologies, including those that sustain the prevailing class hierarchy. As Anne L. Bower suggests in her study of "cookbook culture": "The cookbook reader is frequently consuming the book and its imaginary possibilities, rather than deciding which recipe she'll cook and consume at her table" (2004, 42). An in-depth fan study is needed to discern how fans of Martha and Julia put their recipes to use—whether for constructing dinner or for creating and sustaining an imagined class identity. This analysis of the discourse surrounding the Child and Stewart oeurvres suggests that both avenues are available to the motivated home cook.

Notes

1. While the remainder of this essay focuses on how Child and Stewart, as culinary icons, function to promote and sustain a particular class ideology, we do not want to overlook the extent to which both women can be read through a more progressive lens. In particular, we would classify both women as gender outlaws who deploy, manipulate, and transgress dominant gender ideologies as they establish and sustain their iconic status and economic success. Both women embrace the domestic sphere to which women are traditionally relegated and use this space to catapult themselves beyond such gendered boundaries. Rather than seeing them as victims of an oppressive gender ideology, we can recognize their ability to subvert such ideology as they use it as the foundation for their public identities and successes.

2. One could argue that Child's resistance to cultural imperatives regarding health, dietary practices, and body size is emblematic of her status as a gender outlaw. Rather than chastising her viewers for not conforming to such cultural expectations, Child incites them to resist the dietary practices and fads that require a denial of pleasure and indulgence.

3. Here, we can fully appreciate the contradictory messages that Child and Stewart put forth vis-à-vis gender and class ideologies. While they both resist dominant gender ideology that would restrain women within the domestic sphere of the kitchen, they simultaneously promote a class hierarchy that privileges the cultural cachet of the jet-setting elite over the hum-drum reality of middle-class America.

Works Cited

Adorno, Theodor and Max Horkheimer. 1993. "The Culture Industry: Enlightenment as Mass Deception." In *The Cultural Studies Reader*. 2d ed. Ed. Simon During, 31–41. London: Routledge and Kegan Paul.

Althusser, Louis. 1971. "Ideology and Ideological Apparatuses (Notes towards an Investigation)." In *Lenin and Philosophy*, 127–186. London: New Left Books.

Bower, Anne L. 2004. "Romanced By Cookbooks." *Gastronomica—The Journal of Food and Culture* vol. 4 no.2 (Spring): 35–42.

Byron, Christopher. 2002. *Martha Inc.: The Incredible Story of Martha Stewart Living Omnimedia*. New York: John Wiley & Sons.

Child, Julia, Louisette Bertholle, and Simone Beck. 1966. *Mastering the Art of French Cooking*. New York: Alfred A. Knopf.

Fitch, Noel Riley. 1997. *Appetite for Life: The Biography of Julia Child*. New York: Doubleday.

The French Chef with Julia Child. 2005. Videorecording. WGBH Boston, 432 minutes.

Julia Child: An Appetite for Life. 2005. Videorecording. A&E Biography, 50 minutes.

Martha's Homemade Holidays. 2005. Videorecording. Warner Home Video, 200 minutes.

Mason, Ann and Marian Meyers. 2001. "Living With Martha Stewart Media: Chosen Domesticity in the Experience of Fans." *Journal of Communication*. (December): 801–23.

Moran, Joe. 2005. "Hum, Ping, Rip: The Sounds of Cooking." *New Statesman* 134, issue 4723, No. 2 (January 24): 34.

Oppenheimer, Jerry. 1997. *Just Desserts: The Unauthorized Biography of Martha Stewart*. New York: William Morrow & Co.

Ouellette, Laurie. 1999. "Inventing the *Cosmo* Girl: Class Identity and Girl-Style American Dreams." *Media, Culture & Society* 21: 359–83.

Palmer, Gareth. 2004. "'The New You': Class and Transformation in Lifestyle Television." In *Understanding Reality Television*. Eds. Su Holmes and Deborah Jermyn, 173–190. New York: Routledge and Kegan Paul.

Stewart, Martha. 1982. *Entertaining*. New York: Clarkson Potter.

Strange, Niki. 1998. "Perform, Educate, Entertain: Ingredients of the Cookery Programme Genre." In *The Television Studies Book*. Eds. Christine Geraghty and David Lusted, 301–12. London: Arnold.

Contributors

Nathan Abrams was educated at the Universities of Oxford and Birmingham where he received a PhD in American Studies. He currently lectures in Film Studies at the University of Wales, Bangor. He specializes in American Jewish culture and is the author and editor of numerous books and articles, including: *Containing America: Cultural Production and Consumption in Fifties America* (2001); *Studying Film* (2001); and '*A Journal of Significant Thought and Opinion': Commentary Magazine 1945–1959* (2006).

Annette Cozzi is Assistant Professor of the Humanities at the University of South Florida, where she teaches a range of courses, including Humanities from the Renaissance to the Present, Nineteenth-Century Studies, and Food in Western Culture. She is currently at work on a book manuscript, *Eating English: Food and the Construction and Consumption of Imperial National Identity in the British Novel*, which examines the relationship between food and ideology in the formation of identity.

Marie I. Drews is a doctoral candidate at Washington State University in Pullman, Washington. Her teaching and research interests include multi-ethnic American writers' revisions of American history and the American experience, as well as the literature of American foodways. She is specifically interested in interrogating popular cookbooks from the turn of the century through 1960 to see what food—in eating, preparation, place, and writing—reveals about the politics of race, gender, and sexuality in local and national communities.

Charlene Elliott is an Assistant Professor in Communication, Carleton University. She works in the areas of food marketing, obesity and public health, taste and communication, and intellectual property. Dr. Elliot is co-editor of the (forthcoming) book *Communications in Question: Competing Perspectives on Contentious Issues in Communication Studies* (Thomson-Nelson, with Joshua Greenberg). She has published in journals such as *The Canadian Journal of Communication; M/C Journal; The Senses and Society; Journal for Cultural Research; Consumption, Markets and Culture,* and *Canadian Review of American Studies.*

Lynne Fallwell is Assistant Professor of History at Texas Tech University, where she teaches courses on Germany, the Third Reich/Holocaust, and Comparative Genocide. Her research interests focus on national identity formation, group dynamics, and the construction of social frameworks. She is currently working on a project examining representations of Germany in travel and tourism literature. Her interest in culinary matters comes from growing up in a family business of fish processing.

Celia M. Kingsbury is Associate Professor of English at the University of Central Missouri. Her major research interest is World War I literature and culture, especially war propaganda. She is the author of *The Peculiar Sanity of War: Hysteria in the Literature of World War I* (2002), as well as articles and book chapters on the subject of war and propaganda. She is currently working on a project involving World War I propaganda aimed specifically at women and children and popular fiction that mirrors the propaganda.

Kathleen LeBesco is Associate Professor and Chair of Communication Arts at Marymount Manhattan College, where she teaches classes in media and cultural studies, communication theory, and feminist and queer theory. She is author of *Revolting Bodies? The Struggle to Redefine Fat Identity,* and co-editor of *The Drag King Anthology,* and *Bodies Out of Bounds: Fatness and Transgression.* A former cook and restaurant critic, she team teaches a class on food politics with Peter Naccarato.

Eric Mason is Assistant Professor of English at Nova Southeastern University. His work focuses on how the various modalities of composition—textual, visual, oral, and electronic—intersect with the study of culture. He is currently the online editor of *JAC,* a quarterly journal for the interdisciplinary study of rhetoric, literacy, culture, and politics. His cooking is marginal, in all senses of the word.

Peter Naccarato is Associate Professor of English and Chair of Humanities at Marymount Manhattan College, where he teaches a broad range of classes on literature, literary theory, and cultural studies. He has coauthored several essays on food politics with Kathleen LeBesco and has presented this work with her at a number of national and international conferences. He and Dr. LeBesco also team teach a class on this topic.

Kathleen Banks Nutter earned her PhD in history at the University of Massachusetts in Amherst. She is the author of numerous articles as well as *'The Necessity of Organization': Mary Kenney O'Sullivan and Trade Unionism for Women, 1892–1912* (New York: Garland Press, 2000) and teaches U.S. history at State University of New York Stony Brook on Long Island.

Jean P. Retzinger is a lecturer in the Group Major in Mass Communications at the University of California, Berkeley, where she teaches courses in media and popular culture (including the cultural history of advertising). Her research interest lies in examining environmental implications of food production practices and popular culture representations of food and agriculture.

Index